Film and History

James Chapman

First published 2013 by
PALGRAVE MACMILLAN

Palgrave Macmillan in the UK is an imprint of Macmillan Publishers Limited,
registered in England, company number 785998, of Houndmills, Basingstoke,
Hampshire RG21 6XS.

Palgrave Macmillan in the US is a division of St Martin's Press LLC,
175 Fifth Avenue, New York, NY 10010.

Palgrave Macmillan is the global academic imprint of the above companies
and has companies and representatives throughout the world.

Palgrave® and Macmillan® are registered trademarks in the United States,
the United Kingdom, Europe and other countries

ISBN: 978–0–230–36386–1 hardback
ISBN: 978–0–230–36387–8 paperback

This book is printed on paper suitable for recycling and made from fully
managed and sustained forest sources. Logging, pulping and manufacturing
processes are expected to conform to the environmental regulations of the
country of origin.

A catalogue record for this book is available from the British Library.

A catalog record for this book is available from the Library of Congress.

Theory and History
Series Editor: Donald MacRaild

Theory and History offers lively, comprehensive introductions to the principal theories students encounter while studying history.

'Written by one of our leading film historians, *Film and History* is both accessible and liv' 'y and provides an ideal introduction to the subject.' – **Peter Hutchings**, *Northumbria Univers*

Film is the pre-eminent mass medium of the modern age. It is a valuable source of evidence for the study of both the past and the contemporary world, and is a social practice that has affected the lives of millions. How can historians engage with this important and influential medium?

Written for both students and teachers, *Film and History*:

- provides a concise, accessible introduction to the use of film in historical enquiry and a summary of the main theoretical debates
- charts the development of film history as a subject area and a discipline in its own right
- considers different approaches to film history, including film as an art form, as ideology, as a historical source, and as a social practice
- includes case studies to ground discussion of theories and approaches in specific examples.

Wide-ranging and authoritative, *Film and History* equips students with the methods both to analyse film texts and to understand the place of film in history and culture.

James Chapman is Professor of Film Studies at the University of Leicester and editor of the *Historical Journal of Film, Radio and Television*.

Theory and History
Series Editor: Donald MacRaild

Published

Biography and History	*Barbara Caine*
Film and History	*James Chapman*
Empiricism and History	*Stephen Davies*
Cultural History	*Anna Green*
Gender and History	*Susan Kingsley Kent*
Social Theory and Social History	*Donald M. MacRaild and Avram Taylor*
Narrative and History	*Alun Munslow*
Marxism and History	*Matt Perry*
Transnational History	*Pierre-Yves Saunier*
Postmodernism and History	*Willie Thompson*

Theory and History
Series Standing Order
ISBN 978–1–4039–8526–2 hardback
ISBN 978–0–333–91921–7 paperback
(outside North America only)

You can receive future titles in this series as they are published. To place a standing order please contact your bookseller or, in the case of difficulty, write to us at the address below with your name and address, the title of the series and the ISBN quoted above.

Customer Services Department, Macmillan Distribution Ltd,
Houndmills, Basingstoke, Hampshire, RG21 6XS, UK

For Jeremy Black

Contents

Acknowledgements

This is a book I have wanted to write for a long time. I became interested in the relationship between film and history as an undergraduate at the University of East Anglia where I was often the lone historian in film studies seminars (UEA in those days allowed a major and a minor subject: I majored in English History with a minor in Film Studies). That was where I first acquired a reputation as a trenchant advocate of 'history' against 'theory'. As this is a reputation I have never quite shaken off, I should make it clear here that what I object to is not theory *per se* but rather bad theory – theory that is either not tested against empirical evidence or which is so vague and generalized that it becomes merely a rhetorical tool. I should add that there is nearly as much bad history as there is bad theory, especially in film.

My subsequent academic career has continued to straddle film and history. As a doctoral student at Lancaster University I researched a thesis on film ('Official British Film Propaganda during the Second World War') in the Department of History. My first academic post was as Lecturer in Film and Television Studies in another Department of History, at the Open University, where I was involved in designing the course *Film and Television History* (AA310) and contributed to other courses that included film such as *Total War and Social Change* (AA312) and *Politics, Society and Culture in France and Italy, 1943–1973* (AA304). A decade later I was appointed to the Chair of Film Studies in the Department of History of Art and Film at the University of Leicester, where teaching 'conventional' students has again brought home to me the need for a theoretically rigorous understanding of film and history.

Any book or article represents only the author's current thinking on the subject rather than a definitive and final statement. *Film and History* therefore reflects my current views on the subject (or subjects) that have dominated my academic career to date. These views have taken shape partly through discussions with colleagues in different institutions. These include Charles Barr, Andrew Higson and Peter Krämer, who taught film studies at UEA during my days there; Jeffrey Richards, who supervised my doctoral thesis at Lancaster; Tony Aldgate and the late Arthur Marwick at the Open University; and now colleagues such as Guy Barefoot and David Ekserdjian at Leicester. Through the International Association of Media and History (IAMHIST) I have been able to discuss and debate film with scholars of the calibre of David Culbert, Nick Cull, Leen Engelen, Jo Fox, Tobias Hochscherf, the late Phil Taylor, Richard Taylor, Tony Shaw, Pierre Sorlin, Roel Vande Winkel and David Welch, while the intellectual community offered by the 'Issues in Film History' seminar series at the Institute of Historical Research, particularly Sally Dux, Robert James, Vincent Porter, James Robertson, Justin Smith, Andrew Spicer and Peter Waymark, has undoubtedly influenced the content of this book. A special note of thanks for my two 'critical readers', Mark Glancy and Sue Harper, two of our finest film historians.

I am grateful to Sonya Barker at Palgrave Macmillan and series editor Don MacRaild for their enthusiasm for this book and for the speedy commissioning process. It was at a book launch hosted by Jeremy Black at the Athenaeum Club in October 2010 that the idea for *this* book was first discussed. Jeremy is not only a prolific historian who has consistently championed the cause of good, clear, jargon-free historical writing; he is also a very good friend. It is a pleasure to be able to return a compliment by dedicating this *opusculum* to him.

Introduction

Today there are historians whose interest *is* the movies; increasingly there are also historians interested *in* the movies.

K.R.M. Short[1]

This statement by the founding editor of the *Historical Journal of Film, Radio and Television* makes a useful starting point for a book entitled *Film and History* because it makes a crucial methodological distinction between the subject of film history ('Historians whose interest *is* the movies,' Short amplifies, 'are committed to researching an important international industry which has aspects which are economic, technological, social, psychological and aesthetical') and a broader group who are not necessarily interested in the medium in its own right but who may nevertheless draw upon it in their work ('The historian who is interested *in* the movies is motivated by the question of whether the central line of research can be supported or illuminated by evidence drawn from the world of the movies'). So, while a film historian researching, say, *Gladiator* (2000) would seek to document the making of the film, consider its relationship to other films by its director Ridley Scott, analyse its reception and perhaps speculate on the reasons for its popularity with audiences, other historians might use the film either as evidence of popular views of the society and politics of Ancient Rome at the end of the twentieth century, or perhaps as a reflection of ideological and cultural issues affecting its country of origin, the United States of America, in the year 2000.

Film is still a relatively young academic subject. Although the history of the medium can be traced back to the end of the nineteenth century – the first public exhibition of moving pictures occurred in France and Germany towards the end of 1895 – and while the first recognized film histories were written in the 1920s, in the form of Terry Ramsaye's *A Million and One Nights* (1926) and Paul Rotha's *The Film Till Now* (1930), it was not until the 1960s that film appeared on the academic curriculum. It was in this decade that the first university professors of film were appointed – Thorold Dickinson at the Slade School of Art in London and Jean Mitry at the University of Montréal; that the first professional subject associations for film were formed – the Society for Cinema Studies (North America) and the Society for Education in

Film and Television (Britain); and that the first scholarly journals on film were published – the *Cinema Journal* and *Journal of the University Film Association* in America and *Screen Education* in Britain.[2] The point of critical mass came around 1968–9. In Britain the establishment of the Slade Film History Register in 1968 – intended to serve the same role for film as the National Register of Archives did for manuscript sources – and the landmark conference 'Film and the Historian' held at University College, London, in April of that year marked the emergence of 'film and history' as a distinct subject area.[3] The same period also saw the publication of several of what are now recognized as key foundational texts of film studies – including Andrew Sarris's *The American Cinema* (1968) and Peter Wollen's *Signs and Meaning in the Cinema* (1969)[4] – and the first critical studies of major directors and **genres**. In the United States it is reckoned 'that cinema studies was the fastest growing academic discipline in American universities between 1965 and 1975'.[5]

Why did it take so long for film to gain a foothold in the academy? One reason is that for many years film history was seen as the preserve of collectors and connoisseurs, such as William K. Everson in America and Kevin Brownlow in Britain.[6] It was a pastime rather than a profession: the province of the amateur 'film buff' rather than the academic historian. Another reason for film's belated entry onto the academic curriculum is that there existed for many years a strong intellectual and institutional resistance to the idea that film was a proper subject for academic study. In the preface to his book *Visions of Yesterday*, for example, the cultural historian Jeffrey Richards directed a polemical aside against the prevailing institutional culture in British universities:

> Only now is it being realized – and much more tardily in Britain than in the United States – that a study of the cinema can reveal much about, for instance, popular attitudes and ideals. One of the purposes of this book is frankly propagandist – to hasten the process of acceptance of Cinema Studies in this country ... The birth of this hoped-for day requires a change in attitude by university authorities. Moribund, Oxbridge-orientated university panjandrums are still to be heard up and down the country chuntering that if Cinema Studies is adopted then the next step will be Football Studies (and why not?).[7]

Put simply film was thought too trivial a subject to be taken seriously. The emergence of film (or cinema) studies as an academic subject therefore had to wait for the idea of 'culture' to be transformed from the old **Leavisite** distinction between 'high' and 'low' culture to a more inclusive model that was prepared to take the 'popular' seriously.

The acceptance of film was also not helped by a methodological and ideological rift that opened up quite early in the intellectual history of the fledgling young discipline. On the one hand, emerging principally from an English literature background, was a critical tradition of textual analysis that focused on the 'reading' of film texts, typically classified in terms of the ***auteur* theory** (the films of Alfred Hitchcock, Fritz Lang or Jean Renoir, for example) or **genre** criticism (the Western, the gangster film, the melodrama, the musical, and so forth). In the 1960s this trend coalesced around journals such as *Movie* in Britain and *Film Culture* in America. Many of the first generation of film scholars came from an English Lit. background, and, naturally enough, imported critical tools and methods from that discipline: hence the emphasis on the formal analysis of films and tracing repeated patterns and motifs through the *œuvre* of a particular director or across a genre such as the Western or gangster film. On the other hand, emerging principally from social and cultural history, was another approach that emphasized the institutional and cultural contexts of film-making and considered the relationship between films and the societies in which they were produced and consumed. This tradition also coalesced around particular journals, including *Film and History* and, later, the *Historical Journal of Film, Radio and Television*. Until the 1980s, however, film history was often regarded as something of a poor relation to more theory-based approaches, especially those informed by **semiotics** and **structuralism**. As the American film historian Robert C. Allen has observed: 'Film history was to take a very back seat indeed during the reign of high theory, which is not surprising given its resolutely ahistorical and thoroughly conventionalist underpinnings. All the cool graduate students were analysing texts.'[8]

Since the 1980s there has been evidence of what might be called a 'historical turn' in film studies with the recognition that textual analysis alone is insufficient to understanding films as cultural artefacts, and that all films – including the products of both the mainstream, commercial entertainment cinema and alternative practices such as **art cinema**, documentary, and experimental and avant-garde film-making – all exist within their various ideological, political, social, cultural, economic and institutional contexts. There are now very few critics who cling to what David Bordwell has called 'the sterile notion of the self-sufficient text.'[9] An aspect of the 'historical turn' in film studies has been the emergence of a methodological conversation within the discipline about the nature and purpose of film historical research.[10] As in most other branches of history, the professionalization of film history in the academy has seen a move away from grand narratives of the sort that characterized early histories of film towards an increasing specialization within the discipline. In particular historians began to define the different approaches to writing film history. David Robinson, for example, has observed that 'cinema involves an aesthetic, a technology, and economy and an audience: and all four of these elements will condition what moving images appear on the screen at any particular place and in any particular period.'[11] In their book *Film History: Theory and Practice* (1985) – the first thoroughgoing attempt to lay down a methodological framework for film history – Robert C. Allen and Douglas Gomery defined these approaches as aesthetic film history, technological film history, economic film history and social film history.[12]

So what is the object of film history? Allen and Gomery define the role of the film historian as being to show 'how film as art, technology, social force, or economic institution developed over time or functioned at a given moment in the past'. 'Rather than analyze one film or reflect on the nature and potential of all films,' they add, '*the film historian attempts to explain the changes that have occurred to the cinema since its origins, as well as account for aspects of the cinema that have resisted change.*'[13] A film historian may be interested in films as records of the past (film as a historical source), films as cultural artefacts (the history of film style, form and aesthetics), films as economic commodities (the history of film as a business), the organization of the film-making process (the history of the film industry), the social composition and tastes of cinema-goers (the history of audiences) or films as social documents (the idea that films reflect the attitudes and values of the societies in which they were produced and consumed). To this end film history is both like and unlike other types of history. It shares with other branches of history the aim of showing what has happened and attempting to explain how and why it happened as it did. Where film history differs from other types of history is in the nature of the primary sources on which it is based. While film history makes use of the traditional types of primary source materials – including production records, scripts, trade journals, the diaries and memoirs of film-makers, publicity materials, box-office receipts and film reviews – the main sources are the films themselves. Films are complex cultural texts that are different from traditional historical sources such as letters and diaries, as well as from other cultural texts such as novels and paintings: accordingly their analysis requires specialist methods and skills that are unique to film history.

At this point it is worth reflecting briefly on the extent and nature of the sources for film history. Again, like other types of history, film history is based on an archival record that is fragmentary and incomplete. For such a modern medium there is a surprisingly large number of *lacunae* in the primary sources. It is little appreciated outside film history circles that film itself is a highly perishable medium: celluloid film stock decays more rapidly than paper, and the long-term stability of modern digital formats remains uncertain. Many films, especially from the early history of the medium, are now lost. It has been estimated that up to three quarters of the films made before 1930 no longer survive, while others exist only in fragments. Early works by major film-makers such as F. W. Murnau and John Ford are among those lost to posterity. And even some of the great classics of cinema, including Fritz Lang's *Metropolis* (1926) and Abel Gance's *Napoléon* (1927), exist today only in versions restored through the painstaking efforts of archivists but which may differ from the films as they were originally exhibited. It was not until the 1930s that serious attention was given to film preservation when organizations such as the Museum of Modern Art in New York, the National Film Library in London and the Cinémathèque Française in Paris began collecting prints of films for posterity. Even then archivists have had to contend with the view that film is first and foremost a commodity rather than a historical source or an art form. As Ernest Lindgren, curator of the National Film Archive in Britain, remarked in 1948: 'The word "archive" rings with a deathly sound in the world of cinema, which is so young, vital and dynamic, eager for the future and impatient of the past.'[14]

The dominant approach to film history by far has been aesthetic – the history of film as an art form. This approach tends to privilege the great works of film art – what Allen and Gomery term 'the masterpiece tradition' – and the work of major film-makers who stand out through their creative use of the medium. The film critic Derek Malcolm claims that 'during the hundred or so years of its existence, it [the cinema] has produced as many major artists as any other art form during that time'.[15] This approach has resulted in the creation of a canon of 'classic' films: examples include – but are not limited to – *The Birth of a Nation, The Cabinet of Dr Caligari, The Battleship Potemkin, Napoléon, Sunrise, La Grande Illusion, Modern Times, The Grapes of Wrath, Citizen Kane, Brief Encounter, Les Enfants du Paradis, Bicycle Thieves, Tokyo Story, Pather Panchali, The Seventh Seal, Vertigo, A bout de souffle, L'Avventura, La Dolce Vita, 2001: A Space Odyssey* and *The Godfather.*[16] However, the masterpiece tradition focuses on a tiny handful of films that are by definition exceptional and therefore can hardly be seen as representative of the medium. As the US film scholar David Bordwell observes: 'Film historians have not generally acknowledged the place of the *typical* work. In most film histories, masterworks and innovations rise monumentally out of a hazy terrain whose contours remain unknown.'[17] Other approaches – technological, economic, social – have been less prevalent, certainly in popular histories of film.

The prevalence of predominantly text-based histories has meant that for the most part film history has been understood as the history of films. A consequence of this has been that, until quite recently, the history of cinema as an institution and a social practice has been neglected. Yet, as Richard Maltby avers,

> the history of American cinema is not the history of its products any more than the history of railroads is the history of locomotives...To write a history of

texts and call it a history of Hollywood involves omitting the social process and cultural function of cinema, and denies the contextual significance of the material conditions under which movies were produced and consumed.[18]

An emergent trend in film scholarship recently has been a shift towards broader-based contextual histories of exhibition and cinema-going in which films themselves are no longer the sole focus of attention. It has even been suggested, controversially, that 'movies don't matter': that the important questions in film history are not the development of particular styles or genres, or the production of individual films, but rather the place of cinema in the social and cultural lives of its audiences.[19]

Film and History is neither a history of cinema as a social practice nor another history of film as an art form: in fact it is not a history of film of any kind. It is, rather, a study of the history of film scholarship, focusing on the methodological and theoretical perspectives that have informed the writing of film history. In common with other volumes in the 'Theory and History' series, its subject is the discipline itself. It aims to provide an overview of the intellectual and theoretical contexts in which film history has taken shape and to summarize the main approaches; to chart how the history of film as a popular art form has responded to a shifting cultural and aesthetic agenda over the course of nearly a century; to examine how different theoretical perspectives – including Marxism, feminism and postcolonialism – have influenced the agenda of film history; to consider the nature of film as a historical source; to explore the debate over the idea of film as a 'reflection' or 'mirror' of society; and to show how histories of production, reception and cinema-going can illuminate our understanding of film in its historical contexts. These are the issues discussed in the six chapters that follow. We begin with a short history of the discipline of film history. For, like all types of history, film history is not just about a subject: it is also about the research questions that historians ask and the methodological tools they employ to answer those questions.

1 A Brief History of Film History

For the first time in the history of the world, so far as the author has been able to discover, an art has sprouted, grown up and blossomed in so brief a time that one person might stand by and see it happen.

Terry Ramsaye[1]

Any attempt to identify 'firsts' in a particular field is fraught with problems. Just as there are competing claims for who produced the first moving pictures – including Thomas Edison in the United States, the Skladanowsky brothers in Germany, the Lumière brothers in France and Robert Paul in Britain – so there are various contenders for the first film histories. Allen and Gomery nominate Robert Grau's *The Theatre of Science* (1914) and Terry Ramsaye's *A Million and One Nights* (1926) as marking the origins of film history in America.[2] The preface to a reprint of the latter described it 'the first complete source book on the motion picture' and Ramsaye as 'the first authentic film historian'. The best claimant for the first synoptic history of world cinema is the British critic Paul Rotha's book *The Film Till Now* (1930). This was followed by Benjamin Hampton's *A History of the Movies* (1931), Lewis Jacobs's *The Rise of the American Film* (1939) and Georges Sadoul's multi-volume *Histoire générale du cinéma* (1948–54).[3] It would be fair to say that none of these early histories would meet the standards of academic rigour expected of the discipline today. They were not meant to be scholarly studies: they were written for general readerships and were as much works of journalism as history. Their value, however, as Ramsaye pointed out, is that they were contemporaneous with the history they described. To that extent these works are the film world's equivalents of Thomas Carlyle's history of the French Revolution or Winston Churchill's history of the Second World War. For all their flaws and limitations, they are the foundational texts of film history. They established a narrative that, albeit with many caveats and modifications, continues to inform popular histories of film to this day.

▶ **'Standard Version' histories and the rise of narrative film**

The narratives that emerged from these early histories established what David Bordwell has usefully termed the 'Standard Version' of film history.[4] Standard Version histories all share, to a greater or a lesser, but usually a greater, degree, certain characteristics. Their focus is on the history of film-making and the development of the 'art' of film; this history is presented as a narrative of innovations and advances in film technique by pioneer film-makers who are credited with 'discovering' the language of film; and the underlying story is the rise of what came to be known as the **classical narrative film** that is held to represent the height of film's artistic and technical development. It is also a history that is dominated by American cinema, which represents the model against which other national cinemas are judged.

The Standard Version sees film developing from a sideshow attraction at the end of the nineteenth century to become the dominant popular art form in the Western world within a generation. The first films, such as those of Auguste and Louis Lumière, were short records of everyday events such as workers leaving a factory or a train arriving at a station. These *actualité* films were soon overtaken, however, by short dramatic films that edited together a sequence of **shots** into intelligible stories. The French pioneer Georges Méliès, for example, employed multiple-shot story-telling and optical trick effects in his early fantasy films such as *A Trip to the Moon* (1902). These early films are often described as 'primitive' or 'theatrical': they were typically shot in **tableau** with the camera placed at a front-on angle. In the Standard Version the first significant advances in story-telling were the films of the American pioneer Edwin S. Porter. Lewis Jacobs describes Porter as 'the father of the story film' who 'transformed motion picture art'.[5] Porter's films, notably *Life of an American Fireman* (1903) and *The Great Train Robbery* (1903), marked a major advance in the art of film narration by cutting between scenes that in terms of the film story were taking place simultaneously. This technique, variously known as **crosscutting** or **parallel editing**, was then perfected by D. W. Griffith, an actor turned director who made over 400 one- and two-reel films for the American Biograph Company between 1908 and 1913. It is impossible to exaggerate the importance of Griffith in the Standard Version of film history. Jean Mitry, for example, contends that 'it is to Griffith that it [cinema] owes its existence as an art form, as a means of expression and of signification'.[6] Griffith is credited with pioneering devices such as the **close-up** and **point-of-view** shot, and with developing the system of **continuity editing** which maintains consistent positioning and movement between shots. His supreme achievement was the three-hour epic *The Birth of a Nation* (1915), generally regarded as the first true masterpiece of cinema. Its blatant racism – objectionable to many even at the time let alone in today's more racially-aware climate – is often conveniently overlooked.[7]

In many Standard Version histories film reached the height of its artistic achievement in the 1920s. This period saw the institutionalization of the **studio system** in Hollywood and the ascendancy of the **feature film**. At the same time the emergence of distinct national cinemas and movements in Europe, especially **German Expressionism** and **Soviet montage**, was seen as marking the emergence of an avant-garde. Among the films invariably selected as landmarks of silent cinema are Germany's *The Cabinet of Dr Caligari* (1919) and the Soviet Union's *The Battleship Potemkin* (1925). As silent films crossed boundaries of language and culture, the canon of accepted masterpieces of film art was international. American films were successfully exported to most film-producing nations: the films of Charlie Chaplin, especially, such as *The Kid* (1921) and *The Gold Rush* (1925), were universally admired. The advent of talking pictures following the adoption of sound technology in the late 1920s, however, was seen as retarding the development of film style. The cumbersome technology of early sound recording equipment meant that the camera lost much of its previous mobility: consequently the fluid visual style of the mature silent cinema was lost as films reverted to a more static and 'theatrical' mode.

A few examples must suffice to illustrate this Standard Version. Paul Rotha's *The Film Till Now* was the first attempt to write a comprehensive synthesis of international film history. Rotha, like other early writers, was a cinephile rather than a trained historian, admitting that his chief qualification for writing the book, at the precocious age of 22, was 'having spent an excessive amount of my childhood and schooldays in cinemas'.[8] He begins with an impressionistic survey of 'The Development of the Film', which condenses the first two decades of the medium into a few pages, followed by chapters on each of the major film-producing nations (America, Germany, the Soviet Union, France and, last and least, Britain). Rotha's preferences are clearly for European, especially German and French, films – *The Cabinet of Dr Caligari* is 'the first real aesthetic advance in cinema' – whereas American films represent 'the lowest form of public entertainment'.[9] In this regard *The Film Till Now* is an early example of the familiar cultural distinction between European cinema (equated with 'art') and American cinema (equated with populism). Rotha was writing at the point when sound cinema was displacing the silent film: he disliked 'the usurping dialogue film' and concluded pessimistically that cinema was heading towards 'the abyss'.[10]

Lewis Jacobs's *The Rise of the American Film* offers a slightly different variation on the Standard Version. Jacobs focuses on American cinema: he downplays the importance of European films and suggests that the real impact of films such as *The Cabinet of Dr Caligari* and Soviet montage cinema was that they 'freshened

[the] ambition of American producers [and] led to important innovations in film technique and to an improvement of American films generally'.[11] Jacobs places greater emphasis on the 'social agency' of films than Rotha, whose focus is essentially on film as an expressive art form. And, rather than regretting the arrival of sound cinema, Jacobs sees sound as the final stage in the 'maturity' of the medium. For Jacobs the 1930s mark the culmination of efforts 'to bring the medium to a completeness of expression equal to its artistic and physical possibilities'.[12] Like Rotha, though in different ways, Jacobs's perspective was influenced by the position of the film industry at the time he was writing. *The Rise of the American Film* was published in 1939, a year widely regarded as Hollywood's *annus mirabilis*.[13] This is also suggested by Jacobs's conclusion: 'After almost half a century of progress, the American film has achieved a degree of maturity.'[14]

Rotha and Jacobs, for all their divergent opinions, were nevertheless telling broadly the same story: the similarities between them are more notable than the differences. This is a characteristic of the Standard Version of film history, which is posited on several underlying assumptions. For one thing it is essentially an aesthetic history whose principal focus is on the development of film style and technique. Other factors – technology, economics, industry – are secondary. Developments in film technology tend to be presented as 'discoveries' rather than as a historical process. And there is little awareness of the political economy of the film industry beyond accounts of the 'patent wars' that were fought in the US courts during the early years. The Standard Version also presents a historical narrative that is both linear and teleological. It is based on the notion that the classical narrative film represents the ideal form of the medium. The early history of film is therefore seen in terms of its progress towards that ideal: it privileges film-makers who advanced the art of storytelling (Porter and Griffith) and marginalizes or even ignores developments that do not fit this pattern. Writing in 1955, for example, British critic Roger Manvell prefaced a short history of film in his book *The Film and the Public* as an 'attempt to show how rapidly and effectively the film-makers discovered the great technical and artistic capacities of their chosen medium'.[15]

The Standard Version remained unchallenged for many years: later additions to film historiography expanded it without fundamentally altering its basic tenets. The two major additions to the canon following the advent of sound cinema were French **Poetic Realism** in the 1930s and Italian **Neo-Realism** in the 1940s. These movements were seen within a trend towards a more humanistic cinema providing a greater degree of psychological realism than the commercial products of Hollywood. Rotha, in the preface to a revised edition of *The Film Till Now* in 1949, for example, saw the Italian Neo-Realists in a direct line of descent from previous progressive movements in film when he wrote that 'the most exciting films since the war have come from a small group of film-makers in Italy who, like the Russians in the mid-twenties and the British documentary movement in the thirties, have rediscovered the simple fact that imagination and inventiveness are worth all the technical paraphernalia of the luxury studios if you have something to say'.[16] By now a basic schemata had emerged associating American cinema ('Hollywood') with popular entertainment and European cinemas (mainly France and Italy) with moral seriousness and psychological realism.

So pervasive was the Standard Version of film history that it remained largely intact until the late 1960s. By this time the first film courses had started to appear on the curricula of universities and colleges in the United States. The perpetuation of the Standard Version was due in some degree to the reprinting of early histories – a third edition of *The Film Till Now* was published in 1960, *A Million and One Nights* appeared as a paperback in 1965, followed by a new edition of *The Rise of the American Film* in 1968 – to fill the need for student text books. The emergence of film studies as a university subject also prompted a new wave of general synoptic histories in the 1970s, including Gerald Mast's *A Short History of the Movies* (1971), David Robinson's *The History of World Cinema* (1973), Basil Wright's *The Long View* (1974) and Eric Rhode's *A History of the Cinema from its Origins to 1970* (1976).[17] While the grand narrative now extended to cover the decline of the Hollywood studio system and the rise of European 'new wave' movements in the 1960s, and in some instances even extended beyond the cinema of the West to include Indian cinema (or, rather, the films of Bengali director Satyajit Ray) and Japanese directors such as Akira Kurosawa and Kenji Mizoguchi, the underlying assumptions of these works were largely consistent with those published 40 years before. Basil Wright, for example, even after the innovations of the new wave cinemas, still saw the history of film in conventional terms: 'I do not think that the motion picture – whatever new shapes it may be going to take unto itself – need look much further for its grammar and syntax than those basic principles of **montage** first put forward by Griffith, developed and enlarged by Eisenstein and Dovzhenko, and subsequently elaborated over the years by many directors such as Vigo, Resnais, Godard and Dreyer.'[18]

The final part of the Standard Version to take shape was periodization. The advent of sound had always been seen as a watershed not only because it revolutionized the nature of cinema but because it was achieved so rapidly. The first recognized 'talkie' *The Jazz Singer* was released in 1927; by 1930 silent films had all but ceased to be produced. Now another watershed could be identified in the years either side of 1960. This period witnessed the fragmentation of the US film industry, the world's leading industry both economically and culturally. It also saw the emergence of the **art cinema** movement in Europe and the spread of film-making to the Third World. In his book *A Discovery of Cinema* (1971), for example, Thorold Dickinson divides film history into three phases – 'The Silent Film', 'The Early Sound Film' and 'The Modern Sound Film' – albeit with a caveat that the transition between the second and third phases was a gradual process over the course a full decade (the 1950s).[19] The same basic periodization is also adopted in *The Oxford History of World Cinema* (1995), a scholarly tome edited by Geoffrey Nowell-Smith, which is organized as three sections on 'Silent Cinema' (1895–1930), 'Sound Cinema' (1930–60) and 'Modern Cinema' (1960–95).[20] This periodization is now widely accepted by film historians: its acceptance demonstrates yet again the persistence of the Standard Version.

▶ Revisionist histories: reconsidering early cinema

The Standard Version of film history remained largely unchallenged until the 1970s. The first thoroughgoing revisionist project in film history focused on early cinema. This came about through the efforts of a group of film historians – including Ben Brewster, Noël Burch, André Gaudreault, Tom Gunning, Charles Musser and Barry Salt – who looked afresh at the history of early cinema and began to question some aspects of the Standard Version. This revisionist project was made possible by the efforts of archivists to preserve early films and by the research networks established through the agency of the International Federation of Film Archives (Fédération International des Archives du Film, or FIAF). The landmark in this regard was the FIAF conference held in Brighton in 1978 (as a homage to the 'Brighton School' of British pioneer filmmakers) which included screenings of nearly 600 films made between 1900 and 1906. Many of these had not been widely seen since their original release. The intellectual consequence of the Brighton conference was to redraw the map of early cinema and to prompt new historical and theoretical perspectives that not only challenged many of the received wisdoms about the formative years of cinema but also had implications for understanding the entire history of the film medium.[21]

The picture that emerged post-Brighton was that early cinema was characterized by a greater diversity of styles and practices than previously assumed. There was more, much more, to early cinema than the traditional distinction between the *actualité* films of the Lumières and the fantasy films of Georges Méliès. A major rediscovery was the work of the 'Brighton School' such as G. A. Smith and James Williamson whose films reveal a relatively sophisticated use of the medium. There is a fascination with optical subjectivity in films such as Smith's *Grandma's Reading Glass* (1900), which shows a child looking at its grandmother through a magnifying lens, and Williamson's *The Big Swallow* (1901), which employs trick effects to show a man apparently swallowing both the camera and its operator. Others employed stop-motion techniques, such as Cecil Hepworth's *Explosion of a Motor Car* (1900), and multiple exposures, such as Méliès's *One-Man Orchestra* (1900). Some film theorists made comparisons between early cinema and later avant-garde movements such as Surrealism or the work of experimental film-makers such as Maya Deren and Stan Brakhage: the absence of conventional narrative and the degree of formal experimentation evident in early cinema saw it being claimed as a site of avant-garde practice. While this may seem an absurdly ahistorical judgement, it was nevertheless now abundantly clear that assertions such as Rotha's that 'the birth and early years of the cinema are neither interesting nor particularly brilliant in aesthetic achievement' were in need of significant reassessment.[22]

At a basic level one of the outcomes of this revisionist project has been to nuance the Standard Version's narrative of the pioneers and their discoveries. Porter's landmark films of 1903, *Life of an American Fireman* and *The Great Train Robbery*, for example, begin to look less revolutionary in their own right when seen alongside James Williamson's *Fire!* (1901) or William Haggar's *Desperate Poaching Affray* (1903). British historians have highlighted the 'systematic organisation' of narrative in Cecil Hepworth's *Rescued by Rover* (1905), which can be seen as 'a clear precursor of the films made by D. W. Griffith for the Biograph Company in America between 1908 and 1913'.[23] This is not to debunk the achievements of the pioneers but rather to suggest that the emergence of narrative film-making was more the result of parallel developments in different countries than due solely to individual genius. It was also the case that international traffic in early film was relatively free: films were widely exported, so innovations from one country were quickly assimilated elsewhere.

Charles Musser's archival research concerning the variant prints of Porter's *Life of an American Fireman* is an exemplary case study of micro-level revisionism. This is an early fiction film in which a fire crew is called out to an emergency and a heroic fireman rescues a mother and her baby from a burning house. In one version of the film, held by the Museum of Modern Art, the climactic rescue consists of nine shots alternating between the inside and the outside of the building. In another version of the film deposited with the Library of Congress, however, the same sequence is shown in just two shots: the rescue is seen first from inside the building, and then the same events are repeated as seen from outside the house. It had long been assumed that the Library of Congress print was an early 'rough cut' of the film and that the MOMA print represented the definitive version: this was seen as evidence that Porter understood the technique of cross-cutting or parallel editing as early as 1903. However, Musser established that the Library of Congress print was in fact the 'copyright version' deposited in 1903 – and therefore the film as it was originally released – while the MOMA print was another version that Porter (or possibly someone else) re-edited at a later date. Further evidence of this is that none of Porter's films after *Life of an American Fireman* demonstrated anything like the same amount of cross-cutting, but that he continued to repeat actions between shots as per the 'copyright version' for some years. 'Ironically,' Musser observes, 'the innovations that many historians have attributed to Porter based on the modernized version of *Life of an American Fireman* – parallel editing and matching action – were the very procedures that Porter had the greatest difficulty executing.'[24]

Revisionist scholarship was not limited to reassessments of individual films, however: it also involved reconceptualizing the broad history of early cinema. André Gaudreault, for example, reconsidered the prevalence of tableau framing in early films, arguing that, rather than being dismissed as primitive or theatrical, the device could be understood as a strategy to represent 'the totality of an action unfolding in a homogenous space'.[25] (This perspective was influenced by the work of the French film theorist André Bazin, whose formulation of film aesthetics is discussed in the next chapter.) The most thoroughgoing attempt to theorize the history of early film form came from Noël Burch, who, in contrast to the teleological or evolutionary narrative propagated by the Standard Version, advanced instead a binary model of film practice in which a **Primitive Mode of Representation** (PMR) was superseded by an **Institutional Mode of Representation** (IMR). The IMR, which Burch associates with the Hollywood film after the introduction of sound, is posited on the creation of a fictional world on screen that maintains an illusion of reality: this **verisimilitude** is achieved through making film technique 'invisible' or 'transparent'. Unlike the Standard Version, which saw the early history of cinema as a period of experimental chaos in which the conventions of the classical narrative film took shape through a process of accident and discovery, Burch saw the PMR, which preceded the IMR, as 'a stable system with its own inherent logic and durability'.[26] The characteristics of the PMR included the centrality of the tableau, the prevalance of long shots and the non-closure of narrative. The PMR, Burch argued, persisted until around 1906, after which it was gradually overtaken by the emergence of the IMR.

Again the films of Edwin S. Porter were an important point of reference. In his essay 'Porter, or Ambivalence', for example, Burch argued that, rather than being 'the father of the story film' (as Lewis Jacobs had described him), Porter should be seen as more of a 'Janus' figure whose films exhibit both 'primitive' and 'progressive' elements. Thus the narrational innovations of films like *The Great Train Robbery*, such as the famous close-up of an outlaw firing a revolver at the camera, should be balanced against a film like *Uncle Tom's Cabin*, also made in 1903, and filmed in the 'purely primitive' style of tableau shots. And even in *Life of an American Fireman*, Porter links shots through a dissolve rather than a cut: this was not quite so forward-looking, as in the institutional mode a dissolve would come to represent a temporal rather than a spatial ellipsis. Burch sees Porter's films as emblematic of the co-existence of both the primitive and institutional modes, arguing that they embody 'a locus of contradictions which informed the development of cinema in its beginnings'.[27]

Another influential theorization of early cinema history was offered by Tom Gunning and his concept of a **'cinema of attractions'**. Gunning observes that 'early cinema was not dominated by the narrative impulse that later asserted its sway over the medium' and instead argues that what he terms the 'cinema of attractions' was dominant until around 1906–7.[28] The **genres** of early cinema – travelogues, **phantom rides**, trick films, gag films – had more in common with fairground 'attractions' than with stories. Gunning avers that 'the cinema of attractions directly solicits spectator engagement, inciting visual curiosity, and supplying pleasure through an exciting spectacle – a unique event, whether fictional or documentary, that is of interest in itself'.[29] Added to this was the fact that in the early days of cinema the real attraction was the new technology: early film shows were advertised by the names of the machines (such as the Cinématographe, the Biograph and the Vitascope) rather than the titles of the films. The cinema of attractions prevailed, according to Gunning, until 1906–7, when it was supplanted by a 'cinema of narrative integration'.

Gunning's work has been particularly influential in developing our understanding of early cinema. Its particular merits for the historian are that it does not indulge in evaluative assessments (unlike Burch there is no assumption that one form is necessarily better or worse than the other) and that it does not assume that the transition from the 'cinema of attractions' to the 'cinema of narrative integration' was a linear or even an inevitable process. Gunning points to a film such as Porter's *The Great Train Robbery* as exemplifying both modes in its combination of linear narrative and spectacle (the close up of the outlaw firing his revolver at the spectator). Gunning explains the transition from attractions to narrative not only in terms of film form, seeing the genre of the chase film which proliferated between 1903 and 1906 as 'a synthesis of attractions and narrative', but also in relation to changing exhibition practices with the shift of film from fairground sideshows to dedicated cinemas. Finally, just as aspects of Burch's PMR persisted beyond 1906, so the 'cinema of attractions' did not disappear entirely, but re-emerged occasionally, in epic spectacle films such as *Ben-Hur* (1924), in avant-garde film practice, and in the special effects-driven blockbusters of George Lucas and Steven Spielberg. To this extent the 'cinema of attractions', while originally developed as an explanatory model for early cinema, also has relevance to other periods of film history.

▶ Sociological film histories: Siegfried Kracauer and German cinema

The Standard Version was essentially a text-based approach focusing on matters of form and style: film history as the history of films. It tended to marginalize other approaches – cultural, economic, industrial and technological – which at best were seen as of secondary importance. One of the limitations of the Standard Version was its tendency to detach films from all but their aesthetic contexts: the result was a narrative that seemed to suggest that formal and stylistic developments occur in a vacuum unaffected by wider economic and cultural factors. However, an alternative to aesthetic film history began to take shape in the United States in the late 1940s. This was the sociological approach, which was interested not in the history of film as an art form but rather in what films could reveal about the societies and cultures in which they were produced and consumed. Among the pioneering sociological studies of film were Margaret Thorp's *America at the Movies* (1946), the first thoroughgoing investigation of the tastes, habits and preferences of American cinema-goers, and Hortense Powdermaker's *Hollywood the Dream Factory* (1950), a sociological study of the film industry. However, it was Siegfried Kracauer's history of German cinema – provocatively entitled *From Caligari to Hitler* (1947) – that represented the first application of sociology to the history of film.[30]

Kracauer was an émigré German academic based in the United States, working first at the Museum of Modern Art in New York and later at Columbia University. Although not a member of the **Frankfurt School** (the name applied to a group of émigré German academics previously from the Institute of Social Research at the University of Frankfurt who moved to Columbia in the 1930s, including Theodor Adorno, Max Horkheimer and Walter Benjamin), Kracauer shared their interest in the social effects of modern industrial capitalism and the relationship between mass-produced popular culture and society. In 1942 Kracauer published a pamphlet analysing the techniques of Nazi propaganda films, which in turn led to the award of a fellowship by the Guggenheim Institute to write a history of German cinema. As the first book to apply scholarly principles of evidence and analysis to the study of film history, *From Caligari to Hitler* represented an important historiographical landmark in the field – even if its methods are now regarded as flawed and its conclusions highly questionable.

Although briefly mapping the history of German film-making before and during the First World War, Kracauer focuses on the period between 1918 and 1933, the years of the Weimar Republic when German cinema enjoyed unprecedented artistic and cultural prestige. We have seen how aesthetic film historians such as Rotha regarded German Expressionism as one of the artistic triumphs of the medium. *The Cabinet of Dr Caligari*, generally regarded as the first fully Expressionist film, was released in Germany in 1919. Other films included *The Golem* (1920) *Nosferatu* (1922), *Dr Mabuse, the Gambler* (1922), *Warning Shadows* (1923), *Waxworks* (1924) and *The Last Laugh* (1924). These films are characterized by their extreme stylization: painted backdrops, distorted perspectives, **chiaroscuro** lighting, and actors who make no attempt at naturalistic performance but communicate through gestures. While other critics such as Rotha understood German Expressionism as a stylistic movement, however, Kracauer's approach was very different. He focused not on the artistic qualities of the films but rather on what they revealed about German society in the 1920s. His conclusions were startling: Kracauer saw the distorted perspectives and fragmented *mise-en-scène* of the films as reflecting social disclocation in Germany after the First World War, while the parade of madmen, murderers and insane master criminals who populated these films, he suggested, anticipated the rise to power of Hitler and the Nazis.

Kracauer's understanding of the relationship between film and society is stated at the outset:

> What films reflect are not so much explicit credos as psychological dispositions – those deep layers of collective mentality which extend more or less below the dimension of consciousness. Of course popular magazines and broadcasts, bestsellers, ads, fashions in language and other sedimentary products of a people's cultural life also yield valuable information about prominent attitudes, widespread inner tendencies. But the medium of the screen exceeds these sources in inclusiveness.[31]

Films reflect the 'mental climate' more directly than other media and art forms, Kracauer maintained, for two reasons. First they are collectively produced rather than the work of an individual: consequently individual impulses are subsumed within the dynamics of the group. And second films are produced for the mass audience and therefore can be understood as responding to mass desires: the commercial imperative of film-makers to attract the largest possible audience helps to ensure films reflect the outlook of their audiences.

Kracauer based his analysis of the German cinema between 1918 and 1933 on around a hundred films, which he discussed in terms of their plots, themes and *mise-en-scène*. While the most popular films are 'particularly suggestive of mass desires', he also includes other titles that might have been less successful but which demonstrate the persistence of particular themes and motifs. The key period for Kracauer is between 1918 and 1924, when 'the shock of freedom' following the abolition of censorship by the early Weimar government allowed film-makers to explore subjects, particularly crime and sex, that were hitherto circumscribed. He identifies recurring themes in films such as *The Cabinet of Dr Caligari*, *Nosferatu* and *Dr Mabuse, the Gambler*, particularly the choice between chaos on the one hand or tyranny on the other. The character of Dr Caligari, for example, 'stands for an unlimited authority that idolizes power as such, and, to satisfy its lust for domination, ruthlessly violates all human rights and values'.[32] This thematic articulation, Kracauer suggests, reflects the psychological disposition of the German people towards accepting authoritarian rule as an answer to their political and economic problems. It is no coincidence that the height of visual abstraction in German cinema, between 1918 and 1924, coincided with a period of extreme social and economic dislocation. A period of greater stability, between 1924 and 1929, coincided with the decline of abstraction and the emergence of a 'new realism' in German film. The Wall Street Crash of 1929 ushered in another period of acute social and economic distress, during which some of the motifs of high Expressionism resurfaced. Kracauer concludes that with the election of Hitler in 1933, Germany 'carried out what had been anticipated by her cinema from its very beginning, conspicuous screen characters now came true in life itself'.[33]

From Caligari to Hitler came to be regarded as 'the seminal historical account of the relationship between film and society'.[34] However, Kracauer's methodology has been much criticized. Paul Monaco, for example, takes him to task for 'mixing weak history with flimsy psychology' and for reading 'too much out of the films through hindsight'.[35] His analysis is based on a loose notion of **Zeitgeist** criticism which involves much generalization about such vague ideas as the 'mental climate', 'psychological disposition' and 'collective mentality' of the German people (even sometimes 'the German soul'). His notion of 'collective mentality' is especially problematic: Kracauer seems to regard German society as homogenous (even though this was a period of social and political dislocation) and assumes that all people shared much the same outlook. And his association of megalomaniacs such as Caligari and Mabuse with Nazi leaders such as Hitler and Goebbels is more of a rhetorical strategy than a persuasive historical argument. To suggest that films reflect the psychological orientation of audiences is one thing: to claim that they anticipate later developments is quite another.

There are other more particular flaws in Kracauer's methodology. For one thing his rejection of box-office data as a quantitative index of popularity is problematic. Others who generally accept the reflectionist argument argue that the quantitative popularity of films should be taken into account. As the social historian Arthur Marwick, for example, reminds us: 'There *is* a law of the market; the bigger its commercial success, the more a film is likely to tell us about the unvoiced assumptions of the people who watched it.'[36] Kracauer has also been criticized not only for basing his analysis on barely one-tenth of the approximately 1,000 films produced in Germany between 1918 and 1933 (he does not include any comedies or romantic dramas, which might suggest a different insight into the national psyche), but also for ignoring the fact that German films accounted for only 40 per cent of the market with escapist Hollywood films also faring well at the box office.[37] Finally, Kracauer also ignores the economic and cultural contexts of German cinema in the 1920s. It has since been argued, most comprehensively by Thomas Elsaesser, that the disorienting perspectives and stylized *mise-en-scène* of German films were less a reflection of a collective sense of paranoia than a deliberate and highly conscious strategy of cultural and economic differentiation. They should be understood as an attempt by the leading German film studio UFA (Universum Film Aktiengesellschaft) to establish itself in the international marketplace at a time when chronic inflation in Germany meant that its exports were cheap. In this reading Expressionist cinema was an economically as well as a culturally determined **mode of film practice**.[38]

▶ Institutional, economic and technological histories

Kracauer remained an isolated case of a non-aesthetically oriented approach to film history for nearly three decades. When film belatedly made its entry into the academic curriculum in the 1960s, it was the Standard Version that largely held sway. It was not until the 1970s and 1980s that a group of (mostly) American film historians – including Tino Balio, Rudy Behlmer, Douglas Gomery and Thomas Schatz – turned their attention to the institutional and economic history of the film industry.[39] The emergence of institutional history marked a further shift away from the Standard Version with its focus on film as an art form. Economic histories regard films not as works of art but as commodities: an alternative canon emerges in which the most significant films are not *The Cabinet of Dr Caligari*, *The Battleship Potemkin* and *Citizen Kane* but rather *Gone With the Wind*, *The Sound of Music* and *Avatar*. There are several reasons why the US film industry became the focus of institutional history. One explanation is simply that the US film industry has been the most successful, economically and culturally, in the history of cinema: it is inevitable, therefore, that its institutional and economic organization should demand attention. Another reason is that the US film industry is by some measure the best documented in the world: the paper records of most of the major studios, and of trade organizations such as the Motion Picture Producers Association, have been deposited with research libraries. Other national film industries are not so well served: there are no real equivalents of the Margaret Herrick Library outside America.[40]

Most institutional histories of the US film industry have focused on the hey-day of the studio system during the 1930s and 1940s. Some have documented the production strategies of particular studios, while others consider the wider context of the economic structure of the industry as a whole. The US film industry since the 1920s has been understood as a mature oligopoly in which economic power is exercised by a small group of large companies whose inter-est is to maintain the status quo. The model of economic organization that the US film industry adopted is known as **vertical integration**: the largest cor-porations (MGM, Warner Bros., Paramount, Twentieth Century-Fox and RKO) held interests in all three sectors of the industry – production, distribution and exhibition – meaning that they not only made their own films but also owned their own sales networks and movie theatres. In fact the period of full verti-cal integration was relatively short lived, lasting for barely two decades from the mid-1920s until 1948 when the US Supreme Court passed its historic ruling (known as the **Paramount Decree** because Paramount Pictures was the test case) that the major studios' ownership of first-run movie theatres (account-ing for over half of all box-office receipts) constituted an unfair monopoly and should be dismantled.[41] Other film industries that have achieved some degree of vertical integration include Japan (Nikkatsu, Shochiku and Toho), Germany (UFA), France (Gaumont-Franco-Film-Aubert and Pathé-Natan) and Britain (the Rank Organization and the Associated British Picture Corporation).[42]

Economic histories of the film industry have generally followed one of two models. On the one hand there is a Marxist (or, more pedantically, Marxisant) model of the economic history of film posited on a base–superstructure model in which economic power resides in the hands of a powerful oligopoly who control the industry according to their own interests. Here the argument is that the film industry functions as an agent of American capitalism in so far as it promotes the ideologies underlying that system. Thomas Guback, for example, contends that 'motion pictures naturally support dominant thought patterns and are especially noncritical of the economic system that nurtures them'.[43] One does not have to be a Marxist to realize that what is at stake in films such as *Mr Smith Goes to Washington* (1939) or *Wall Street* (1987) is not the political or economic system *per se* but rather the abuse of the system by corrupt and self-interested individuals. Another characteristic of Marxist histories is their view of the relationship between the industry and its consumers as entirely one-sided. Kerry Segrave's study of the overseas distribution of American films, for example, concludes:

> Hollywood integrates its consumers from the top down; producing a product for mass consumption, then creating a demand for it. There is no common demand from the bottom up, forcing the cartel to produce certain types of movies. The

US industry is not subject to public demand, rather the public is the subject of calculation and manipulation by the industry.[44]

On the other hand the business history model argues, contrary to the Marxist view, that the film industry is led entirely by market forces and that producers are only responding to popular demand. As Nick Roddick observes in his study of the production strategies of the Warner Bros. studio in the 1930s: 'This is, after all, a normal industrial pattern: the market determines what is manufactured, not vice versa. And only by denying the basically industrial nature of film production can film criticism manage to ignore this fact.'[45] It has been shown time and again that no amount of advertising and marketing can sell a film if the public is not interested: otherwise *Heaven's Gate* (1980) and *Raise the Titanic!* (1980) would not have lost their producers millions at the box office. Kristin Thompson's historical study of overseas trade in the 1920s and 1930s provides a counterweight to the work of Guback and Segrave. Thompson documents how the US film industry adopted an aggressive overseas marketing campaign following the disruption of European film production during the First World War. However, she concludes that the success of American films in maintaining their pre-eminent market position when indigenous European production revived in the 1920s was due essentially to market forces. Put simply audiences preferred Hollywood films because of their superior production values: 'American films were longer and had popular stars, lavish *mise en scène* and skilful cinematography; during the war these changes in the Hollywood film gained for it a definite following and other national industries would have difficulty in creating films as attractive.'[46]

The history of film technology is another approach that has developed largely due to the availability of archive materials. Most technological histories focus on key moments in the history of the industry and the adoption of new technologies such as sound, colour and **widescreen**. Much technological history is overtly deterministic in so far as the technology to make films has to exist before the artistic possibilities of the medium can be explored. Thus, for example, Raymond Fielding asserts: 'All my work as an historian has proceeded from the premise that the history of the motion picture – as an art form, as a medium of communication, and as an industry – has been determined principally by technological innovations and considerations.'[47] However, the history of technology alone does not explain the history of the medium. Quite often there has been a considerable time lag between technological innovations and the adoption of that technology by the industry. **Widescreen** cinematography is an oft-cited example: **anamorphic** lenses had been developed in the 1920s but it was not until the 1950s that anamorphic widescreen processes were adopted by the film industry when, faced with declining audiences, it turned to widescreen spectaculars as a means of differentiating cinema from the rival medium of television.[48] And film-makers have responded to technological change in different ways. Charlie Chaplin, for example, resisted the arrival of talking pictures, filming *City Lights* (1931) and *Modern Times* (1936) with synchronized soundtracks but no dialogue, until finally succumbing to the inevitability of talkies in *The Great Dictator* (1940). Here, clearly, aesthetic considerations outweighed technological determinism. At the other extreme modern film-makers such as George Lucas, Steven Spielberg, James Cameron and Peter Jackson have been quick to adopt new technologies. Here there are both economic and aesthetic imperatives at work: the production discourses of films such as Jackson's *The Lord of the Rings* trilogy (2001–3) and Cameron's *Avatar* (2009) emphasize the role of state-of-the-art special effects in order to realize their imaginative visions of fantasy worlds.

The complex relationship between institutional, economic and technological histories is nowhere better demonstrated than in accounts of the arrival of talking pictures at the end of the 1920s. This case study also shows how archival research has challenged the Standard Version of film history. The old histories of Hollywood saw the adoption of talking pictures as a desperate gamble by one studio, Warner Bros., which was facing bankruptcy and needed a gimmick to draw audiences into its recently (and expensively) acquired movie theatres. This was the version of its own history mythologized by Hollywood in the musical *Singin' in the Rain* (1952) in which the rest of the industry expected Warners to 'lose their shirts' and were taken aback by the unexpected success of *The Jazz Singer*. Lewis Jacobs describes the chaos that beset the industry in the wake of *The Jazz Singer*: 'The entire industry, now in a panic, rushed into the production of sound pictures, hoping to make up for lost time; overnight Hollywood became frantic with the mad race to catch up with Warner.'[49]

This narrative has been challenged by revisionist historians, led by Douglas Gomery, who have argued that, rather than being a gamble, the adoption of sound was part and parcel of a planned strategy by Warner Bros. to establish itself as one of the leading film companies alongside the likes of industry giants MGM and Paramount. Warner Bros. embarked upon an ambitious, and risky, but carefully executed expansion strategy that included the acquisition of the First National theatre chain and the formation, in partnership with Western Electric, of a subsidiary called the Vitaphone Corporation to market sound equipment for producers and exhibitors. Warner Bros., always a thrifty studio, was bankrolled by the investment bank Goldman Sachs, which was impressed by the studio's strict accounting and tight budgetary control. The studio was not facing bankruptcy: its investments in movie theatres and sound technology led to a loss in 1926 but this 'was simply a case of well-financed, well-planned short-run indebtedness'.[50] The success of this strategy can be seen in the fact that the Stock Market value of Warner Bros. increased from $5 million in 1925 to $230 million in 1930.

There were other factors at play too. Warner Bros. was not an isolated example. The Fox Film Corporation, a culturally ambitious studio, also invested in sound technology and, like Warner Bros., tested the market with shorts before releasing its first feature-length talking pictures, *Sunny Side Up* and *In Old Arizona*, in 1929. Again this can be seen as part of a commercial strategy by the studio – a strategy that also included hiring the acclaimed German director F. W. Murnau to direct the 'artistic picture' *Sunrise* (1928), with synchronized soundtrack but no dialogue, an expensive film that demonstrated a significant degree of cultural ambition on the studio's part.[51] In this context the 'gamble' taken by Warner Bros. was consistent with developments across the industry at large.

The most recent account of the arrival of talking pictures sees 'the transition to sound as partly rational and partly confused'.[52] While Warner Bros. was the first studio to take the plunge, it had opted for a sound-on-disc system whereby sound was recorded on wax records. This was the system used for *The Jazz Singer*, but it proved technically cumbersome and was soon abandoned: it is ironic that the 'first talking picture' *The Jazz Singer* was also the last hurrah for this process. It was the rival sound-on-film system, utilizing a photo-electric cell, adopted by Fox that would become the industry standard. Warner Bros. and Fox were the first studios to convert wholesale to the production of sound films, followed by MGM and Paramount. There were two notable industrial consequences of the conversion to sound. One was the formation of a new vertically integrated company when the Radio Corporation of America patented its own sound-on-film system and acquired its own chain of movie theatres (Radio-Keith-Orpheum) to form RKO Radio Pictures. And another was the forging of alliances between Hollywood and Wall Street as the studios had to find the capital investment (estimated at a total of $500 million across the industry) necessary to convert their stages and movie theatres to sound. Unknown to the studios at the time, this relationship would ensure their survival following the Wall Street Crash.

▷ The rise and fall of 'Screen theory'

Gomery concludes his article on Warner Bros. and the introduction of talking pictures with a call 'to search out new sources of primary data'. 'Only then,' he suggests, 'can the type of history of the American film industry emerge that Buscombe demands, and Cripps, Comolli and other film-and-ideology analysts so vitally need'.[53] Gomery's article had been published in the journal *Screen*: his mild dig at the work of Edward Buscombe (whose article 'Notes on Columbia Pictures Corporation' had been published in the same journal the previous year) and Jean-Luc Comolli (whose co-authored article 'Cinema/Ideology/ Criticism' had appeared in English translation in *Screen*) needs to be understood in the context of a methodological and ideological schism that emerged in the 1970s between film history on the one hand and a new brand of film theory on the other. Much of this theory was associated with *Screen*: hence **'Screen theory'** became a catch-all term that defined a particular approach to the study of cinema as (in the Althusserian sense) an **'ideological apparatus'**.[54]

So much ink and fury has been spilled over 'Screen theory' that it is worth taking a moment to consider its contribution to the history of film scholarship. And in order to do this properly it is necessary to consider the ideological and intellectual contexts in which 'Screen theory' took shape. Essentially it emerged from a polemical dissatisfaction with the existing approaches to film analysis – *auteur* **theory** and **genre** criticism – in the early 1970s. *Screen*, published by the Society for Education in Film and Television (SEFT), was an outgrowth of *Screen Education*, which in the 1970s departed from the film-educational remit of its sister journal and embraced new theoretical perspectives, particularly **structuralism** and **semiotics**, which were seen as offering a more analytical, even scientific, method of analysis than the aesthetic criticism that had hitherto held sway. 'Screen theory' can be seen as an outcome of the radicalization of intellectual culture in the late 1960s – witnessed most dramatically in France in May 1968 – as well as a strategy to legitimate film studies by adopting the language of high theory. It advanced the idea of cinema as an 'apparatus' rather than an art form, drawing upon perspectives informed by Marxism (particularly its Althusserian variant) and psychoanalysis (the Lacanian variety especially). However, it would be misleading to see 'Screen theory' as a homogenous practice: indeed the editorials in *Screen* itself often allude to profound theoretical differences within the editorial board.[55]

To its critics (of whom there were many even within film studies) 'Screen theory' represented an elitist intellectual clique whose worst feature was its recourse to obtuse and jargon-riddled language that could be understood only by fellow initiates.[56] (This tendency gave rise to many jokes at its expense. My favourite is the one about the poststructuralist Godfather: he's the one who makes you an offer you can't understand.) It also seemed to be a project whose aim was to construct a totalizing theory of cinema as an ideological apparatus – a theory in which neither history nor aesthetics had any place. If we leave aside the resort to theoretical jargon, there are two major criticisms that can be levelled against 'Screen theory'. The first is that its search for an all-encompassing explanatory framework led to a tendency to homogenize the nature of cinema and to overlook the very real differences between film texts. Indeed one will search in vain for references to actual films in some articles, while one of the shortcomings of an essay such as Laura Mulvey's widely-cited 'Visual Pleasure and Narrative Cinema' is that it makes a series of broad assumptions based on a brief analysis of films by two directors (Josef Von Sternberg and Alfred Hitchcock) neither of whom can be said to be representative of classical Hollywood.[57] The second criticism is that advocates of 'Screen theory' detached cinema from its historical contexts. There is a tendency to see films as autonomous 'texts' and to regard the ideological structure of the cinematic apparatus as fixed and unchanging. Accordingly there is no real engagement with cinema as either a historical or a social process. Yet even Marx understood that capitalism was not a fixed structure but one that underwent a process of historical transformation.

It would be fair to say that 'Screen theory' shared little common ground with the sort of film history being practised by British and American scholars in the 1970s. The result was a rift that opened up along ideological and methodological fault lines and led to a generation of unproductive hostility between the two rival schools. This has particularly been the case in Britain, where ideological differences perhaps also reveal a continued sense of unease over the academic legitimacy of film studies: rival methodologies become rhetorical strategies through which different groups claim intellectual ownership of the discipline. One example must suffice to illustrate these differences. In 1983 the publication of an anthology volume, *British Cinema History*, prompted a quite extraordinary exchange between one of the editors, Vincent Porter, and Andrew Higson, who had reviewed the book, appropriately enough, in *Screen*.[58] Higson was highly critical of what he saw as the 'essentially sociological model of cinema' offered by the contributors to *British Cinema History* on the grounds that they reveal 'a fairly traditional sociological approach to representation and ideology, which tends too often to reproduce the dominant realist aesthetic of British film criticism'. He saw the book as redolent of 'orthodox film criticism' and felt that its failure to address either the nature of independent cinema or the existing critical framework for studying British cinema meant that it had little to offer for 'the radical film theorist'.[59] Porter complained that Higson's review 'imposes a reading of *British Cinema History* which is not substantiated by the text' and that 'he is not only in danger of misrepresenting *British Cinema History* to your readers, but, perhaps more seriously, of implying that film theory can offer more to film history than it has yet achieved and that its potential for developing an independent cinema and film culture is more significant than is in fact the case.'[60] Higson in turn replied that Porter's letter 'is very much within the same terms of reference as that volume's editorialising' and pointed to 'his refusal to accept that the editorial structuring of *British Cinema History* serves only to reproduce those ideologies'.[61]

It will be clear that what is at stake here is much more than a difference of opinion over the nature of British cinema or the pedagogic value of one particular book. The dispute also reveals deep-rooted ideological differences over the purpose of film criticism. On this point Higson highlights a fundamental difference between film history and film theory:

> Porter may think that the purpose of the film historian is 'to understand and assess the role of film in British society and its historical development'. *Screen's* task, however, must be to work towards transforming the role of film in society, to help build an independent cinema and film culture. This involves thoroughly challenging the traditional ways in which, for instance, British cinema has been conceptualised.[62]

While the dispute itself was unproductive, merely serving to embed further what were clearly entrenched attitudes on both sides, it did nevertheless throw into sharp relief very different understandings of the role of film scholarship. On the one hand film historians saw their task as being to explore the institutional, economic, cultural, aesthetic and technological contexts of cinema and in so doing to shed light on its historical role in reflecting and shaping society. On the other hand 'Screen theory' was committed to a radical project to challenge prevailing approaches and in so doing to bring about a transformation in film culture itself.

By this time, however, 'Screen theory' had run its course. It had never been – and to be fair had never really claimed to be – a homogenous critical practice. 'Screen theory' drew upon such a diverse range of theoretical ideas – including Althusserian Marxism, Lacanian psychoanalysis, structural linguistics and radical feminism – that it was never able to establish a secure intellectual framework for its analysis of cinema as an ideological apparatus. The totalizing theory of cinema that for a while it had seemed to promise remained elusive. In the 1980s 'Screen theory' fractured under the weight of its internal theoretical and ideological contradictions. Several of the key proponents, such as Stephen Heath and Colin MacCabe, shifted into literary and cultural studies. Others, including Laura Mulvey and Steve Neale, embraced the 'historical turn' that followed the high point of film theory.[63] And *Screen* itself matured into a more inclusive journal, embracing new methodological developments such as gender studies in the 1980s and reception theory in the 1990s. It is important to note, moreover, that even during its 'theoretical turn' in the 1970s *Screen* remained more catholic in its contents than some of its critics have alleged. It included, for example, in addition to Gomery's article on Warner Bros. and sound, important historical pieces by Charles Barr (whose study of the critical response to *Straw Dogs* and *A Clockwork Orange* was an early example of reception studies), Edward Buscombe (on the history of Columbia Pictures), Patrick Ogle (on the aesthetic and technological contexts for the development of **deep-focus cinematography**) and John Ellis (exploring how British critics in the 1940s set the discursive terms for British film culture that were not properly challenged until the 1970s).[64]

▶ New Film History

The period since the mid-1980s has seen the emergence of what has come to be called 'New Film History'. The term was first used by Thomas Elsaesser in a review essay in 1985, where he suggested that New Film History was the outcome of two pressures: on the one hand 'a polemical dissatisfaction with the surveys and overviews…that for too long passed as film history', and on the other hand 'sober arguments among professionals now that…much more material has become available, for instance on the early silent period'.[65] Other developments in the 1980s included the widespread availability of video recorders and players, meaning that old films no longer had to be seen in archives or revival cinemas, and which made easier the close textual analysis of films, and the increasing expansion, and diversification, of film studies programmes at university level. New Film History also marked a *rapprochement* of sorts between the extremes of empirical history and high theory. Elsaesser saw in New Film History the possibility 'that what I have described as the history of the cinema may reconcile itself with the concerns of film theory'.[66] Jeffrey Richards, himself a staunch defender of empirical methods, also detected 'a rewarding convergence between the two approaches, as cinema historians have taken on board some of the more useful and illuminating of the theoretical developments, such as gender theory, and the Film Studies scholars have been grounding their film analysis more securely in historical context'.[67]

The foundational text of New Film History – and undoubtedly one of the landmarks of modern film scholarship – is David Bordwell, Janet Staiger and Kristin Thompson's highly influential book *The Classical Hollywood Cinema* (1985), a *magnum opus* that explores both the historical development of film style and the institutionalization of working practices in the US film industry between the late 1910s and *c.*1960. The primary focus of *The Classical Hollywood Cinema* is on the relationship between film style on the one hand (characterized as a set of norms and conventions) and the mode of production (how films are made) on the other: the institutionalization of style and mode of production are mutually reinforcing and each helps to perpetuate the other. In this analysis **classical Hollywood cinema** between 1917 and 1960 is understood as a mode of film practice characterized by 'a set of widely held stylistic norms sustained by and sustaining an integral mode of production'.[68] The authors show how 'style and industry came to be so closely synchronized by 1917': the classical narrative film become the dominant style, while the studio-based mode of production, based on a hierarchical management system and a specialized division of labour, was firmly established.[69] This mode of film practice remained in place for the next four decades. Later technological developments – sound, colour and widescreen – did not fundamentally alter the style of films but were assimilated into the classical style. The introduction of sound, for example, did not retard film style as severely as some advocates of the Standard Version maintained: the early technological problems were soon overcome and the camera regained its mobility so that by 1933 'shooting a sound film came to mean shooting a silent film with sound'.[70] Bordwell, Staiger and Thompson argue that 1960 marks the end of the classical period because 'it was widely believed that at the end of the decade Hollywood had reached the end of its mature existence' and 'a certain technological state of the art had been reached'.[71] While the classical film did not disappear – the authors suggest that a modified version of the classical film has continued to be the norm for Hollywood – its ascendancy was 'reduced somewhat' by structural changes in the film industry and by the dissemination of 'alternative' modes of film practice (such as European art cinema) in the 1960s.

The Classical Hollywood Cinema exemplifies a method known as **historical poetics**: the analysis of a group style in its historical contexts. There are two particular features that align it with New Film History. The first is that the methodology is analytical rather than evaluative: the authors are concerned to describe and explain changes in film style but do not indulge in making aesthetic or cultural judgements about the value of particular films. Their stylistic analysis is based on an 'unbiased sample' of 100 films selected in such a way that they were 'not biased by personal preferences or conceptions of influential or masterful films': thus 1941 is represented not by *Citizen Kane* or *How Green Was My Valley* but rather by *Appointment with Love*, *King of the Zombies*, *Play Girl* and *We Go Fast*.[72] The second distinguishing feature is that as well as the films, the authors examine what they term 'trade discourses' – production materials, scripts, technical manuals, trade journals – in order to show how the classical style was institutionalized by the working practices of the studios.

The Classical Hollywood Cinema is not above criticism, of course. The notion of an 'unbiased sample' is problematic – silent films are under-represented as fewer have survived, and a statistical fluke means that more Warner Bros. films are included than other studios' – while a dozen indexed references to *Citizen Kane*, including a three-page discussion of Gregg Toland's use of **deep-focus cinematography** in the film, demonstrate that the authors range beyond their sample when it suits them. It has been argued that the idea of an 'invisible' or 'transparent' style of narration being institutionalized during this period ignores genres such as comedy and the musical where a more self-reflexive style was the norm.[73] The tendency to see directors with a recognizable personal style such as Alfred Hitchcock or Orson Welles, and particular movements such as **film noir**, as operating within the 'bounds of difference' of classical film perhaps downplays the significance of their departures from the norm: *film noir*, for example, has been understood as representing a fracture in classical Hollywood.[74] Above all *The Classical Hollywood Cinema* can be criticized on the same grounds as 'Screen theory': that it attempts to create a holistic model and a totalizing explanatory framework that claims it can account for all films produced within the studio system.

'The historical hegemony of Hollywood makes acute and urgent the need to study film styles and modes of production that differ from Hollywood's,' Bordwell remarks.[75] It is perhaps an indication of the massive (and intimidating) work of historical scholarship that is *The Classical Hollywood Cinema* that its methods have not been widely applied to other film industries. Colin Crisp's *The Classic French Cinema 1930–1960* (1993), Thomas Elsaesser's *New German Cinema* (1989) and Bordwell's own *Planet Hong Kong* (2000) are perhaps the closest equivalents.[76] Instead the main trend within New Film History has been towards the investigation of historically specific genres or movements rather than whole film industries. Sue Harper's *Picturing the Past: The Rise and Fall of the British Costume Film* (1994) is exemplary in this regard: Harper explores the 'social function of historical film' at the height of its popularity during the 1930s and 1940s and through a combination of archival research and textual analysis demonstrates how the genre mobilized history as a means of articulating discourses around class and gender. Unlike Bordwell & Co., however, she opts for depth of analysis rather than breadth of coverage, suggesting that 'the historian ought to produce a geology of culture in a specific period and medium…It seemed to me that such a project, though broad in its implications, had to be narrowly focused to have any credibility.'[77]

There is sometimes a danger that New Film History will become an overarching term to cover all film histories written since the 1980s. It should rather be understood as a broad methodological trend in the discipline: some would even consider it a methodology in its own right.[78] In recent years the term has been adopted particularly by British film historians – including Melanie Bell, Laurie Ede, Mark Glancy, Lawrence Napper, Justin Smith and Andrew Spicer – who, while writing on a wide range of subjects, share some common methodological assumptions.[79] There are several characteristics of New Film History. One is its emphasis on the central importance of primary sources in documenting the production and reception histories of films: thus the film historian spends as much time in libraries and archives as watching films. Such sources include government records (for example the papers of the US Department of Commerce or the British Board of Trade), studio archives, personal papers, memoirs, scripts, press releases, publicity materials, censors' reports, trade papers, fan magazines, reviews and social surveys of cinema-going. It is only through the analysis of primary sources that the historical conditions and processes which shape the production and reception of films can be ascertained. This archival rigour is complemented by the cultural competence to 'read' films not only through their narrative and content but also through their formal properties and visual style. In particular the historian is alert to the 'look' and 'sound' of films and is able to analyse the representational discourses at work within them (direction, camerawork, art direction, costume design, sound effects, and so on).

All this adds up to a greater methodological sophistication in our understanding of the relationship between text and context. No longer is film understood as a 'reflection' or 'mirror' of its historical context *à la* Kracauer, but nor is it seen in the abstract theoretical terms of 'semiotic codes' and 'signifying practices'. Rather film is understood as a complex cultural artefact whose form and content are the outcome of the many processes – ideological, industrial, economic, technological, social, aesthetic – that shape the final product. The film text itself can be understood as the residue of the production process: the outcome of all the decisions taken and compromises made during its journey to the screen. Quite often the travails of production are embedded in the finished film: an uneven film often indicates a troubled production history (Orson Welles's *Othello* or Michael Cimino's *Heaven's Gate*, for example), while a well-constructed film is generally the outcome of a smooth production process (such as Hitchcock's *Rear Window* or – contrary to received wisdom – *Casablanca*). The key concepts are agency (the role of individuals including producers, writers, directors, cinematographers, editors and actors) and process (including scripting, costing, shooting, post-production, and interventions from external agencies such as censors).

One of the underlying assumptions of New Film History is that film is a medium and an industry in a constant state of flux: production cycles come and go, and styles change as film-makers negotiate structural change in the industry and respond to changes in audience tastes. Film history itself is also constantly changing, adapting and evolving in response to a changing intellectual landscape: new sources come to light, new research questions arise, new methodological problems are addressed. Like all history, film history is – or at least it should be – a constant process of discovery, evaluation and re-evaluation.

2 Film as an Art Form

The history of the movies is, first of all, the history of a new art.

Gerald Mast[1]

The most common approach by far to film history is aesthetic – the history of film as an art form. It is quite common for works of film history to describe themselves in this way. Terry Ramsaye, for example, begins his book *A Million and One Nights* with the statement that it 'endeavours to cover the birth of a new art'.[2] Mark Cousins, writing nearly 80 years later, similarly avers that his book *The Story of Film* 'tells the story of the art of cinema'.[3] To describe film as an art form – or an individual film as a work of art – assumes that a degree of cultural or aesthetic value is being attached to it. We should acknowledge from the outset that not all cultural commentators would necessarily accept Mast's assertion that film is an art form. Marxist critics, such as those associated with the **Frankfurt School** in the 1930s and 1940s, have argued that film cannot be considered an art because it is, first and foremost, a commercial product. Theodor Adorno and Max Horkheimer, for example, in their influential *Dialectic of Enlightenment* – a sustained polemic against what they termed the 'culture industry' – claimed that 'all mass culture is identical'. 'Movies', they asserted, 'no longer pretend to be art. The truth that they are just business is made into an ideology in order to justify the rubbish they deliberately produce.'[4] A less polemical, and more common, position is to accept that some films might be deemed works of art whereas others are not, while many critics distinguish between an **art cinema** on the one hand and a commercial or mainstream cinema on the other.

Aesthetic film history has largely concerned itself with two major questions. The first is what are the qualities or properties unique to the medium of film that define its 'essence'? This is the project of **classical film aesthetics** as it emerged in the early and mid-twentieth century. Classical film aesthetics is concerned with the nature of film as a medium of representation and expression. It revolves around the relationship between film and the 'real' world and concerns the degree to which film can or should be a realistic representation of external social and physical conditions. The other major concern of aesthetic film history has been how to resolve the tension at the heart of the medium between art and industry, between culture and commerce. How can we reconcile the

Romantic idea of the film-maker as a creative artist with the institutionalized nature of the film-making process? One answer to this conundrum is offered by advocates of the *auteur* **theory**, who maintain that, despite the industrial context of film production, creative agency resides with the director who should be regarded as the 'author' of the finished film. Another approach, known as **Neoformalism**, applies the method of **historical poetics** in order to examine the relationships between film style (often in the form of nationally and culturally specific movements) and the historical conditions in which films are produced. Finally, all these approaches are explored through a short case study of *Citizen Kane*, a film that has regularly featured in polls of the 'best' films ever made and which holds a privileged place in aesthetic histories of film.

► Classical film aesthetics

Classical film aesthetics as it developed in the first half of the twentieth century can be split into two major schools or traditions: what, following J. Dudley Andrew, are generally termed 'formative' and 'realist'.[5] On the one hand **realist film theory** asserts that the unique formal property of film is its ability to reproduce life-like images of people, places and objects: the art of film therefore rests upon it achieving a close representation of external physical reality. On the other hand **formative film theory** maintains that film becomes art only when it goes beyond the photographic reproduction of external reality and uses the formal properties of the medium for expressive effect. A similar distinction informs classical aesthetics in art. On the one hand there is the view, deriving from Aristotle, that 'art imitates life' and that the role of the artist is to record nature – a tradition that informed painting from the Renaissance to the Impressionists. On the other hand there is the tradition of abstract, non-naturalist art – exemplified by movements such as Cubism, Dadaism, Expressionism and Surrealism – which rejects the tenets of naturalism and believes that the role of the artist is to express ideas, moods or feelings, and that this might be done in abstract form. The same distinction is also made in relation to the history of the novel between realists such as Austen, Dickens, Balzac and Tolstoy, and modernists such as Conrad, Joyce, Proust and Woolf.

The intellectual parallels between classical film aesthetics and other artistic practices assume particular significance when we consider the historical development of film as an art form. On the one hand film turned to literature, especially the nineteenth-century novel, as a source for both cultural legitimacy and formal structure. The desire for cultural legitimacy is seen in the proliferation of adaptations of classic literature during the early 1900s: there were numerous short adaptations of the works of Dickens, Tolstoy, Ibsen and Scott, for example. In France the Société Film D'Art was founded in 1908 to produce adaptations of stage plays featuring well-known theatre performers of the day. At the same times the realist conventions and formal structure of the novel were adapted into film: the basic principles of the **classical narrative film** such as **verisimilitude** (preserving the appearance of being 'real') and the formal organization of the story (beginning – middle – end) are largely based on the nineteenth-century novel. On the other hand, however, film also embraced **modernism**, in which the forms of story-telling and representation assume precedence over the story itself. This is evident in the emergence of stylistic abstraction – Expressionism and Surrealism both crossed over into film in the 1920s, for example – and in the self-conscious narration that characterized European art cinema after the Second World War.

The distinction between realist and formative aesthetics was inherent in film from the outset, exemplified on the one hand by the *actualité* films of the Lumière brothers and on the other by the magic films of Georges Méliès. David Bordwell has suggested that Lumière and Méliès represent 'the two founts of cinema'. 'Since Lumière,' he amplifies, 'motion pictures have been attracted to the detailed reproduction of external reality.' 'From Méliès' theatrical stylization and cinematic sleight-of-hand,' in contrast, 'come the distorted décor of Caligari and the camera experimentation of the European avant-garde.'[6] While this distinction may seem somewhat over-schematic, as in practice there is significant formal interaction between the two modes – *Citizen Kane*, for example, has been claimed by advocates of both schools – the two traditions have nevertheless been highly influential in the cultural appreciation and artistic evaluation of film. The formative school privileges film styles and movements where the formal aspects of *mise-en-scène* take prominence over narrative, such as the cinema of **German Expressionism**, and films structured around **montage**, such as the Soviet films of the 1920s. It also champions film-makers who reveal their mastery of the techniques of montage, such as D. W. Griffith, Sergei Eisenstein, Abel Gance, Alfred Hitchcock, John Ford and Akira Kurosawa. The realist school, in contrast, prefers movements such as French **Poetic Realism** and Italian **Neo-Realism** and the films of directors who favour slow narration or who demonstrate a 'poetic' visual style, such as Jean Renoir, Robert Bresson, Yasujiro Ozu, Satyajit Ray, Michelangelo Antonioni and Andrei Tarkovsky. The evolution of the canon of film art and the changing critical reputations of certain films and film-makers owe much to the ascendancy of these different theories of film aesthetics.

▶ The formative tradition

The first tradition to achieve intellectual ascendancy, during the 1920s and 1930s, was the formative school. Its chief proponents were the German intellectuals Hugo Munsterberg and Rudolf Arnheim, the Hungarian theorist and film-maker Béla Belázs, and the Soviet-Russian directors Lev Kuleshov, Vsevolod Pudovkin and Sergei Eisenstein. The formative theorists drew a distinction between the raw material of film (the image recorded by the camera) and the formal principles that turned the raw material into cinema. Belázs used the analogy of sculpture: 'A stone on the hillside and the stone of one of Michelangelo's sculptures are both stone … It is not the substance but the form that constitutes the difference between them.'[7] The underlying principle of the montage theories of the Soviet school was that it was not the raw film but its assembly into a sequence that mattered. According to Kuleshov: 'It was now perfectly clear to us that individual shots, the separate parts of a film, were only filmic material but not cinema proper … It was not important how the separate shots were taken. What mattered was how they were arranged, how the motion picture was assembled.'[8]

There are several characteristics of most formative theory. One is its emphasis on the uniqueness of film. While film shares certain features with painting, photography, literature and theatre, it is nevertheless distinct from other art forms by virtue of the formal properties unique to the medium. These include cinematography, editing and *mise-en-scène*. Formative theory often speaks about film in terms of its 'plasticity' – the idea that the image is moulded and shaped. Another characteristic is its teleological view of film style: the idea that film developed as it did due to a process of 'discovery'. This perspective is exemplified by Rudolf Arnheim's *Film as Art* (published in German in 1932 and later translated into English):

> It is easy to understand that film directors only very gradually arrived at making use of these means … What had hitherto been merely the urge to record certain actual events, now became the aim to represent objects by special means exclusive to film. These means obtrude themselves, show themselves able to do more than simply reproduce the required object; they sharpen it, impose a style upon it, point out special features, make it vivid and decorative. Art begins where mechanical reproduction leaves off, where the conditions of representation serve in some way to mould the object.[9]

This is a characteristic statement of the formative school: Arnheim goes on to list the ways in which film differs from reality, including the two-dimensional nature of film, the framing of the image, and the use of editing to disrupt spatial and temporal continuities.

The development of formative film theory was in part a response to developments in the medium during the 1920s. In particular German Expressionism and **Soviet montage** were held up as **paradigm**s of formative aesthetics. These movements demonstrated how film was able to transcend the photographic reproduction of reality either through visual abstraction (German Expressionism) or through editing (Soviet montage). The 'plastic' *mise-en-scène* of Expressionist films such as *The Cabinet of Dr Caligari*, *Nosferatu* and *Warning Shadows* with their distorted perspectives, acute camera angles and **chiaro-scuro** lighting creates a fictional world that is far removed from reality. The visual style of Expressionist cinema has been understood as a means of reflecting the psychological and emotional state of the characters and creating a mood of paranoia and nightmare.[10]

It was Soviet cinema, however, that most fully embraced formative aesthetics, both in theory and as practice. In the mid-1920s a series of 'Jubilee' films were commissioned by the new Soviet state to commemorate the revolutionary struggle and to promote the ideology of Bolshevism. These films included Sergei Eisenstein's *Strike* (1925), *The Battleship Potemkin* (1925), *October* (1928) and *The General Line* (1929), Vsevolod Pudovkin's *Mother* (1926), *The End of St Petersburg* (1927) and *Storm Over Asia* (1928), Alexander Dovzhenko's *Zvenigora* (1928) and *Arsenal* (1929), and Esfir Shub's *The Fall of the Romanov Dynasty* (1927). These films were all characterized by their use of montage – rhythmic editing, short shots, rapid cutting – and by their representation of historical events as mass movements rather than as personal stories in the style of **classical Hollywood cinema**.[11]

The principal tenet underlying Soviet montage theory was the belief that meaning in film arose not so much from the individual shot as through the way in which the sequence of shots were edited together. Lev Kuleshov, who headed an Experimental Film Workshop in the 1920s, argued that montage 'is the most important thing in the overall construction of a picture'. 'Montage', he added, 'is the means of mastering and organizing the filmic material, and of mastering and organizing the viewer's impressions and emotions. Montage makes film different from the theatre and saves it from the dreary role of a moving photograph.'[12] This reminds us that montage was not only a theory of film form (what made film different from other arts) but also a device of film propaganda (to influence the responses of the spectator). Much of the subsequent discussion of montage has focused on its theoretical application and has tended to overlook its propagandistic intent. The famous **Kuleshov Experiment** is taken as the starting point of montage theory in practice. Kuleshov filmed actor Ivan Mozhukhin looking at the camera and edited it together with other images that according to the written accounts (the original film experiment does not survive) included a bowl of soup, a dead body and a baby. Audiences who saw the test reportedly praised Mozhukhin's acting, registering hunger as he looked at the bowl of soup, sorrow for the dead friend and love for the baby, even though on each occasion the shot of his face was the same.[13]

Although Kuleshov directed only a handful of films – his best known was the satire *The Extraordinary Adventures of Mr West in the Land of the Bolsheviks* (1924) – his students, including Pudovkin and Eisenstein, embraced his teaching and proceeded to put theory into practice. The narrative structures and formal components of Soviet montage films are highly distinctive. They downplay the role of the individual and focus instead on representing revolutionary movements as social and historical processes. They employ a device known as **typage** to represent different character types on a symbolic level rather than as individuals. And in contrast to the classical style, which relied on **continuity editing** and 'invisible' cuts, Soviet montage films use devices such as **elliptical editing** and **jump cuts** that jar and shock the spectator. The Soviet school acknowledged its debt to D. W. Griffith, whose films *The Birth of a Nation* and *Intolerance* demonstrated an embryonic form of montage in practice, but theorized the technique and took it much further. In particular the Soviet films of the 1920s feature more shots and have a shorter average shot length than other films of the time: hence the spatial and temporal relations within the films are more complex.[14]

Yet Soviet montage was not a homogeneous practice: there were subtle but important differences between practitioners. Pudovkin and Eisenstein are associated with two, opposing theories of montage. Pudovkin advocated what he called 'structural montage' in which individual shots were put together like building blocks. He argued that the sequence of shots 'must correspond to the natural transference of attention of an imaginary observer' and should demonstrate 'a special logic that will be apparent only if each shot contains an impulse towards transference of attention to the next'.[15] So, for example, if one shot shows a person turning their head and looking, the next shot should show what they are looking at. Eisenstein, in contrast, promoted what he called the 'montage of attractions' where effects are created through the juxtaposition of images. For Eisenstein 'montage is an idea that arises from the collision of independent shots – shots even opposite to one another'.[16] Eisenstein saw this oppositional or dialectical form of montage in relation to Marxist political thought: he believed that art, like politics, was based on conflict.

The most famous example of montage in practice is the 'Odessa Steps' sequence of *The Battleship Potemkin*. This sequence is one of a handful – other examples include the chase over the salt flats in John Ford's *Stagecoach* (1939) and the shower murder in Alfred Hitchcock's *Psycho* (1960) – that have been analysed in forensic detail by film historians.[17] *The Battleship Potemkin* was commissioned to commemorate the twentieth anniversary of the Revolution of 1905: it is a reconstruction of events surrounding the Odessa naval mutiny. The Odessa Steps sequence – where Tsarist troops shoot down a crowd of civilian protestors – is among the most famous in film history. Its special quality is to be found not only in the rhythmic structure of the editing but also in the way that Eisenstein disregards normal spatial and temporal continuities: events are stretched out longer in 'film time' than in 'real time' and there are discontinuities between shots. During the carnage, for example, a baby's pram rolls down the steps: but in different shots it is shown moving from left to right and then from right to left – thus disregarding a basic principle of continuity editing – and in some shots it appears to move upwards across the screen even as it is rolling down the steps. Another famous image is the jump cut from a close up of a woman's face to the same woman with broken glasses and blood pouring from her eye. This is an example of Eisenstein's 'montage of attractions'. He explained the effect thus: 'Representation of a spontaneous action... Woman with pince-nez. Followed immediately – without a transition – by the same woman with shattered pince-nez and bleeding eye. Sensation of a shot hitting the eye.'[18]

Eisenstein stands out among his contemporaries both for the formal complexity of his films and for the sheer volume of his writing. His essays were translated into English as *The Film Sense* (1942) and *Film Form* (1948): they came to be regarded as virtual manifestos of film practice. Like his films, Eisenstein's writing is complex. His essays are characterized by digressions into philosophy, religion, politics and art, while his tendency to write in short, elliptical segments can sometimes makes his arguments elusive. Yet it is evident that his ideas continued to develop over the next 20 years until his premature death in 1948. Eisenstein's theory of montage was not static but continually evolving. His writings include references to a bewildering variety of types of montage. These include 'metric montage' (an editing pattern based on the number of frames per shot), 'rhythmic montage' (maintaining continuity between shots), 'tonal montage' (creating an emotional effect on the part of the spectator), 'overtonal montage' (a combination of metric, rhythmic and tonal effects) and 'intellectual montage' (soliciting an intellectual response from the spectator).[19] An example of intellectual montage is the famous scene in *Strike* where Eisenstein cuts between troops shooting striking workers and the massacre of a bull in an abattoir: while there is no narrative link between the two images their juxtaposition prompts the spectator to make an associative connection. Other variations include 'vertical montage' (linking all the formal components of montage simultaneously), 'horizontal montage' (linking formal components continuously), 'polyphonic montage' (the linking of image and sound which Eisenstein explored in his 1938 film *Alexander Nevsky*) and 'chromophonic montage' (the integration of colour and sound for psychological rather than aesthetic effect which Eisenstein experimented with in his last completed film *Ivan the Terrible Part 2*).[20] The role of montage, Eisenstein argued, was to being about a 'synchronization of the senses': to this end he welcomed the advent of new technologies which he saw as enhancing the formal possibilities of the medium.[21]

It is no coincidence that the ascendancy of formative film theory coincided with the late silent cinema: this period was held by many to mark the maturity of film as an art form. Alfred Hitchcock, for instance, whose approach to film-making was heavily influenced by the Soviet school, felt that 'the silent pictures were the purest form of cinema'.[22] This reflects a view that the essence of film art was defined by its visual properties, including cinematography and editing. The arrival of talking pictures at the end of the 1920s, however, would have a major impact not only on film-making practices but also on aesthetic debates around film. The addition of sound – once the early technical difficulties had been overcome – enhanced film's potential for **realism** and naturalism. This would lead to a reformulation of film aesthetics as the formative school lost ground to new realist-based theories.

▶ The realist tradition

A challenge to the formative approach emerged during the 1940s and 1950s in the form of a realist-based theory of film whose chief proponents were the German sociologist Siegfried Kracauer – whom we have already encountered in Chapter 1 in relation to his landmark history of German cinema – and the French film critic André Bazin. The emergence of realist theory was again to some extent a reflection of historical developments in film style. The advent of talking pictures had signalled the end of a certain 'international style' – the sense that silent films crossed boundaries of nation, culture and language on account of their perfection of the visual art of cinema and the absence of spoken dialogue – and accelerated the rise of national cinemas with their own distinct characteristics. The trend in the 1930s was towards films that dealt more directly with contemporary social reality, exemplified by the films of Jean Renoir, Marcel Carné and others in France, by the British documentary movement, and by certain American films such as *I Am A Fugitive from a Chain Gang* (1933) and *The Grapes of Wrath* (1940). The trend towards realism was enhanced in British and American cinemas during the Second World War and reached perhaps its peak in the late 1940s with the international acclaim lavished upon the Italian Neo-Realists.

A congruence of stylistic and intellectual developments, therefore, brought about a reformulation of film aesthetics in which **realism** was now championed over formalism. This was exemplified by Kracauer, who followed his *From Caligari to Hitler* with *Theory of Film* (1960), a *magnum opus* whose subtitle ('The Redemption of Physical Reality') effectively sums up his thesis. Kracauer began from the proposition that what differentiated film from the other arts was that film 'is uniquely equipped to record and reveal physical reality'. He then argued, contrary to the formative school, that because film *can* reproduce reality, therefore it *should* reproduce reality. He elaborated thus:

> When calling the cinema an art medium, people usually think of films which resemble the traditional works of art in that they are free creations rather than explorations of nature. These films organize the raw material to which they resort into some self-sufficient composition instead of accepting it as an element in its own right. In other words, their underlying formative impulses are so strong that they defeat the cinematic approach with its concern for camera-reality... Yet such a usage of the term 'art' in the traditional sense is misleading. It lends support to the belief that artistic qualities must be attributed precisely to films which neglect the medium's recording obligations in an attempt to rival achievements in the fields of the fine arts, the theatre, or literature. In consequence, this usage tends to obscure the aesthetic value of films which are really true to the medium.[23]

Kracauer asserted, furthermore, that those films which hitherto had been claimed as art, such as German Expressionism, 'frequently ignore physical reality or exploit it for purposes alien to photographic veracity'. He argued, instead, for an appreciation of films 'which incorporate aspects of physical reality with a view to making us experience them'. He identified in particular documentary films such as the American anthropologist Robert Flaherty's *Nanook of the North* (1922) and the Dutch film-maker Joris Ivens's *Rain* (1929).

The French critic André Bazin was the leading advocate of the realist school. Bazin had started out as a critic for *Le Parisien Liberé* after the Second World War and was one of those who found much to admire in the influx of American films that had not been available in France during the German Occupation. In 1947 he founded *La Revue du Cinéma*, followed in 1951 by *Cahiers du Cinéma* ('Cinema Notebooks'), which under his editorship became the most influential of the new wave of specialist film magazines that emerged after the war. Bazin wrote extensively about film, including books on Jean Renoir and Orson Welles, though much of his work was in the form of articles. Unlike Kracauer there is no *magnum opus* summarizing his position: instead his views can be gleaned from short articles on a wide range of topics. Bazin died in 1958: a representative selection of his work was published posthumously under the title *What Is Cinema? (Qu'est-ce que le cinéma?)*.

Bazin's major contribution to aesthetic film theory was the concept of the objective reality of the filmic image. To this extent his ideas belong within the Aristotelian tradition of classical aesthetics: that art imitates life. Bazin saw film not as a radical departure from other art forms, as the formative critics believed, but as an extension of what had gone before. In 'The Myth of Total Cinema', for example, he argued that film represented the fulfilment of a trend 'which dominated in a more or less vague fashion all the techniques of mechanical reproduction of reality in the nineteenth century, from photography to the phonograph, namely an integral realism, a recreation of the world in its own image…unburdened by the freedom of the artist or the irreversibility of time.'[24] In 'The Ontology of the Photographic Image' he emphasized the connection between photography and cinema as 'discoveries that satisfy, once and for all and in its very essence, our obsession with realism'.[25] Bazin reacted against the emphasis on montage that characterized formative theory and distanced himself from the extreme stylization of German Expressionism which 'did every kind of violence to the plastics of the image by way of sets and lighting'.[26] He preferred the Italian Neo-Realist cinema of the post-Second World War period because of its achievement 'in stripping away all expressionism and in particular the total absence of the effects of montage'.[27]

Bazin's view of the aesthetic history of film is summarized in 'The Evolution of the Language of Cinema'. He avers that in the late 1920s 'the silent film had reached its artistic peak'.[28] Unlike the formative school, however, who saw the advent of sound as a decisive break that retarded the further artistic development of the medium, Bazin identifies a greater degree of continuity between silent and sound cinema, particularly in relation to editing practices. He asserts that by the late 1930s 'the talking film, particularly in France and in the United States, had reached a level of classical perfection as a result, on the one hand, of the maturing of different kinds of drama developed in part over the past ten years and in part inherited from the silent film, and, on the other, of the stabilization of technical progress'.[29] This 'classical perfection' (an idea that recurs throughout Bazin's work) was reached through a combination of 'well-defined styles of photography and editing perfectly adapted to their subject matter' and technological developments such as panchromatic film stock that enabled directors to embrace the technique of composition in depth.[30]

For Bazin the major stylistic development during this period was the advent (or rather rediscovery, as it had been a feature of silent cinema) of **deep-focus cinematography**. This is a technique wherein objects in the background of the image are in equally sharp relief as those in the foreground: it creates an illusion of depth in contrast to the blurring of images in the background that characterizes **soft-focus cinematography**. Bazin favoured deep-focus because it 'brings the spectator into a relation with the image closer to that which he enjoys with reality' and because it implies 'a more active mental attitude on the part of the spectator and a more positive contribution on his part to the action in progress'.[31] Unlike montage, which imposed meaning on the spectator, deep-focus allowed greater scope for the spectator to see and inter-pret the image as he saw it. Bazin therefore championed those film-makers who embraced deep-focus, including Jean Renoir in France (*La Grande Illusion*, 1937; *La règle du jeu*, 1939) and William Wyler in Hollywood (*The Little Foxes*, 1941).

The realism achieved through deep-focus cinematography was further enhanced when combined with long takes. Long takes were preferable to montage because they did not break up the scene but instead allowed events to unfold as if they were happening in real time. This is one of the features that distinguishes Orson Welles's first two films, *Citizen Kane* (1941) and *The Magnificent Ambersons* (1942), which Bazin saw after the end of the Second World War. Discussing *The Magnificent Ambersons*, for example, Bazin argued that 'his [Welles's] refusal to break up the action, to analyse the dramatic field in time, is a positive action the results of which are far superior to any-thing that could be achieved by the classical "cut"'.[32] Another example of this technique that Bazin admired was William Wyler's *The Best Years of Our Lives* (1946). He identified three pivotal scenes – the reunion of Al (Fredric March) and his wife Milly (Myrna Loy), the scene where Fred (Dana Andrews) tele-phones Peggy (Teresa Wright) to break off their relationship, and the wedding of Homer (Harold Russell) and Wilma (Cathy O'Donnell) where Fred and Peggy are reunited – where the 'real action' of the scene takes place in the background while the foreground detail is incidental.[33]

Bazin's theory of film therefore represented a shift away from montage and placed the emphasis on *mise-en-scène*: he saw the instrinsic quality of film in the composition of the individual shot rather than in the relationship between shots. Bazin accepted that a 'total cinema' which fulfilled his ideal of realism was a 'myth' that could not be achieved. Perhaps the closest to his ideal were the Italian Neo-Realist films. Bazin admired the Neo-Realists for their 'perfect and natural adherence to **actuality**' and for their 'fundamental humanism'.[34] He praised the 'objective social reality' of Vittorio De Sica's *Bicycle Thieves* (1948), which he considered 'one of the first examples of pure cinema'.[35] However, it was *Umberto D* (1951) which, for Bazin, marked the apotheosis of Neo-Realism. *Umberto D* – an account of a day in the life of an old man and his dog – was an attempt by director Vittorio De Sica and writer Cesare Zavattini to strip away all spectacle and melodrama. Bazin's reading of one particular scene sums up his view of film aesthetics:

> One wonderful sequence – it will remain one of the high points of film – is a perfect illustration of this approach to narrative and thus to direction: the scene in which the maid gets up. The camera confines itself to watching her doing her little chores: moving around the kitchen still half asleep, drowning the ants that have invaded the sink, grinding the coffee. The cinema here is conceived as the

exact opposite of that 'art of ellipsis' to which we are much too ready to believe it devoted.[36]

In a Hollywood film, as Bazin points out, such a scene would have been condensed and dealt with as quickly as possible, especially since the maid is a relatively minor character. Instead the film stretches it out into a sequence that shows the maid's mundane everyday routine in minute detail. Bazin sees the effect of *Umberto D* as being 'to make cinema an asymptote of reality – but in order that it should ultimately be life itself that becomes spectacle'.[37]

Bazin's contribution to the aesthetic history of film was enormously important: he is widely regarded as the most important critic of the post-war decade. Of course his theory of film is open to debate. Bazin's critics have pointed out the unvoiced moral and political assumptions of his work, particularly his commitment to humanism: Marxist theorists would later reject humanism as a symptom of the ideological limitations of bourgeois thinking. Another criticism is that Bazin's ideal of realism as an unmediated reflection of social reality is naïve in that it ignores the extent to which the sort of realism he advocates is itself a formal and aesthetic construct.[38] It could be argued, for example, that techniques such as deep-focus cinematography and long takes are just as manipulative in their own way as montage as they direct the spectator's attention to particular aspects of *mise-en-scène* arranged by the director. Yet Bazin is more subtle than he has often been given credit for. In particular he frequently highlights the tension between his ideal of realism and the limits of film practice: hence his use of terms such as asymptote – a curve which gradually approaches a straight line but will meet it only at the point of infinity. In light of later technological developments, however, Bazin's ideal of realism perhaps seems more prescient: a film such as Alexander Sokurov's *Russian Ark* (2002), which uses digital video to record uninterrupted time, might be seen as finally marking the infinity point where theory and practice meet.

▶ *Auteur* theory and its variants

While classical film aesthetics focused on the nature of film as an art form, it had little to say about the role of the film-maker as an artist. Yet a work of art is usually understood not only as an exemplar of its formal properties but also as the expression of the creativity and vision of the artist. Masterpieces are, by definition, created by the masters: they are the works that stand apart from the rest by dint of their special qualities and distinctive characteristics. This idea is prevalent in histories of art and literature: Michelangelo and Shakespeare are regarded as great artists because their use of the medium is deemed more original, more complex and more creative than their contemporaries. This idea has also informed aesthetic film histories. Gerald Mast, for example, contends that 'no great film has ever been made without the vision and unifying intelligence of a single mind to create and control the whole film'.[39] This is far from being a new idea. In 1947, for example, the British critic C. A. Lejeune remarked that 'on the rare occasions on which you do come across a film of character, it is ten to one you will find a single creative intelligence behind it'.[40]

Auteur theory – also referred to variously as *la politique des auteurs*, auteurism and authorship – emerged during the 1950s and 1960s.[41] Put simply *auteur* theory asserts that, regardless of the collaborative nature of film-making and the industrial contexts of film production, it is the director of a film who, by dint of his control over the film-making process, should be regarded as the true 'author' of the finished film. It maintains that films reflect the thematic interests and stylistic preferences of their directors: films express the 'vision' or 'world view' of their director in much the same way as a novel or play does for the writer or dramatist. The idea first gained intellectual currency in the pages of *Cahiers du Cinéma* in the 1950s, where a group of young critics – including François Truffaut, Jean-Luc Godard, Eric Rohmer and Claude Chabrol, all of whom would become film-makers themselves a few years later as major figures in the French **Nouvelle Vague** – began to articulate *la politique des auteurs* in film reviews and in articles on directors whom they particularly admired. At the heart of *la politique des auteurs* was the Romantic concept of the artist as a creative individual. To some extent the *politique* can be seen as a response to the critique of mass culture by the Frankfurt School. In contrast to the mass-culture critics, who averred that film was not art, the project of *la politique des auteurs* was to legitimate film as a popular art form. Hence the privileging not only of European art cinema (represented by directors such as Roberto Rossellini and Jean Cocteau) but also Hollywood (particularly the films of Alfred Hitchcock and Howard Hawks). Rohmer's article 'Rediscovering America', for example, mounted a passionate defence of what he saw as the 'efficacy and elegance' of American cinema, challenging the prevalent idea of Hollywood as a philistine commercial industry by likening it instead to 'that haven which Florence was for painters of the Quattrocento or Vienna for musicians in the nineteenth century'.[42]

The critical 'policy' advocated by the *Cahiers* critics developed ideas from both the formative and realist aesthetic traditions. Like formative critics they rejected the 'theatrical' in favour of the 'filmic': they emphasized the central importance of *mise-en-scène* as the defining formal component of film that distinguished it from other arts. They differentiated between, on the one hand, directors whose mastery of *mise-en-scène* allowed them to express a consistent stylistic vision throughout their films and therefore could be regarded as *auteurs*, and, on the other hand, directors who were essentially arrangers but lacked the stylistic vision of the true *auteur* and whom they called *metteurs-en-scène*. But they were also influenced by Bazin (who, after all, was editor of *Cahiers du Cinéma*) and championed some 'old school' directors such as Jean Renoir whose humanist view of the world and deceptively simple style based around fluid camera movement and deep-focus cinematography could also be seen as the mark of an *auteur*. Bazin, interestingly, distanced himself from the polemical extremes of his younger colleagues and never fully embraced *la politique des auteurs*.[43]

The chief beneficiaries of *la politique des auteurs* were Hollywood directors such as Alfred Hitchcock and Howard Hawks. For the *Cahiers* critics Hitchcock was the example *par excellence* of an *auteur*: a director whose films exhibited recurring thematic preoccupations (paranoia, guilt, innocence) and visual motifs (particularly his emphasis on **point-of-view** and subjective narration). It was the intervention of the *Cahiers* critics that saw the elevation of Hitchcock from a technically gifted but superficial director – John Grierson once called him 'the world's best director of unimportant pictures'[44] – to a major film-maker whose films explored serious existential and psychological issues. Rohmer and Chabrol published the first book-length study of Hitchcock in 1957, while the first English-language auteurist study, by British critic Robin Wood, followed in 1965. Wood argued that Hitchcock's 'mature' films of the 1950s and 1960s demonstrated 'a consistent development, deepening and clarification' and that it was this continuing development which 'seems to me the mark of an important artist – essentially, that which distinguishes the significant from the worthless'.[45]

In the 1960s *la politique des auteurs* was taken up by Andrew Sarris, a film critic for small magazines like *Film Culture* and *Village Voice*, and sometime editor of an English language version of *Cahiers du Cinéma* (1966–7), who refashioned it as the '*auteur* theory'. For Sarris, *auteur* theory was more than just an evaluative idea: it was a critical tool for the reassessment of American cinema. He set out his manifesto in these terms:

> After years of tortured revaluation, I am now prepared to stake my critical reputation, such as it is, on the proposition that Alfred Hitchcock is artistically superior to Robert Bresson by every criterion of excellence, and, further, that, film for film, director for director, the American cinema has been consistently superior to that of the rest of the world from 1915 through 1962. Consequently I now regard the *auteur* theory as a critical device for recording the history of American cinema, the only cinema in the world worth exploring beneath the frosting of a few great directors at the top.[46]

This was polemical stuff, particularly in the pages of a progressive journal like *Film Culture*, which only a year before had published a 'revolutionary manifesto' arguing in favour of a new independent cinema in opposition to the dominance of Hollywood. Nevertheless Sarris's ideas had much currency, especially at a time when the decline of the **studio system** seemed to offer the possibility of greater creative freedom for film-makers.

Sarris's key work was his book *The American Cinema: Directors and Directions* (1968), in which he claimed that 'the *auteur* theory is not so much a theory as an attitude, a table of values that converts film history into directorial autobiography'.[47] The method Sarris adopted was to construct a critical hierarchy of directors starting at the top with a 'Pantheon' ('the directors who have transcended their technical problems with a personal version of the world', including the likes of Charles Chaplin, John Ford, D. W. Griffith, Howard Hawks, Alfred Hitchcock, Fritz Lang, Josef Von Sternberg and Orson Welles) and then descending through other categories including 'The Far Side of Paradise' ('directors who fall short of the Pantheon either because of a fragmentation of their personal vision or because of disruptive career problems': these included Frank Capra, George Cukor, Cecil B. De Mille, Vincente Minnelli, Otto Preminger, Nicholas Ray, Douglas Sirk, George Stevens, King Vidor and Raoul Walsh) and 'Expressive Esoterica' (Budd Boetticher, Andre de Toth, Allan Dwan, Arthur Penn, Don Siegel, Jacques Tourneur) down to 'Oddities, One-Shots and Newcomers' (including Ida Lupino, the only woman director in a list of 200) and 'Miscellany'.[48]

Sarris's critical hierarchy was, necessarily, highly personal and subjective. Some of his assessments now seem somewhat perverse. While few would argue with the rationale for selecting his pantheon directors, he relegates other potential candidates for the pantheon to lesser status. John Huston, Billy Wilder and William Wyler, for example, are all placed in the category 'Less Than Meets the Eye' reserved for 'the directors with reputations in excess of inspirations'.[49] Others, such as Gregory La Cava and Frank Tashlin, now appear overrated. However, the crucial question is not whether Sarris's verdicts on individual directors stand up to scrutiny but whether this approach to film history is a useful one. The idea of film history as 'directorial autobiography' is essentially a 'great man' interpretation of history, and there is a certain tautology in the suggestion that the great films are those made by the great directors. Sarris attributed creativity to the director's ability to impose his own stamp on his films: 'There were (and are) weak and strong directors as there were weak and strong kings, but film history, like royal history, concerns those who merely reign as well as those who actually rule…The strong director imposes his own personality on a film: the weak director allows the personalities of others to run rampant.'[50]

Yet in other respects Sarris's intervention did make an important contribution to film history. For all its flaws, his critical hierarchy represented a step towards a film history that privileged not only the 'great directors' but also the lesser lights ('those who merely reign as well as those who actually rule'). In this sense we might see Sarris as moving away from the 'masterpiece tradition' and taking into account a wider range of films and film-makers than previous histories. Most critiques of Sarris have focused on his construction of the pantheon and have therefore seen him as privileging the same handful of film artists: but in fact the book includes 200 film-makers of whom only 14 make it into the pantheon. Sarris was one of the first critics to accept that ordinary films as well as masterpieces were also part of film history. No less a scholar than David Bordwell even considers *The American Cinema* as 'the best guide to what is lasting in Hollywood studio filmmaking'.[51]

The American Cinema marked the high point of the *auteur* theory. In the early 1970s the Romantic idea of the film-maker as creative artist was challenged by new theories based on **structuralism** and **semiotics**. Other challenges to the *auteur* theory came from the emergence of **genre** theory and criticism, signalled by books such as Jim Kitses's *Horizons West* (1969), Colin McArthur's *Underworld USA* (1972) and Will Wright's *Sixguns and Society* (1975),[52] which argued that the visual and narrative codes of film genres were more significant in understanding the links between groups of films than who directed them, and from poststructuralism, especially the work of Roland Barthes, whose influential essay 'The Death of the Author' argued that the meaning of a text arose from the relationship between the text and the reader rather than from the intention of the author.[53] New Film History has stressed the idea of 'agency' rather than 'authorship', exploring the influence that producers, screenwriters, and even actors have over the film-making process. Peter Krämer, for example, has shown how a powerful star such as Jane Fonda was able, for a period in the late 1970s, to pursue her own liberal, feminist agenda in films such as *Coming Home*, *The China Syndrome* and *Nine to Five*. Krämer argues that Fonda can be considered the *auteur* of her films in that she 'was able to initiate her own projects and to have overall control of their realization'.[54]

Nevertheless the *auteur* theory, or a variant of it, continues to exert considerable influence over aesthetic film history. This is evident, for example, in the work of Gilles Deleuze, whose two books, *Cinema 1: The Movement-Image* (1983) and *Cinema 2: The Time-Image* (1985), have been afforded significant intellectual currency in theories of film aesthetics. Deleuze's *Cinema* books are an attempt to combine philosophy – particularly the work of the French philosopher Henri Bergson and the American semiotician Charles Sanders Peirce – with practical film criticism. What Deleuze offers 'is not a history of cinema. It is a taxonomy, an attempt at the classification of images and signs.'[55] Deleuze sees a correspondence between cinema and Bergson's notion that our perceptions of time and movement cause affections which in turn cause actions. In *Cinema 1*

Deleuze charts what he terms the 'movement-image' through the films of directors including D. W. Griffith, Sergei Eisenstein, Fritz Lang, John Ford, Howard
Hawks and Alfred Hitchcock. For Deleuze the 'movement-image' is a cinema of
narrative drive structured around actions and reactions. He further differentiates (in a manner that recalls Eisenstein's varieties of montage) between various
sub-categories including 'perception-image', 'affection-image', 'impulse-image'
and 'action-image'.[56] In *Cinema 2* Deleuze describes the process whereby, during and after the Second World War, 'a cinema of seeing replaces action'.[57] The
'time-image' is exemplified by the films of Orson Welles, Robert Bresson, Max
Ophüls, Federico Fellini, Alain Resnais, Yasujiro Ozu, the Italian Neo-Realists
and the French *Nouvelle Vague*. For Deleuze the 'time-image' is a different type
of filmic expression which, while not necessarily better than the 'movement-
image', could not have existed before the other.

It will be clear from this brief summary of what are in fact very complex arguments that, for all the philosophical apparatus in which he couches his work,
Deleuze is basically an unreconstructed auteurist. To quote from the conclusion
of *Cinema 2*:

> The great cinema authors are like the great painters or the great musicians: it is
> they who talk best about what they do. But, in talking, they become something
> else, they become philosophers or theoreticians – even Hawks who wanted no
> theories, even Godard when he pretends to distrust them. Cinema's concepts
> are not given in cinema. And yet they are cinema's concepts, not theories about
> cinema.[58]

It seems to me that, when shorn of the dubious philosophical baggage
(Bergson, for example, was an anti-Darwinist whose work carries little weight
in modern philosophy), what Deleuze offers to aesthetic film history is simply
a more theoretically complex way of differentiating between a cinema of montage (the 'movement-image') on the one hand and a modernist art cinema (the
'time-image') on the other. And like many theorists Deleuze writes about film
aesthetics in a vacuum: there is no consideration of the role of social, economic
or technological factors in shaping the medium.

Auteur theory in its purest form did not persist beyond the 1970s. Yet the
director remains a focal point of film-historical research: and the net has been
extended to include not only the 'great' directors but also the lesser lights. A
current series of monographs on 'British Film Makers' published by Manchester
University Press, for example, includes studies of key British directors such as
Anthony Asquith and Carol Reed but also figures such as Roy Ward Baker, J.
Lee Thompson and Lance Comfort whose names will be familiar only to the
most ardent cinephiles. While the director's *œuvre* continues to be the focus

of research, however, the series is also concerned to place the individual film-makers in the contexts of the film industry and film culture of which they were part. No longer is the director placed in an authorial vacuum, but rather is seen within 'the wider social contexts which helped to shape not just that particular film-maker but the course of British cinema at large'.[59]

▶ David Bordwell and the historical poetics of cinema

The work of US film historian David Bordwell represents the most complete attempt by one critic to attempt not only a systematic history of film style (rather than film art) but also to establish a critical and methodological framework for writing such a history. We encountered Bordwell in the previous chapter as one of the authors of *The Classical Hollywood Cinema*. Bordwell has written over a dozen other books on film, most of them weighty tomes, along with countless articles in film journals. He has written studies of Carl-Theodor Dreyer, Yasujiro Ozu and Sergei Eisenstein along with more general works including *Narration in the Fiction Film* (1985), *Making Meaning* (1989), *On the History of Film Style* (1997), *The Way Hollywood Tells It* (2006) and *Poetics of Cinema* (2008).[60] Bordwell's work encompasses an extraordinarily wide range of styles and film-making practices, from highly formalist and 'poetic' directors such as Dreyer and Ozu to modern blockbusters and Far Eastern martial arts cinema. This breadth is possible in part because Bordwell's method is not subjective and evaluative, as per Sarris, but assertively empirical and analytical.

Bordwell is one of the most methodologically conscious of scholars, and his work is invariably presented in terms of systematic research questions (even 'research programmes') in the exploration of which he deploys various critical tools. He claims to be neither historian nor theorist 'because I do not accept any hard-and-fast distinctions among theory, criticism, and history'.[61] He distances himself from '**Screen theory**' with its interpretative frameworks derived from Saussurean linguistics, Lacanian psychoanalysis, Althusserian Marxism and the structural narratology of Barthes – calling these approaches collectively 'SLAB theory' – on the grounds that it is more concerned with justifying the theoretical apparatus than with a systematic analysis of actual films.[62] And when Bordwell does draw upon theory it is always grounded in empirical analysis. In *Narration in the Fiction Film*, for example, he adopts the terms of Russian Formalist critics such as Mikhail Bakhtin and Viktor Shklovsky and their distinction between *fabula* (often translated as 'story') and *syuzhet* ('the actual arrangement and presentation of the fabula in the film', in other words the 'plot').[63] So, for example, the *fabula* or story (for example that Rick and Ilsa were lovers in Paris in 1940) is inferred through the organization of *syuzhet* (a flashback sequence including scenes of Rick and Ilsa in romantic situations). This is combined with the use of cognitive psychology in an attempt to explain how spectators actually 'read' films by constructing a story from what they see and hear. None of these concepts are followed slavishly: a key feature of Bordwell's work is the extent to which he seeks to test theoretical perspectives against empirical data.

The concept that very much is Bordwell's own – though others have adopted it in their own work – is the notion of historical poetics. Bordwell understands historical poetics as seeking answers to two general questions about film: 'What are the principles according to which films are constructed and by means of which they achieve particular effects? How and why have these principles arisen and changed in particular empirical circumstances?'[64] This approach (Bordwell shies away from claiming it as a methodology) involves the analysis of group style: the norms and practices that characterize film-making in particular historical contexts. This approach places Bordwell's work within an intellectual tradition that includes E. H. Gombrich's *The Story of Art* and extends back to Aristotle's *Poetics*. The crucial point here is that the norms and practices of one film culture will vary from another: films should be considered in relation to the norms of the film industries and film cultures of which they are part. To describe a three-hour Hindi melodrama such as *Mother India* (1957) as a 'long' film, for example, would be to assess it in relation to the norms of **classical Hollywood cinema**, where a normal length is usually between 90 minutes and two hours, rather than in relation to the conventions of Hindi cinema, where three-hour films are not unusual.

Two examples must suffice to illustrate Bordwell's critical practice: these have been chosen because they demonstrate how the same methods can be applied to very different film cultures. One is the case of Japanese cinema. While the organization of Japan's film industry along studio-based mass-production lines has inevitably drawn comparison with Hollywood, the formal structure and editing conventions of Japanese films differ in several important respects from classical cinema. For example, Japanese films do not observe the **180-degree rule** (the invisible 'line' which the camera does not cross) or the pattern of **shot/reverse shot** (typically employed when two characters are in discussion). Bordwell does not see this as 'breaking' the rules of classical film-making but rather as evidence that Japanese cinema operates by different spatial conventions (including 360-degree space). He argues, furthermore, that from the 1930s Japanese cinema gradually (and not uniformly) asserted its difference from Hollywood by a tendency toward slower narration and pictorialism, reaching its fullest extent in the films of Kenji Mizoguchi and Yasujiro Ozu in the 1950s.[65]

The second example is European **art cinema** after the Second World War. Bordwell sees art cinema – exemplified by the films of directors such as Federico Fellini, Michelangelo Antonioni, Ingmar Bergman, Alain Resnais, Jean-Luc Godard and Luis Buñuel – as 'a distinct **mode of film practice**, possessing a definite historical existence, a set of formal conventions, and implicit viewing procedures'.[66] Its norms and conventions include narrative ambiguity, psychological realism and authorial expression. In particular art cinema films have a looser narrative structure than Hollywood films and are often left open-ended without the sense of closure that characterizes the classical film. There is an important distinction here from the work of auteurist critics who assign the psychological complexity and stylistic flourishes of art cinema to authorial expressivity: Bordwell in contrast sees authorial expressivity itself as one of the defining characteristics of art cinema.

Some critics have described historical poetics as a Neoformalist approach to cinema. **Neoformalism** understands modes of film practice such as classical Hollywood, art cinema or Soviet montage as 'formal systems' each with their own **paradigm**. It distinguishes 'between stylistic or narrative *devices* (e.g. the cut or the motif) and *systems* (e.g., spatial continuity or narrative causality) within which they achieve various *functions*'.[67] A criticism that has been made of Neoformalism and historical poetics is that in emphasizing norms and formal systems they downplay the differences between individual film-makers. At is most reductive level historical poetics regards all films as variations on a norm or paradigm. Consider, for example, the place of the *auteur* director under the studio system. Bordwell suggests that 'authorial presence in the Hollywood cinema is usually consistent with classical norms...Since the classical style is a paradigm, a filmmaker may habitually and systematically choose one alternative over another.'[68] So, for example, John Ford would choose to stage scenes around doorways, whereas Douglas Sirk would do so around mirrors. Another criticism that has been made of Neoformalism is that its emphasis on the analysis of form and style ignores the role of culture and ideology in shaping the film text. There is a tendency to explain stylistic change in relation to formal practices alone without considering factors external to the 'formal systems' of film. Bordwell, however, dismisses this criticism out of hand: 'In no other domain of enquiry I know...is there such unremitting insistence that every significant research project should shed light on society. Scholars can freely study iambic pentameter, baroque perspective, and the discovery of DNA without feeling obliged to make vast claims about culture's impact on said subject.'[69] This curt dismissal of an entire body of historical and theoretical enquiry is uncharacteristic for Bordwell. But the examples he cites also point to the chief limitation of historical poetics: that its application as a critical tool is restricted to the analysis of form and style rather than the content or themes of films. So, for example, historical poetics would help us to understand a film like *The Birth of a Nation* in relation to the development of the formal systems of Hollywood (the **feature film**, classical narration, **continuity editing**) but it would not help us to shed light upon the question of its historical accuracy or understand why its racial politics provoked such controversy. In other words it raises one of the big questions about any form of artistic and cultural practice: how far can art be detached from the social contexts in which it is produced?

▷ Case study: *Citizen Kane* (1941) and the masterpiece tradition

Citizen Kane provides an ideal case study of the issues discussed in this chapter. It is a film squarely within the masterpiece tradition of film history. Andrew Sarris, for example, averred that '*Citizen Kane* is still the work that influenced the cinema more profoundly than any American film since *Birth of a Nation*'.[70] It has often been voted the best or most influential film ever made by critics and film-makers. To understand why the film has been privileged in this way we need to consider not only the qualities of the film itself but also how the film relates to the cultural and aesthetic discourses around film. To some extent the special place of *Citizen Kane* in aesthetic film history is because it 'fits' so many different approaches.

In fact the special status of *Citizen Kane* can be traced back to the circumstances of its production and the publicity discourses circulating around it at the time. Orson Welles, who had achieved notoriety with his radio production of *The War of the Worlds* in 1938, had been hired by RKO Radio Pictures with a contract that offered an unprecedented degree of creative autonomy for an untried film-maker. The recruitment of Welles and his Mercury Theatre group should be seen as a bold gamble by RKO, the smallest and least prestigious of the 'Big Five' studios, to produce 'prestige' films that would bring critical kudos to the studio. The release of *Citizen Kane* in May 1941 was accompanied by a publicity campaign designed to arouse interest in the film as being unusual and different. It was enthusiastically reviewed: the *New York Times* thought it was 'one of the most sensational films ever made in Hollywood', while *Commonweal* called it simply 'one of the outstanding films of all time'.[71] It was voted the best film of the year by the National Board of Review of Motion Pictures and the New York Critics, and was nominated for eight Academy Awards ('Oscars'), though in the event it won only in one category for best screenplay.

Robert Carringer's study of the production and reception of *Citizen Kane* has shown how the reputation of the film declined somewhat in Anglo-American film criticism during the 1950s but that its standing was resurrected by the French cinephile culture of *Cahiers du Cinéma* for whom it was one of the American films seen after the Second World War. André Bazin was the principal cheerleader for a film that he felt 'marks more or less the beginning of a new period…a revolution in the language of the screen'.[72] For Bazin the film's use of long takes and deep-focus cinematography accorded with his ideal of realism. Bazin admired the 'stylistic unity' and 'formal brilliance' of *Citizen Kane* (and *The Magnificent Ambersons*) and argued that 'the *découpage* on depth becomes a technique which constitutes the meaning of the story'.[73] The 1960s saw the resurrection of *Citizen Kane*'s critical reputation in America, where it was championed by Sarris, and in Britain, where it topped *Sight and Sound*'s second poll of the best films of all time in 1962 – a position that it held unchallenged for five decades until it was finally usurped by Alfred Hitchcock's *Vertigo* in 2012.

By the 1970s *Citizen Kane* had become the pre-eminent example of the masterpiece tradition of film history. David Bordwell, in an article published in 1971, argued that the real significance of *Citizen Kane* was not that it demonstrated the realist aesthetics of Bazin, but rather that it seemed the perfect fusion of both realist and formative techniques. (To be fair to Bazin he had recognized this: 'It is not that Welles denies himself any recourse whatsoever to the expressionistic procedures of montage, but just that their use from time to time in between one-shot sequences in depth gives them new meaning.')[74] On the one hand there are sequences where the combination of long takes and staging in depth creates the effects Bazin admired: famous examples are the scene in the office of the *Inquirer* newspaper where we first meet Charles Foster Kane as an adult and, later, the attempted suicide of his second wife Susan. On the other hand there are examples of formative effects: the camera flourishes, expressionist framing and elliptical editing that Bordwell calls 'moments of sheer cinematic pluck'. Examples include shots such as the nurse reflected in the glass as she enters Kane's bedroom near the start of the film (an effect that recalls the distorted perspectives of German Expressionism) and the 20 years between the young Kane's 'Merry Christmas' and Mr Thatcher's response of 'Happy New Year' (elliptical editing). For Bordwell the combination of realist and formative techniques 'coalesce into a unified style by expressing the film's juxtaposition of reality and imagination'.[75]

The growing critical status of *Citizen Kane* also coincided with the rise of art cinema in Europe. *Citizen Kane* exemplifies many characteristics that would become associated with art cinema: psychological complexity, narrative ambiguity, authorial expressivity. It stands out from the norm of classical Hollywood by dint of its open-ended narrative (Kane's dying word – 'Rosebud' – remains as much of an enigma at the end of the film as the beginning) and its complex formal structure that uses multiple narrators and flashbacks. It is a film with an exceptionally complex relationship between *fabula* (the life of media magnate Charles Foster Kane) and *syuzhet* (a series of interviews with Kane's surviving friends and colleagues by a reporter seeking to discover the meaning of 'Rosebud'). The ambiguity and highly subjective narration of the film was ahead of its time: *Citizen Kane* is seen as anticipating films such as Akira Kurosawa's *Rashomon* (1950) and Alain Resnais's *Last Year at Marienbad* (1960). Deleuze contends that *Citizen Kane* marked 'the first occasion on which a direct time-image was seen in the cinema'.[76] He elaborates: 'If montage...remains the cinematographic act *par excellence* in Welles it none the less changes its meaning: instead of producing an indirect image of time on the basis of movement, it will organize the order of non-chronological coexistences or relations in the direct time-image.'[77] (Translation: the plot is non-linear.)

Finally, *Citizen Kane* can also be seen as a test case for the *auteur* theory. Welles's career after *Citizen Kane* was fragmented and uneven. *The Magnificent Ambersons* was drastically re-edited by the studio before release. Welles began, but did not complete, a third film for RKO, and spent the rest of his career as a freelance actor and occasional director in Europe and America. He made some other good films – the thrillers *The Lady from Shanghai* (1948) and *Touch of Evil* (1958) both demonstrated some of the stylistic brilliance of *Citizen Kane* – but there were also many unrealized projects, including a film of Don Quixote, while his film of *Othello* (1952) was filmed in numerous locations over several years as and when Welles had funding to continue with it. Welles is therefore a rare, possibly unique, example of a director who achieved his greatest success with his very first film. Unlike other 'greats' of American cinema such as John Ford and Alfred Hitchcock, each of whom has a long list of classic films to their name, Welles's status in film history rests largely on the one film. 'The conventional American diagnosis of his career is decline, pure and simple, but decline is never pure and never simple,' writes Sarris. 'Welles began his career on such a high plateau that the most precipitous decline would not affect his place in the Pantheon.'[78]

The special status of *Citizen Kane* in the history of film perfectly exemplifies the masterpiece tradition. This is an idea of film history that privileges individual works of film art: it also explains the film's significance in terms of its aesthetic qualities that are seen to transcend its historical conditions of production and reception. It will be clear from this chapter that aesthetic histories of film are generally based on a narrow selection of films and film-makers: by definition a masterpiece-based approach excludes the majority of films. And, as aesthetic histories account for the majority of film histories, this means that film history in general has been built on a narrow and (by dint of their special status) unrepresentative selection of films. However, to understand *Citizen Kane* only as a great work of film art is limiting as it excludes other approaches. *Citizen Kane* can also be placed within technological histories (as a 'state-of-the-art' example of film technique *c.*1941), institutional and industrial histories (as one of 47 films released by RKO in 1941 and one of 379 produced in Hollywood that year) and social histories (as a thinly disguised portrait of real-life newspaper magnate William Randolph Hearst and a statement about the corrupting effects of wealth and power). Let us now consider some of these alternatives – approaches that do not necessarily privilege either the 'best' films or films as individual works of art.

3 Film and Ideology

> Cinema is one of the languages through which the world communicates itself to itself. They [films] constitute its ideology for they reproduce the world as it is experienced when filtered through the ideology...Once we realize that it is the nature of the system to turn the cinema into an instrument of ideology, we can see that the filmmaker's first task is to show up the cinema's so-called 'depiction of reality'.
>
> Jean-Luc Comolli and Jean Narboni[1]

The 1970s saw the emergence of a radical, polemical and highly theorized new style of film criticism that rejected many of the tenets of **classical film aesthetics** and embraced instead the notion of cinema as an **ideological apparatus**. This trend began in France, where in 1969 the new editors of *Cahiers du Cinéma* turned their back on the Romantic notion of the film-maker as an artist represented by *la politiques des auteurs* and declared their commitment to what Jean-Luc Comolli and Jean Narboni in a polemical editorial-manifesto referred to as 'scientific criticism' with 'a clear theoretical base to which to relate our critical practice and its field'.[2] This radical shift of editorial direction was a consequence of the upheavals within French intellectual culture in 1968 which had seen, among other things, a fierce popular backlash against the sacking of Henri Langlois as curator of the Cinémathèque Française – a protest led by film-makers including Jean-Luc Godard, François Truffaut and Alain Resnais – and the establishment of a self-proclaimed 'Estates General of the French Cinema' to call for state support for film production and education.[3] *Cahiers du Cinéma* no longer subscribed to the critical evaluation of film as an art form but rather to the analysis of cinema as an instrument of ideology. A similar trajectory was followed in Britain by the journal *Screen*, which in the early 1970s declared its intention 'to go beyond subjective taste-ridden criticism and to try to develop more systematic approaches over a wider field'.[4] In particular *Screen* set itself against other journals such as *Movie* (a British magazine established in 1962 that followed a broadly auteurist line) and the narrower educational remit of its predecessor *Screen Education*. The rise of what came to be known as **'Screen theory'** was nothing less than a critical project to construct a totalizing theory of cinema as an ideological tool. It was a project in which traditional notions of aesthetic value had no place. It was also a project that at times seemed avowedly a-historical: indeed the ascendancy of high theory in film studies arguably retarded the development of film history. In 1977, for example, Geoffrey Nowell-Smith noted that 'a loss of confidence in traditional historiographic procedures and the turn towards non-historic modes of theorisation has produced a severe hiatus in the study of the cinema'.[5]

▶ Cinema as an ideological apparatus

At the heart of the new theories of cinema in the 1970s was the view that cinema was – in the terms of the French political scientist Louis Althusser – an 'ideological apparatus'. This idea marked a radical departure from previous understandings of the role of ideology in cinema. It was generally accepted that while some films were clearly ideological in their intent – most obviously in the case of propaganda films such as *Triumph of the Will* or *Alexander Nevsky* – the products of the commercial film industry were merely 'entertainment' or 'escapism'. The promotional discourses of Hollywood averred that cinema was a 'dream factory' and that films were about people rather than politics. The only consistent challenge to this view came from the **Frankfurt School** and from American mass-culture critics such as Dwight Macdonald who saw cinema in explicitly Marxist terms as a reflection of the economic structures and institutions that produced it. For Macdonald: 'Mass Culture is imposed from above. It is fabricated by technicians hired by businessmen; its audiences are passive consumers... The Lords of *kitsch*, in short, exploit the cultural needs of the masses in order to make a profit and/or to maintain their class rule.'[6]

Althusser argued for a more subtle and complex understanding of ideology than that offered by so-called 'vulgar' Marxism. Rather than seeing ideology as something imposed on citizens from above, Althusser believed that ideology arose from 'the *lived* relation' between the individual and society: 'Ideology is *inscribed in* discourse in the sense that it is literally written or spoken *in it*; it is not a separate element which exists independently in some free-floating realm of "ideas" and is subsequently embodied in words, but a way of thinking, speaking, experiencing.'[7] Althusser saw institutions such as the church and the educational system as 'ideological state apparatuses' whose role was not so much to indoctrinate citizens in approved thinking and behaviour as to encourage their identification with institutions and practices that were themselves part of the dominant ideology in society. This idea could also be readily applied to art and cultural practices – including cinema.

Comolli and Narboni's article 'Cinema/Ideology/Criticism' – which first appeared as an editorial in *Cahiers du Cinéma* in October 1969 before appearing in English translation in *Screen* in 1971 – was the foundational text of the new ideological film criticism. Comolli and Narboni drew upon an Althusserian concept of ideology in their assertion that '*every film is political*, inasmuch as it is determined by the ideology which produces it' and in their focus on cinema as an 'ideological system'. Their rejection of conventional aesthetic criticism, and particularly the Bazinian notion of **realism**, was explicit in their statement that 'the tools and techniques of film-making are a part of "reality" themselves, and furthermore "reality" is nothing but an expression of the prevailing ideology'. 'Seen in this light,' they went on, 'the classic theory of cinema that the camera is an impartial instrument which grasps, or rather is impregnated by, the world in its "concrete reality" is an eminently reactionary one.'[8]

This is not to say that Comolli and Narboni saw cinema as some sort of ideological monolith as the Frankfurt School did. Rather, they recognized that ideology was inscribed in film texts in different ways. The main body of their article was concerned with establishing a set of categories in which the relationship between film and ideology could be understood. Category A – the largest in their view – 'comprises those films which are imbued through and through with the dominant ideology in pure and unadulterated form, and give no indication that their makers were even aware of the fact'. Categories B and C consisted of 'films which attack their ideological assimilation on two fronts' either by 'direct political action' (B) or 'against the grain' (C). Category D were films 'which have an explicitly political content...but which do not effectively criticize the ideological system in which they are embedded because they unquestioningly adopt its language and its imagery': they cited the example of the little-known *Le Temps de Vivre*. Category E comprized 'films which seem at first sight to belong firmly within the ideology and to be completely under its sway, but which turn out to be so only in an ambiguous manner'. Finally categories F and G covered what Comolli and Narboni termed 'live cinema' – more commonly known as **Direct Cinema** or *Cinéma Vérité* – which 'are films arising out of political events or reflections but which make no clear differentiation between themselves and the non-political cinema because they do not challenge the cinema's traditional, ideologically-conditioned method of "depiction"'.[9]

Comolli and Narboni stated their own formal and political preferences in suggesting that films of categories B and C 'constitute the essential in cinema' and should therefore be the main focus of the critical project. However, it was their category E, which to some extent cut across their schemata, that would feature most prominently in this ideological criticism. These were films which 'throw up obstacles in the way of the ideology, causing it to swerve and get off course...This is the case in many Hollywood films for example, which while being completely integrated in the system and in the ideology end up partially dismantling the system from within.'[10] The suggestion that a film could operate both within but also to an extent against the dominant ideology offered an avenue for the reclamation of Hollywood cinema in particular. It is no accident that it was in the 1970s that the films of Douglas Sirk, for example, became an important point of reference in film studies. Sirk was claimed as a 'progressive' *auteur* whose films – particularly his melodramas of the 1950s such as *All That Heaven Allows* and *Written on the Wind* – could be read as a critique of the social values and patriarchal ideology of American society.[11]

The most influential examples of this form of ideological criticism in practice were a series of close readings of individual films presented as collective texts by the editors of *Cahiers du Cinéma*. The first of these essays – on John Ford's *Young Mr Lincoln* (1940) – has become canonical. The underlying assumption of the *Cahiers* editors was that the film text was constituted through the relationship between a historically specific set of codes and that the aim of criticism was to explore 'the relation of these films to the ideology which they convey, a particular "phase" which they represent, and to the events (present, past, historical, mythical, fictional) which they aim to represent'.[12] They proceed to offer a systematic reading of the film that first locates it in relation to its various historical contexts (Hollywood in the late 1930s, the United States in the late 1930s, the production strategies of Twentieth Century-Fox) and then analyse key scenes in the film (including Lincoln's electoral speech, his soliloquy at the grave of his sweetheart Ann Rutledge, his arrival in Springfield where he sets up as a lawyer, the Independence Day celebrations leading to the murder of Scrub White, the dance where Lincoln meets Mary White, and the climactic trial in which Lincoln defends Adam Clay against the charge of murder and exposes the real culprit). They highlight the tensions within the film between its 'ideological project' (to present Lincoln as the 'great reconciler' and – in their analysis – to support the Republican cause in the forthcoming US presidential election of 1940) and his role as 'bringer of the truth' which involves harassing a witness in order to prompt a confession. And they conclude that, while ostensibly advocating non-violence, *Young Mr Lincoln* shows that the repression of violence 'turns into exorcism, and gives to its signifiers, in the murder and the lynching scenes, a fantastic contrast which contributes considerably to the subversion of the deceptively calm surface of the text'.[13]

It has been suggested that there as many ideological contradictions within the *Cahiers* editors' reading of *Young Mr Lincoln* as they identify in the film itself. In particular they set out to detach the film from an authorial context but paradoxically their analysis of the tension between the 'generic code' and the 'Fordian code' suggests that the latter subverts the former and so 'seems to confirm the intuition, if not the theory and method, of author criticism'.[14] It would also be fair to say that their historical contextualization of *Young Mr Lincoln* is very thin and that they pay scant regard to the economic factors involved. Nevertheless the reading of *Young Mr Lincoln* – which was translated for *Screen*, where it was published in 1972 – was highly influential on the early development of 'Screen theory'. Stephen Heath's analysis of Orson Welles's *Touch of Evil* (1958), for example, employs a similar critical vocabulary as he talks about different 'orders of discourse' within the film text, and how it 'constructs the ideological subject'.[15] Like the *Cahiers* critics, Heath is unable to distance himself entirely from ***auteur* theory**: his answer, though, is to suggest that Welles's authorship is 'an effect of the text' rather than an external agency that determines its meaning.

There are several criticisms that can be levelled against this type of ideological film criticism. One is that in focusing on ideology as embedded in the text through such ideas as 'signifying structures' and 'orders of discourse' it entirely ignores the industrial contexts of production which also might influence the ideological effect of the film. Edward Buscombe, for example, pointed out the limitations of 'the study of film texts viewed as autonomous, self-sufficient entities' and complained that criticism 'has tended to take the film as "given" and has ignored questions of how the organisation of a film text might relate to the organisation of an industry or to specific working practices'.[16] Another point is that if one analyses films closely enough looking for their internal ideological contradictions then many of them will end up lumped in *Cahiers'* category 'E'. The fact is that most films will expose some form of contradiction or tension – even if they are ultimately resolved. As Robin Wood observed: '*All* the genres can be profitably examined in terms of ideological oppositions, forming a complex interlocking pattern...It is probable that a genre is ideologically "pure" (i.e. safe) only in its simplest, most archetypal, most aesthetically deprived and intellectually contemptible form – such as the Hopalong Cassidy films or Andy Hardy comedies.'[17]

▶ The Gramscian turn

An alternative to the Althusserian notion of cinema as an ideological apparatus was provided by the adoption of Gramsci's theory of hegemony in the 1980s. Antonio Gramsci, an Italian communist imprisoned by the Fascists, had recognized that even totalitarian regimes depend upon consent to maintain their rule. In his 'Prison Notebooks' (published posthumously in 1947) Gramsci outlined his notion of 'hegemony': that the dominant groups in society can only establish and maintain their dominance by winning the consent of others. This involves a process of 'negotiation' and 'transaction' whereby dominant groups address the interests and aspirations of other groups and make concessions to them. Like Althusserian Marxism, Gramsci's theory of hegemony offers a more sophisticated understanding of the relationship between ideology, political process and social institutions. It was also adopted into the study of popular culture, particularly in the work of the Centre for Contemporary Cultural Studies at the University of Birmingham which pioneered the study of popular culture as an instrument of hegemony.[18]

A few examples must suffice to illustrate the application of Gramscian theory to film and cultural studies. Tony Bennett and Janet Woollacott's *Bond and Beyond* (1987) – a highly theorized study of the James Bond phenomenon in literature, cinema and popular culture – asserts that 'in order to become significantly popular, fictional forms must in some way relate to and connect with popular experience and, rather than simply imposing dominant ideologies, must therefore make concessions to the opposing or different values and ideologies of subordinate social groups'.[19] Bennett and Woollacott argue that the orthodox critical view of Bond – that the character is reactionary, sexist and racist (a view from which, incidentally, they do not dissent themselves) – does not account for the huge global popularity of the films: therefore the films cannot be understood as straightforward reflections of dominant ideology but rather as texts that respond in some way to the tastes, interests and aspirations of their consumers. (A characteristic of this approach – not shared by some ideological criticism – is its recognition that the consumption of cultural texts is a matter of choice. One cannot force unwilling audiences to pay at the box office to see a Bond movie – any movie for that matter.) Bennett and Woollacott characterize the Bond of Ian Fleming's novels as 'a political hero for the middle classes', while the Bond of the films became 'a hero of modernisation' as the films 'both significantly broadened the social basis of Bond's popular appeal in Britain and extended the horizons of his popularity internationally'.[20]

Gramsci similarly informs the work of the prolific US film historian Marcia Landy, whose books include studies of Italian and British cinema and of **genres** such as melodrama and the historical film. Landy's analysis of British film genres – including historical, empire, war, melodrama, comedy, horror, science fiction and social problem films – 'is predicated on the assumption that the films are particularly revealing of the contestation over hegemony which expresses itself as much in the private sphere as in the public arena'.[21] An example of this process is how the British social problem films of the 1950s (such as *The Blue Lamp*, *I Believe in You*, *Cosh Boy*, *The Weak and the Wicked*, *Yield to the Night*, *Sapphire* and – extending to the early 1960s – *Victim*) highlight the disjuncture between the desires of their protagonists and the values of the community into which the films seek to assimilate them. Landy's analysis of Italian historical films similarly draws upon Gramsci's discussion of the Italian Risorgimento (which he regarded as a failed revolution) to make sense of the politics of Luchino Visconti's *Senso* (1954) and *The Leopard* (1963): 'Gramsci's analyses of the social and cultural history of the Risorgimento provide a grid to challenge the monolithic nature of traditional and academic forms of historicizing that elide the importance of the everyday, of the subjective, and of the nature and power of common sense.'[22] She interprets *The Leopard*, for example, where the central relationship is between an aristocratic and a bourgeois family, through Gramsci's argument that the rise of the Italian bourgeois class was characterized by a desire to conform to the existing social values and structures.

The Gramscian turn in cultural studies was all too much for historian Arthur Marwick, who declared that 'from the point of view of the pragmatic historian the fanciful metaphor of processes of negotiation taking place in the formation of cultural hegemony carries too heavy a freight of untested assumptions about dialectical conflict'. He adds: 'To me such assertions as that Carol Reed's film *The Stars Look Down* (1938) "proved that cinema was maturing as a hegemonic instrument, becoming more clearly an area of exchange and negotiation rather than a patronising instrument of political coercion" simply restates a predetermined position without saying anything of real interest about this fascinating film.'[23] As ever the proof of the theory is in the application. It seems to me that while the analysis of individual films as sites of 'negotiation' and 'transaction' are as problematic in their way as ideological analysis, the Gramscian model does nevertheless offer a means of understanding the relationship between the film industry and its consumers. Unless one agrees with Dwight Macdonald that audiences are 'passive consumers', then the film industry needs to provide a product that will meet the entertainment needs and cultural tastes of cinemagoers. As with much theoretical work at this time, however, the cinema audience is largely absent from these studies.

▶ Structuralism and semiotics

'Screen theory' would soon become synonymous with theories of **structuralism** and **semiotics** imported from French intellectual culture. Structuralism – which owed its intellectual origins to the work of French social anthropologist Claude Lévi-Strauss and Russian Formalist critic Vladimir Propp – was posited on the notion that all forms of social organization are based on a set of underlying patterns and relationships which give them structure and form. This could be applied to film in the sense that the meaning of a film arises not from surface details (such as plot, characterization and *mise-en-scène*) but rather from the ideological structures embedded in the text at a deeper level. Typically this is constructed as a series of binary oppositions: good/bad, male/female or young/old, for example. The related field of semiotics (or semiology) is an approach to linguistics pioneered by the Swiss linguist Ferdinand de Saussure. Semiotics differentiates between the 'sign' (for example a word), the 'signifier' (its sound or appearance) and the 'signified' (the concept attached to it).

Peter Wollen's book *Signs and Meaning in the Cinema* (1969) marked the entry of structuralism and semiotics into English-language film theory. Wollen adopted structuralist methodology to offer a reformulation of *auteur* theory away from the idea of the film-maker as a creative individual and to consider instead the thematic patterns embedded in the films. 'What the *auteur* theory does,' Wollen argued, 'is to take a group of films – the work of one director – and analyse their structure. Everything irrelevant to this, everything non-pertinent, is considered logically secondary, contingent, to be discarded.'[24] Wollen compared the films of John Ford and Howard Hawks, concluding that Ford was a 'much richer' film-maker than Hawks because the thematic structures (or as Wollen preferred it 'antinomies') of his films were deeper and more complex in their relationships to each other.[25] In the postscript to a second edition of *Signs and Meaning in the Cinema* published in 1972, Wollen argued that the *auteur* should be understood as an 'unconscious catalyst' rather than a creative artist:

> *Auteur* analysis does not consist of retracing a film to its creative source. It con-
> sists of tracing a structure (not a message) within the work, which can then *post*
> *factum* be assigned to an individual, the director, on empirical grounds. It is
> wrong, in the name of a denial of the traditional idea of creative subjectivity,
> to deny any status to individuals at all. But Fuller, or Hawks, or Hitchcock, the
> directors, are quite different from 'Fuller' or 'Hawks' or 'Hitchcock', the struc-
> tures named after them, and should not be methodologically confused.[26]

This idea came to be known as '*auteur*-structuralism' and represented an attempt to combine the new type of ideological criticism with the still prevalent *auteur* theory. However, as was soon pointed out, *auteur*-structuralism was posited on a theoretical contradiction. On the one hand it attempted to preserve a place for the director with a personal vision, while on the other hand it asserted that the meaning of a film could not be reduced to authorial intent. It therefore detached the director from a creative role while maintaining the director as the link between the films.

Structuralism seemed on more secure ground when applied to **genre**. Will Wright's *Sixguns and Society* (1975) was a structuralist study of the American Western film that took Lévi-Strauss as its principal 'idea and inspiration'. Wright argues that 'the Western, like any myth, stands between human consciousness and society'. 'If a myth is popular,' he continues, 'it must somehow appeal to or reinforce the individuals who view it by communicating a symbolic meaning to them.'[27] Wright proceeds to analyse the structure of what he terms the 'classical' Western through a set of narrative conventions and motifs: the hero enters a social group; the hero is unknown to the society; the hero is revealed to have an exceptional ability; the society does not entirely accept

the hero; there is a conflict of interest between society and the villains; the
villains are stronger than society; the hero initially avoids involvement in the
conflict; the villains endanger a friend of the hero; the hero fights and defeats
the villains; society is safe; society accepts the hero; the hero loses or gives up
his special status.[28] These functions 'describe the narrative structure of the classical Western, which presents a dramatic model of communication and action
between characters who represent different types of people inherent in our con-
ceptualization of society'.[29] Wright suggests – in language that recalls Comolli
and Narboni – that the Western 'has become part of the cultural language by
which America understands itself.'[30]

The principal criticism of structuralist analysis of this sort is that it becomes
overly reductive: in searching for the underlying structuring patterns between
films it emphasizes the similarities between them at the expense of their differences. A further specific criticism of Wright's approach is that he bases his study
on the top-grossing Westerns on the grounds that box-office success alone is
the best indicator of a film's impact. This is problematic, however, as the box
office 'is neither a barometer of significant developments within the Western
nor an infallible guide to the genre's interaction with the social and political
realities of twentieth-century America'.[31] Wright never satisfactorily explains
the interaction between the social and ideological function of myth on the one
hand and film production trends on the other: the relationship between the
two processes remains implicit.

Semiotics has proved an even more problematic methodology than structuralism in its application to film. For one thing semiotics tends to deal in broad
generalizations rather than specific examples. The most striking feature of the
English translation of Christian Metz's 'The Imaginary Signifier' that appeared
in *Screen* in 1975 is that in the course of its 62 pages it makes passing reference to only three films.[32] For Metz 'the cinematic institution is not just the
cinema industry … it is also the mental machinery – another industry – which
spectators "accustomed to the cinema" have internalised historically and which
has adapted them to the consumption of films'.[33] Yet this concept remains
entirely untested historically. Instead Metz resorts to a theoretical framework
derived from psychoanalysis (Sigmund Freud and Jacques Lacan) that because
it assumes an unconscious process is resistant to any kind of empirical testing.
'We do not yet have the kind of general agreement over basic principles which
would permit convincing semiological studies of individual films,' Peter Wollen
observed in 1969: and this has remained the case.[34] Semiotics represented perhaps the most extreme instance of the tendency within 'Screen theory' to
search for totalizing explanatory frameworks of the cinematic apparatus. This is
not to dismiss it outright. The one redeeming feature of Metz's work is that, for
all its broad generalizations and psychoanalytical baggage, it was, nevertheless,

a theory of cinema based on an extensive study of films. The same cannot be said of other theorists – Lacan, Barthes, Foucault, Derrida – who would be co-opted to provide theoretical ballast for film studies.

▶ **Feminist film theories**

The emergence of feminist film criticism can be dated quite precisely to the early 1970s with the publication of Molly Haskell's *From Reverence to Rape* (1973) and Marjorie Rosen's *Popcorn Venus* (1973), two books charting the representation of women in American cinema and finding the films wanting for their sexist and stereotyped images of women.[35] Haskell, for example, avers that films were guilty of promoting the 'big lie' of the inferiority of women. Hollywood, as 'the propaganda arm of the American Dream machine', promoted stereotypes of femininity – love goddesses, sex kittens, virgins, spinsters, martyrs, mothers – but 'was not interested in sponsoring a smart, ambitious woman as a popular heroine'.[36] Ironically these books – both quite journalistic in content and both widely reviewed – were soon followed by a number of films that were praised for offering more psychologically realistic characterizations of women, notably Martin Scorsese's *Alice Doesn't Live Here Any More* (1974), Herbert Ross's *The Turning Point* (1977) and Paul Mazursky's *An Unmarried Woman* (1978). However, these films could be seen either as exceptions that proved the rule, distinctive only because they stood out from the norm, or in Gramscian terms, as illustrating how Hollywood would take up issues raised by the women's movement in order to appease its critics while at the same time recasting the issues in the conventional form of melodrama.

Feminism is a social movement whose focus is on gender inequality and, especially, on how women have been oppressed through the ideological discourses of **patriarchy**. This transfers to film both as a theory of power (the recognition that women by and large do not hold positions of authority in the film industry) and as a theory of representation (that women are presented in films in such a way that reinforces sexist attitudes and does not correspond to social reality). As the editorial in the first issue of *Camera Obscura*, a journal devoted to feminist theory, put it: 'Women are oppressed not only economically and politically, but also in the very forms of reasoning, signifying and symbolical exchange of our culture. Cinema is a privileged place for an examination of this kind in its unique conjuncture of political, economic and cultural modes.'[37] Even so-called 'women's films' – a term applied, often in a derogatory way, to films either featuring women as principal protagonists and/or assumed to be produced for a mostly female audience – are ultimately conditioned by the patriarchal discourses of society in general and the film industry in particular. Pam Cook summarizes the position of most feminist critics when she suggests that even in female-centred melodrama 'the feminine is defined in traditional terms: "feminine" virtues of caring, compassion and sensitivity are set against "masculine" aggression, violence and destruction'.[38]

The most influential – and controversial – intervention in feminist debates around film was Laura Mulvey's seminal 1975 article 'Visual Pleasure and Narrative Cinema'. This article can be placed in the intellectual context of 'Screen theory': it signalled a shift away from the prevailing methodology of Althusserian Marxism and towards the adoption of a (specifically Lacanian) psychoanalytical perspective. Mulvey's aim was explicitly ideological: she sought to use psychoanalysis 'as a political weapon, demonstrating the way the unconscious of patriarchal society has structured film form'.[39] She argues that the act of spectatorship in the cinema 'has been split between active/male and passive/female' and that a 'determining male gaze projects its phantasy [sic] on to the female figure which is styled accordingly'. 'In their traditional exhibitionist role,' she avers, 'women are simultaneously looked at and displayed, with their appearance coded for strong visual and erotic impact so that they can be said to connote *to-be-looked-at-ness*'.[40] Mulvey understands the act of cinema spectatorship as a process of voyeurism and **scopophilia** (gaining pleasure through looking). And, drawing upon psychoanalytical theory, she contends that 'the meaning of woman is sexual difference, the absence of the penis as visually ascertainable, the material evidence on which is based the castration complex essential for the organisation of entrance to the symbolic order and the law of the father.'[41]

The intellectual currency afforded to Mulvey's article is evident from the fact that it is probably the most widely anthologized piece of critical writing in film studies. However, it is also one of the most problematic and tendentious. Quite apart from the somewhat dubious psychoanalytical framework – one does not need to import ideas of the Oedipus complex and castration anxiety to recognize that men and women are sexually different – the article makes a series of general statements about cinema based on a brief discussion of a narrow selection of two films by Josef Von Sternberg (*Morocco, Dishonoured*) and three by Alfred Hitchcock (*Rear Window, Vertigo, Marnie*), neither of whom could be said to be representative of either Hollywood or narrative cinema in general. More fundamentally, Mulvey's division between active/male and passive/female and her assertion that the organization of **point-of-view** invites the spectator to identify with the male protagonist has the unfortunate effect of casting all spectators as male. This tendency to homogenize the audience as an undifferentiated mass is a characteristic of much 'Screen theory' – and one of its chief limitations. Nevertheless the idea of the 'male gaze' continues to inform feminist film theory even though it accounts for only one half of the audience.

'**Queer Theory**' has since pointed out that Mulvey's male spectator is also assumed to be heterosexual: again this cannot be taken for granted.

Mulvey responded to the absence of the female spectator in a follow-up article, based on a reading of *Duel in the Sun* (1946), in which she speculated that the female spectator may either identify with the passive femininity which has been assigned for her or associate with the male gaze.[42] This argument has in turn been criticized for the apparent assumption that female spectators can gain pleasure only through accepting a subordinate position or through a transgendered identification with the male spectator. Of course the denial of a female gaze might itself be taken as an example of the oppressive operation of patriarchy. Other feminist theorists, however, have argued for the recognition of the female gaze. Tania Modleski, for example, responds to Mulvey's active/ male passive/female dichotomy by highlighting the salient point that in *Rear Window* – 'a movie that all critics agree is about the power the man attempts to wield through exercising the gaze' – not only is the male protagonist passive throughout (he is confined to a wheelchair) but that the concluding shot of the film shows the man asleep (and therefore not looking at anyone) while the woman has 'the last look'.[43] This is in the context of a re-evaluation of Hitchcock's films in which Modleski seeks 'to save his female viewers from annihilation at the hands not only of traditional male critics but of those feminist critics who see woman's repression in patriarchal cinema as total, women's "liking" for these films as nothing but masochism'.[44]

But is there any scope for films that break free from patriarchal ideology? One of the developments in feminist film theory has been to examine the films of women directors (of whom there are relatively few in relation to film-making as a whole) in order to see whether they conform to the conventional mode of gendered spectatorship. The films of Dorothy Arzner – along with Ida Lupino one of only two women who enjoyed significant directorial careers within the **studio system** – have been seen as problematizing the operations of patriarchal ideology. In particular her musical *Dance, Girl, Dance* (1940) has been seen as an 'explicitly feminist film'.[45] In a key scene in the film the heroine Judy (Maureen O'Hara), an aspiring serious ballerina obliged to perform in a burlesque show, turns on the male audience who have been jeering her and delivers an impassioned response during the course of which the point-of-view switches from the (male) spectators in the film to the (female) protagonist. Claire Johnston sees this – and other Arzner films such as *Merrily We Go To Hell* (1932) and *Christopher Strong* (1933) – as examples of how 'the woman...determines her own identity through transgression and desire in a search for an independent existence beyond and outside the discourse of the male'.[46]

It could be argued that with the films of Dorothy Arzner – and, also, the work of the British director Muriel Box – we are again in the realm of *Cahiers du Cinéma*'s category 'E': films which ostensibly belong within an ideological discourse but which on examination can be seen as problematic. A more radical alternative is offered by feminist **counter-cinema**, as exemplified by avant-garde films such as Chantelle Akerman's *Jeanne Dielman* (1975), Laura Mulvey and Peter Wollen's *Riddles of the Sphinx* (1977) and Sally Potter's *Thriller* (1979). Counter-cinema – a term first coined by Peter Wollen in an analysis of Godard's *Vent d'est* (1969) – is a film practice conceived in dialectical opposition to **classical Hollywood cinema**: ambiguity instead of transparency, estrangement instead of identification, unpleasure instead of pleasure, and so forth.[47] Mulvey argues that feminist cinema as an avant-garde practice is the only way to 'free the look of the camera into its materiality in time and space and the look of the audience into dialectics and passionate detachment'.[48] Perhaps the best one can say about *Riddles of the Sphinx* – a film that remains mercifully unseen except on university film studies courses – is that it not only exhibits all the tendencies one could ever conceive of as being 'counter' to classical cinema but that it also represents the practical fulfilment of Mulvey's aim of the 'destruction of pleasure as a radical weapon'.[49]

▶ Postcolonialism and cinema

Postcolonialism, like feminism, is both a theory of power and a theory of representation: it is a critical framework for understanding relations between colonizers and colonized (political, economic, social) and for analysing the images of colonized subjects produced both by the colonizers and by the colonized themselves. The 'post' of postcolonialism locates the theory historically – it tends to be associated with the nations of the so-called 'Third World' that achieved independence after the Second World War – though postcolonialist discourse has also been applied retrospectively to earlier periods. Hollywood's Tarzan films of the 1930s and 1940s, for example, have been attacked for their racist representations of Africans as primitive, tribal, savage and superstitious: yet for many years this was the only image of Africa circulating in popular cinema.[50] The Tarzan films can therefore be seen as representing an ideological process through which Hollywood assumed control of the filmic representation of Africa. It was not until the 1960s that the rise of indigenous film-making allowed Africans to take ownership of their own images in film.

The intellectual foundation of much postcolonial theory is Edward Said's *Orientalism* (1978). Said argues that the idea of 'the Orient' was 'a European invention' created by and within Western culture and that 'Orientalism' became a cultural discourse to describe the relationship between Europe and the Orient. He explains: 'Orientalism can be discussed and analyzed as the corporate institution for dealing with the Orient – dealing with it by making statements about it, authorizing views of it, describing it, by teaching it, settling it, ruling over it.'[51] The intellectual significance of Said's work is that it has shed light on the cultural dimension of colonialism, which can no longer be understood only as a political or economic institution. Yet, while the theory of Orientalism has been influential in literary and cultural studies, its application to film has been limited to analyses of the promotion of the idea of the 'Yellow Peril' in representations of the Chinese or – to take a less offensively racist example – the 'exotic' appeal of stars such as the Indian-born Sabu for Western audiences.

Postcolonial discourse has been applied in various ways in film studies. On one level it has provided a theoretical framework for understanding the emergence of national cinemas outside the West: these include not only the cinemas of Africa, Asia and Latin America but also those of former 'white' colonies such as Australia and New Zealand where an indigenous production industry of any significant size did not emerge until the 1970s. It has also been applied to the study of **sub-state cinemas**: minority cinemas within nation states such as Aboriginal cinema in Australia, Maori cinema in New Zealand, Bengali cinema in India, Québécois cinema in Canada or Welsh cinema in Britain.[52] On another level it has been adopted as a critical tool for analysing the cultural politics and representational discourses of films addressing aspects of the colonial/postcolonial experience. These range from national epics such as Australia's *Gallipoli* (1981) or India's *Lagaan* (2001) to more personal, intimate films such as Tracey Moffatt's *Nice Coloured Girls* (1987) or Gurinder Chadha's *Bhaji on the Beach* (1993) – films by, respectively, an Australian Aboriginal and a British Asian director which explore the hybridity of cultural identities in multicultural societies.

A significant feature of the work on postcolonial cinemas is that it refocuses attention on aesthetics in a way that is less evident in some other theoretical approaches. This can be explained in several ways. On the one hand the absence of mass-production film industries in much of the Third World (Africa, principally, but also parts of Latin America and the Middle East) and the consequent weakness of institutional structures makes the idea of cinema as an ideological apparatus rather less applicable. (This is not to say that cinema has not been an instrument of state ideology: Cuba and Algeria are the foremost examples of Third World nations that adopted film as an instrument of propaganda in the 'anti-colonialist struggle'.) And on the other hand the narrative and formal strategies of much Third World film-making have often been consciously 'alternative'. Fredric Jameson argued, somewhat tendentiously, that all

Third World 'texts' are 'necessarily allegorical' and 'project a political dimension in the form of national allegory': he exemplifies this with films such as *Xala* (1975) by the Senegalese director Ousmane Sembene which offers a particularly critical perspective on the postcolonial experience by showing how the power structures of colonialism are preserved as an African elite emerges to take the place of Europeans following decolonization.[53] Finally, an understanding of production contexts is, once again, necessary for a full understanding of postcolonial cinemas. *The Battle of Algiers* (1965), for example, problematizes the idea of a dialectical relationship between Europe and the Third World. *The Battle of Algiers* was sponsored by the newly independent Algerian government as a semi-documentary account of the role of the Algerian National Liberation Front in its campaign against the French military. Regarded by many as the foundational film of Algerian cinema, it has also been described as 'a European film about the Third World' because many of those involved in its production, including its director (Gillo Pontecorvo), were Italian.[54]

▶ Case study: Third Cinema

The example of 'Third Cinema' – a term applied to a radical, alternative form of film theory and practice that emerged in the late 1960s – highlights many of the issues around film and ideology discussed in this chapter. Third Cinema was an attempt to provide both a radical alternative to mainstream or classical cinema and to reconceptualize the dominant paradigm within film studies between a commercial or entertainment cinema on the one hand and an **art cinema** on the other. The term was first used by Argentinian film-makers Fernando Solanas and Octavio Getino in their polemical manifesto entitled 'Towards a Third Cinema' in 1968.

   Third Cinema is not, as often assumed, synonymous with Third World cinema, but rather represents a particular historical and ideological phase within the cinema of the Third World. Teshome Gabriel, one of the leading theorists of Third Cinema, has argued that the history of film-making in the Third World has gone through three distinct phases. The first – which he terms 'the assimilation phase' – involves a close identification with Hollywood.[55] These films – exemplified by Egyptian cinema of the 1930s and Brazilian films of the 1940s – often imitate the genres and entertainment patterns of Hollywood, while adapting them to meet local cultural circumstances. The musical, for example, became one of the staple genres of Third World cinemas: the *ranchera* in Mexico, *chanchada* in Brazil and *tanguenara* in Argentina all adapted the conventions of the Hollywood musical to the local idiom. Gabriel's second phase – 'the remembrance phase' – involves the 'indigenisation and control of talents, production, exhibition and distribution' and 'a movement for a social institution of cinema in the Third World'.[56] Examples of this phase include the Mexican films of Luis Buñuel in the 1950s and the *Cinema Nôvo* movement in Brazil during the 1960s which demonstrated the influence of **Neo-Realism** in their use of real locations and their more complex spatial relationships. The third phase – which Gabriel terms 'the combative phase' – is characterized by 'film-making as a public service institution' in which the film industry 'is not only owned by the nation and/or government, it is also managed, operated and run for and by the people'. A particular feature of this phase is 'an ideological point-of-view instead of that of a character as in dominant Western conventions'.[57] This is exemplified by Cuban cinema of the 1960s and by films such as *The Battle of Algiers*.

Gabriel's taxonomy of Third World cinemas maps onto Solanas and Getino's concept of First, Second and Third Cinema. 'First Cinema' encompasses not only Hollywood but also the commercial cinemas of other countries (including the Soviet Union). 'Second Cinema' is an 'author's cinema' that allows space for artistic expression but which is still essentially conceived within a commercial context. 'Third Cinema', however, marks 'the revolutionary opening towards a cinema outside and against the System – a cinema of liberation'.[58] Third Cinema is radical, militant, oppositional, politicized, experimental and anti-imperialist. For Solanas and Getino it was a product of 'revolutionary struggle':

> The anti-imperialist struggle of the peoples of the Third World and of their equivalents inside the imperialist countries constitutes today the axis of the world revolution. Third Cinema is, in our opinion, the cinema that recognizes in that struggle the most gigantic cultural, scientific, and artistic manifestation of our time, the great possibility of constructing a liberated personality with each people as a starting point – in a word, the decolonization of culture.[59]

Towards a Third Cinema' was one of several such manifestos – others included Glauber Rocha's 'Aesthetics of Hunger' and Julio Garcia Espinoza's 'For an Imperfect Cinema'[60] – that were published in progressive film journals in America and Europe, such as *Cineaste*, *Jump Cut*, *Afterimage* and *Framework*. It is not difficult to see how the radical, Marxist orientation of these manifestos fitted with the intellectual concerns of film theory at the time.

Solanas and Getino's *Hour of the Furnaces* (1968) is the paradigmatic film of Third Cinema. It has been described as 'a Marxist historical analysis of neo-colonialism and oppression in Argentina'.[61] The four-hour film is structured in three parts. The first part ('Neocolonialism and Violence') is dedicated to Che Guevara and shows how Argentina has been exploited not only by Europe and the United States but also by its ruling elites (the film was made during a period of military rule in the country). The second part ('An Act for Liberation') focuses on the government of Juan Perón and examines its legacy, while the third section ('Violence and Liberation') is a series of interviews with political activitists discussing the potential for revolution. It will be clear that *Hour of the Furnaces* is very far from being a conventional film: one of the reasons why it was so well received within radical film culture was because it conformed to the view of some theorists that a genuine revolutionary cinema necessarily entailed formal innovation. The film includes an eclectic mixture of form and styles: it is both documentary and fiction and includes aspects of both *Cinéma Vérité* and Surrealism. It employs associative **montage** in the manner of Sergei Eisenstein (shots of prize bulls at a cattle show in Buenos Aires are intercut with the faces of the Argentinian bourgeosie) and uses captions and inter-titles in the manner of Godard to break up the narrative. Solanas and Getino intended that screenings of the film should be interrupted so that members of the audience could debate among themselves. They considered this 'a new facet of cinema: the participation of people who, until then, were considered spectators'.[62]

Third Cinema arose from a particular set of historical and ideological circumstances. Solanas and Getino, like many left-wing intellectuals, believed that the 1960s had witnessed 'the development of a worldwide revolution whose moving force is to be found in the Third World'.[63] In the eyes of some radicals, events such as the Cuban Revolution, the Algerian War of Liberation and the Vietnam War seemed to point towards a global revolution against First World colonialism. The rallying cry of Third Cinema was 'revolution': its heroes were Che Guevara, Ho Chi Minh and Mao Tse-tung. However, the moment of Third Cinema was short lived. Its influence and appeal declined in the 1970s. There were several reasons for this. For one thing the economic downturn of the 1970s caused many Third World countries to become more inward-looking and less internationalist. Nor was the advent of reactionary military regimes in much of Latin America and Africa conducive to radical film-making. And on another level the intellectual appeal of Marxism was diminished by events such as Mao's 'Cultural Revolution' in China and the atrocities of Idi Amin in Uganda and the Khmer Rouge in Cambodia. In hindsight, as Jonathan Buchsbaum points out, '[the] precondition for *third cinema* – the worldwide uprising of the masses – sounds like a rhetorical anachronism, soggy with Marxist internationalism'.[64] Nevertheless it remains – like the **Soviet montage** cinema of the 1920s and Wollen's notion of counter-cinema – a rare example of the formal interaction between film theory and film practice.

This has been a necessarily brief overview of the broad area of film and ideology. The shift away from theories of aesthetics towards theories of ideology marked a paradigm shift in the discipline of film studies whose effects are still being felt. The project of 'Screen theory' was twofold: to show that cinema was an instrument of ideology, and to find a methodology that would enable progressive critics to counter its ideological effects. The failure of 'Screen theory' to establish the totalizing theory of cinema that had seemed for a while to be its aim can be explained by the diverse – and in some respects incompatible – theoretical perspectives that it had adopted to this end. Structuralism was too reductive, semiotics simply too opaque, and, while feminism and postcolonialism are both able to provide nuanced readings of films, these are approaches based on the examination of specific social and cultural discourses that account for only part of the ideological work of any film. As the intellectual limitations of 'Screen theory' became apparent from the early 1980s, however, film scholars were finally beginning to ask the historical questions about the institutional, economic and cultural contexts of film-making that hitherto had been marginalized. This would, in time, see a shift away from the view of films as autonomous, self-sufficient texts and the emergence of an approach to film analysis that was much more securely grounded in historical context.

4 Film as a Historical Source

Ever since the invention of cinematography the question has been raised again and again whether and to what extent it would be possible to use film as a way of documenting contemporary history.

Fritz Terveen[1]

The role of film as a historical source involves a very different set of questions and debates to those involved in analysing it either as an art form or as an ideological apparatus. Yet the idea of film as a historical record predates the emergence of both theories of aesthetics and cinema as a social practice. Indeed, as Terveen indicates, it is as old as the medium itself. As early as 1898, for example, the pioneer Polish cinematographer Boleslas Matuszewski, whose films included records of state occasions such as the Coronation of Tsar Nicholas II (1897) and the Diamond Jubilee of Queen Victoria (1897), declared that film was 'a new source of history' and predicted that 'animated photography...will give a direct view of the past'.[2] The notion of film as a historical source attaches a very different evidential value to film than aesthetics: in this approach the value of film is not to be found in its artistic or formal properties but in what it reveals about social and historical conditions at the time at which it was made. The discourse around film as a historical source has tended to focus on actuality and non-fiction films rather than on the fictional feature films that dominate aesthetic histories. However, the discursive terms are similar to those we have seen in Chapter 2. Matuszewski's notion of the 'truth' of the filmic image anticipated André Bazin by over half a century:

> Perhaps the cinematograph does not give history in its entirety, but at least what it does deliver is incontestable and of absolute truth...One could say that animated photography has a character of authenticity, accuracy and precision that belongs to it alone. It is the ocular evidence that is truthful and infallible *par excellence*...In short, one wishes that other historic documents had the same degree of certitude and clarity.[3]

Like other pioneers, of course, Matuszewski was seeking to promote his own business, and to this end he made somewhat exaggerated claims for the cinematograph. In particular his faith in the 'absolute truth' of the filmic image does not stand scrutiny. Indeed, never has there been a more misleading dictum than 'the camera never lies'. Early cinematographers were not averse to recreating scenes for the camera if they were not able to capture the event itself: Georges Méliès, for example, made films of the sinking of the battleship USS *Maine* (1898) and the Coronation of Edward VII (1901) that were shot entirely in the studio – the latter film was even released before the coronation![4] However, this fact should not detract either from Matuszewski's far-sightedness in recognizing the need for film preservation – he called for the establishment of a 'Depository of Historical Cinematography' to archive 'all scenes … of historical interest' – or from his suggestion that 'animated photography will … become an agreeable method for studying the past' and 'a singularly efficacious teaching process'.[5] As we will see Matuszewski remained a prophet without honour for many decades: it would be 70 years before historians were ready to embrace film in the manner he advocated.

▶ From 'film and history' to 'film history'

It would be fair to say that for many years professional historians remained resistant to film, which, especially following the ascendancy of the **feature film**, was regarded as a medium of popular entertainment rather than as a historical source. It was not until the interwar period that historians began to show an interest in film; and, even then, those who did were small in number and cautious in their approach. At this time discussion focused on the way in which the film industry represented – or, rather, misrepresented – history in films. The grandiosely named International Iconographical Commission, for example – an organization that emerged from a series of meetings of the International Congress of the Historical Sciences between 1926 and 1934 – asserted that the term 'historical film' should specifically be limited to films 'which record a person or period from the time after the invention of cinematography and without dramaturgical or "artistic" purposes: those films which present a visual record of a definite event, person or locality, and which presuppose a clearly recognisable historical interest inherent in the subject matter.'[6] In other words it was only **actuality film** that had any value as a historical source and not the fiction film or 'so-called historical films' such as *Ben-Hur* (1924) which took too much dramatic licence in their treatment of the past.

A similar conservatism was evident in Britain, where the Films Inquiry Committee of the Historical Association took a distinctly jaundiced view towards the 'falseness' of feature films and warned that it was 'gravely concerned at the effect on children and adults of films purporting to represent historical personages which are being shown in picture palaces'.[7] Typical of the narrow-mindedness of the historical establishment's attitude towards feature film is one historian's detailed critique of Alexander Korda's *The Private Life of Henry VIII* (1933). This was the first major international success for the British film industry during the talkie era, with Charles Laughton winning the Academy Award for Best Actor for his lusty and irreverent performance in the title role. However, historian Charles Beard took the film to task on the grounds that 'it is feeble history, bad psychology and worse archeology' and that it 'displays a lamentable lack of knowledge of the manners, customs and practices of the Court in the third and fourth decades of the sixteenth century'. Beard was a specialist in arms and heraldry, and he went on to describe the many historical errors, some of them absurdly pedantic, such as the king's shoes being buckled on the wrong side ('Mr Laughton wears his spurs like a cowboy'), the Earl of Essex not wearing his Lesser George Garter, the Gentlemen of the Court wearing their swords within the palace precincts, and the executioner of Anne Boleyn wielding a German fighting sword of 1580 ('He would, moreover, never have sharpened his instrument on a grindstone; he would have honed it').[8]

This was the level at which historical engagement with film would remain for several decades. For, despite various initiatives such as the formation of the British Universities Film Council in 1948 and the Institut für den Wissenschaftlichen Films in Göttingen in 1949, most historians remained deeply sceptical of the value of film for either teaching or research. It was left to film-makers, such as Sir Arthur Elton, a leading light of the pre-war documentary movement, to make the case that 'films can be used, as other historical source material can be used, for various and different historical purposes'. Unlike Matuszewski, however, Elton did not ascribe to film any quality of 'absolute truth' in the representation of events. As a film-maker himself he was only too aware of the medium's capacity for manipulation and misrepresentation. If Matuszewski had anticipated Bazin's notion of film as an objective representation of reality, Elton recalled the advocates of **formative film theory** such as the **Soviet montage** school: 'Let one piece of film be joined to another, and something new comes into existence, some quality shared by neither piece alone.'[9]

It was not until the late 1960s, however, that 'film and history' emerged as a subject of serious discussion and debate. In 1968 issues of the French historical journal *Annales* and the BUFC's *University Vision* called for historians to pay greater attention to filmic sources.[10] It was also in 1968 that the Inter University History Film Consortium was established at the University of Leeds in order to produce archive compilations for teaching modern history – its first was *The Munich Crisis* (1968) – and that the Slade Film History Register was set up by Thorold Dickinson at the University of London. The major landmark event, however, was the conference 'Film and the Historian', held at University College, London, in April 1968. Chaired by A. J. P. Taylor, the conference brought together professional historians, including J. A. S. Grenville, Nicholas Pronay and Paul Smith, different generations of film-makers, including Sir Arthur Elton and Andrew Mollo, film researchers such as Lisa Pontecorvo and archivists such as Ernest Lindgren from the National Film Archive. In his opening remarks, Taylor described the purpose of the conference as being akin to 'propaganda to convince the doubters and inexperienced of how effective film can be for the use of modern historians'.[11]

The 'film and history' movement gathered momentum in the 1970s through a series of international conferences – including in London, Göttingen, Koblenz, Utrecht, Brandbjerg, Tutzing and Copenhagen – and through the adoption of film for teaching modern history by organizations such as The Open University and the Inter University History Film Consortium.[12] In America the Historians' Film Committee was set up in 1970 and the following year founded its journal *Film and History* in order 'to disseminate information to historians and teachers regarding the use of film, television, and other visual fixations [*sic*] in teaching and research for all historical periods'.[13] The production of television series such as *The World at War* (1973), which made extensive use of archive film, also added to the growing legitimacy of 'film and history'.[14] While the focus remained largely, at this stage, on non-fiction film, particularly newsreels and documentaries, there was now evidence of a more sophisticated, and certainly much less jaundiced, attitude towards the use of film as a historical source than in previous generations. No longer did the simple idea of historical 'truth' hold sway. In his professorial inaugural lecture at the University of Birmingham in 1970, for example, J. A. S. Grenville emphasized 'the essential and simple point…that a piece of film is not some unadulterated reflection of historical truth captured by the camera'.[15]

Indeed the emphasis of the 'film and history' movement was now on understanding the highly mediated nature of film as a historical source. A recurring theme is the distinction between 'reality' or 'actuality' on the one hand and 'illusion' or 'artifice' on the other. This is one of the themes that emerges in *The Historian and Film* (1976), an edited collection that represented the first thoroughgoing attempt to lay down a methodological framework for the use of film as a historical source. Thus, for example, William Hughes: 'For historians, the great value of film is its capacity for recording actuality. But the medium has equal potential for distorting reality, and for disguising discontinuities in its recording of events.'[16] In the same volume Nicholas Pronay's essay on newsreels differentiates between 'the illusion of actuality' (actuality films 'which created the illusion that the viewer was actually witnessing an event, which in reality took place far away both in terms of *distance* and in terms of *time*') and 'the illusion of reality' ('trick' films, such as cartoons, 'which created the illusion of witnessing episodes in the life of creatures which in fact could only exist as images on the screen').[17] This aspect of the 'film and history' discourse has often been overlooked by those who insist that historians do not engage with theory. However, in distinguishing between the object of a film and its visual representation, historians were in fact engaging with the same broad ideas as contemporary theories of **semiotics** – albeit expressed in a different discursive language. (The distinction between the subject of a film and its visual representation can be understood by looking at a film such as the Lumières' *Arrival of a Train at La Ciotat* [1895]. The contemporary audiences who reportedly jumped out of the way as the train approached the camera were reacting not to a real train but rather to its image in the film.)

Another idea that has informed the 'film and history' discourse is Arthur Marwick's distinction between 'witting' and 'unwitting' testimony. 'Witting testimony' refers to 'the deliberate or intentional message', while 'unwitting testimony' is 'the unintentional evidence that it also contains'.[18] Danish historian Karsten Fledelius has applied this idea specifically to film: 'Often the most interesting evidence is the "unwitting testimony" of the cinematographic recordings, all those incidental aspects of reality which have just "slipped" into the camera without being consciously recorded by the cameraman.'[19] This distinction assumes that films, like other historical sources, have been produced for a particular reason – this is the 'witting testimony' – but that they may also contain other information that was not included deliberately or consciously by the film-makers. Consider, as an example, the short documentary *London Can Take It!* (1940), an account of a night during the Blitz produced by the GPO Film Unit. The 'witting testimony' of this film is that the morale of the British people remained high and they were able to withstand the nightly air raids by the Luftwaffe: this was the propaganda message that the film-makers wanted to put forward. But the film also contains 'unwitting testimony' of historical conditions during the Blitz: its impact on the urban environment, how social routines and patterns of behaviour changed, and the material conditions of working-class Londoners at the time. None of these points are highlighted by the commentary, suggesting that they were not intended by the film-makers.

The 'film and history' movement came of age with the formation of a professional society in 1977 – the International Association for Audio-Visual Media in Historical Research and Education, which later changed its name, though not the acronym of IAMHIST, to the International Association for Media and History – which has provided a forum for historians and practitioners interested in the use of film and other mass media in historical teaching and research. This was followed in 1981 by the launch of IAMHIST's own journal, the *Historical Journal of Film, Radio and Television*, which describes itself as 'an interdisciplinary journal concerned with the evidence produced by the mass media for historians and social scientists, and with the impact of mass communications on the political and social history of the twentieth century', and which has become the leading forum for both (to use K. R. M. Short's distinction quoted in the introduction) 'historians interested *in* the movies' as a historical source and 'historians whose interest *is* the movies' in their own right.[20]

▶ Actuality, authenticity, realism

At this point it will be useful to discuss three key terms that figure prominently in discussion of film as a historical source – terms that have sometimes been used interchangeably, though they each really mean different things. **Actuality** refers to film that provides a record of real people, events or locations – such as the early 'topicals' (records of newsworthy events) and 'scenics' (travelogues of foreign places and landscapes). **Authenticity** refers to films that are understood as being 'true to life' or 'true to history' even if they are not actuality. So, for example, a historical feature film such as *A Night to Remember* (1958) about the sinking of the *Titanic* could claim authenticity in so far as the film-makers went to great lengths to get their historical facts correct, whereas a comedy like *Carry On Cleo* (1964) makes no claim to period authenticity. **Realism** is better understood as a social or aesthetic construct in which a film represents characters and situations in a manner that conforms to our experiences of real life. Film theorists further differentiate between social realism (representing 'true-to-life' characters and situations), psychological realism (where characters behave according to plausible psychological motivations), and aesthetic realism (representing the external world according to the formal codes and conventions of realism such as long takes and **deep-focus cinematography**).[21] These distinctions are best illustrated through specific examples.

The Battle of the Somme (1916) has been a particularly central film in debates around 'film and history' as it was the first feature-length documentary film compiled from actuality footage. *The Battle of the Somme* was compiled from footage shot at the front by two British War Office cinematographers, Geoffrey Malins and J. B. McDowell, on the first day of the major British offensive against the German lines (1 July 1916). Malins and McDowell shot film of the opening artillery bombardment, the explosion of a giant mine under Hawthorn Ridge, British troops on their way to the front, scenes at a first aid station showing wounded British and captured German soldiers, and captured German trenches. When the rushes were shown to the Topical Committee for War Films in London, it was decided that the footage should be edited into a feature film. *The Battle of the Somme* was first shown in London on 21 August 1916, followed by a general release across the country.[22]

The reception of *The Battle of the Somme* has been well documented: it evidently had a powerful impact on the British public and there are reports of hundreds of thousands of people flocking to see it. Reviews in both the national and the trade press were much impressed by its vivid and authentic pictures of the front. One sequence in particular was much commented on: where a platoon of soldiers goes 'over the top' and two of the men fall dead. Among those who saw the film was the author Sir Henry Rider Haggard, who recorded in his diary that the film 'does give a wonderful idea of the fighting'. 'The most impressive to my mind,' he added, 'is that of a regiment [*sic*] scrambling out of a trench to charge and of the one man who slides back shot dead. There is something appalling about the instantaneous change from fierce activity to supine death.'[23]

However, as film archivist Roger Smither has conclusively demonstrated, the scenes in *The Battle of the Somme* that so impressed contemporaries were in fact staged for the camera behind the lines. There are numerous visual clues. The trench is too shallow for the front line and there is no barbed wire on the parapet; the troops themselves are lightly equipped and are not wearing field backbacks; and the position of the camera is too exposed for this to have been taken under enemy fire. The clinching detail is that one of the 'dead' soldiers who falls onto barbed wire in No Man's Land can then be seen crossing his legs. How far does this staged or reconstructed footage compromise *The Battle of the Somme* as an authentic historical record? Smither points out that 'the proportion of such film to the whole work is actually quite small' and that the vast majority of *The Battle of the Somme* is indeed the real thing.[24] In this sense the inclusion of a small amount of 'fake' material in *The Battle of the Somme* does not significantly detract from its value as a historical source: but of course the historian needs to be aware of which **shots** are authentic and which are not.

Contrast the actuality and authenticity of *The Battle of the Somme* with the Omaha beach sequence of Steven Spielberg's *Saving Private Ryan* (1998). This film is widely held to have set new standards of realism in the representation of combat. One reviewer described it as 'Hollywood's most grimly realistic and historically accurate depiction of a World War II battlefield'.[25] And for the military historian Stephen E. Ambrose it was 'the most accurate and realistic depiction of war on screen that I have ever seen'.[26] The publicity materials for the film attest to the extraordinary lengths to which Spielberg and his collaborators went in order to achieve authenticity. These included consulting service veterans and employing real amputees in the parts of men who lose limbs in the carnage. In order to simulate the noise of machine-gun bullets ripping into bodies the sound editor recorded rounds being fired into meat carcasses wrapped in cloth, while Spielberg and cinematographer Janusz Kaminski used **desaturated colour** to replicate the 'look' of authentic combat footage.

Yet this 'most realistic' of combat movies is, of course, a work of fiction (contrary to some accounts it is not based on a true story) and its graphic war footage is the work of a master film-maker with all the technical resources of Hollywood at his disposal. It is realistic – albeit that the impression of realism is created entirely through artifice – but it is not strictly authentic. Toby Haggith of the Imperial War Museum Film and Video Archive has compared *Saving Private Ryan* to actuality footage shot under combat conditions. He shows that, in fact, Spielberg over-egged the pudding, creating effects that would have been impossible for the cameraman to achieve. For example, the shot of the first fatalities, machine-gunned as the ramp of their landing craft is lowered, is taken from an 'impossible' camera position outside the landing craft and looking back towards it. Furthermore, combat cameramen were trained to keep the camera steady in contrast to the **jump cuts** and out-of-focus shots in the feature film. Haggith concedes that 'the Spielberg version of D-Day is a more impressive account of the event' than the existing film of the landings – taken by cameramen of the British Army Film and Photographic Unit at Sword beach – but nevertheless points out 'the artificial and manipulative technique with which the battle has been recreated'.[27]

▶ The nature of filmic evidence

It is worth taking time to consider the nature of film as a historical source. The word 'film', of course, covers a wide range of forms ranging from short actuality scenes and home movies at one end to big studio blockbusters at the other. All films, however, essentially consist of moving images recorded through a process of photo-mechanical reproduction: and most films comprise multiple images edited together in a sequence. It will immediately be apparent – as recognized by the 'film and history' scholars and despite the claims to the contrary by Bazin and Matuszewski – that film is a highly mediated source. No film is ever 'an unadulterated reflection of historical truth': decisions have been made about what to film, where to position the camera, which shots to select, and the sequence in which those shots are edited together. This is true even of the most straightforward actuality films. The Lumières' films *Workers Leaving the Factory Gate* and *Arrival of a Train at La Ciotat* both consist of one shot under a minute in length. In both films the camera is placed in a position that approximates the point of view of a spectator watching the event: but whereas the first film is shot as a **tableau**, the second is from an angle that makes it seem the locomotive is heading towards the camera.

In general it is possible to distinguish between two types of filmic evidence. On the one hand there are films where the nature of the historical evidence is directly related to the empirical content of the film. These tend to be non-fiction films – actuality films, newsreels, documentaries – that represent a particular person or event. And this is true no matter how heavily mediated the source is. Thus, for example, a newsreel of the liberation of Belsen will provide a record of the event itself and also has some value as evidence of the extent of the Nazi extermination programme and of the physical condition of the survivors. On the other hand there are films, mostly fiction films, where the value as a historical source is detached from the empirical content of the film. For example, neither *The Birth of a Nation* nor *Gone With the Wind* are sources for the American Civil War and its aftermath: but what they do reveal is evidence of American attitudes towards race and gender in the 1910s and 1930s, respectively, as well as a sense of how the Civil War was understood in hindsight.

It will be clear that the different types of film offer up different sorts of evidence. The conventional distinction is between fiction and non-fiction film: but even here there is need to differentiate further, especially in the latter category. For the historian interested in, say, social conditions or leisure activities, the most useful type of filmic evidence is likely to be unedited actuality film. This will range from 'home movies' to semi-professional local news films. Amateur film-making was a popular pastime between the 1920s and 1960s, though it tended to be the more prosperous families who could afford cine-cameras (usually small gauges such as 8-millimetre or 9.5-millimetre) and so the available material is weighted disproportionately in favour of the middle classes. The evidential value of such material depends partly on its subject matter and partly on its provenance. The most famous 'home movie' footage, for example, is probably that shot by Eva Braun, which shows Adolf Hitler relaxing at his mountain retreat at Berchtesgaden. While it provides a fascinating insight into the 'home life' of the Führer, however, it is of little use in understanding the wider historical conditions of the Third Reich as it is, by its nature, restricted to the elite group around Hitler. Another example of amateur film that has acquired particular historical significance is Abraham Zapruder's cine-camera footage that caught the moment of the assassination of President John F. Kennedy in Dallas on 22 November 1963. The Zapruder footage has been analysed in forensic detail to the extent that it has been able to identify which was the fatal shot that killed the president: what it does not reveal is the identity of the assassin.[28]

Perhaps the type of film most used by the social historian, however, is the edited non-fiction film. This provides visual evidence of material conditions, working practices, social customs and behaviour, though it has gone through an additional layer of mediation than raw unedited footage. (And even unedited footage is mediated of course: choices have been made about what to film and where to place the camera.) The most extensive collection of this sort of material anywhere in the world is believed to be that of the Lancashire film-makers

Sagar Mitchell and James Kenyon, which comprises over 800 non-fiction subjects shot between the late 1890s and 1913. The Mitchell and Kenyon films were mostly actuality films of local events shown in cinemas under the banner: 'See yourself as others see you.'[29] The interest of these films lies in their representation of commonplace events: football matches, fairgrounds, seaside trips and so forth. Like home movies they document the activities of ordinary people, who otherwise tend to be invisible, or at best a marginal presence, in film.

These early 'topicals' can be seen as precursors of the newsreel film. The first regular weekly newsreels were introduced *c*.1910 and thereafter became institutionalized with the emergence of major newsreel producers such as Pathé, Gaumont and Movietone. The chief value of the newsreels is in documenting what topical events were reported to the public and how those events were represented. The newsreel is a more heavily mediated source than edited non-fiction film: editorial choices have been made about what to report, the film has been edited into a sequence, and, from the late 1920s, music and commentary were added as an additional layer of exposition. In the United States the style of the sound newsreel was defined by Louis de Rochemont's *March of Time*, characterized by its quick tempo, snappy editing and strident commentary (the style is imitated perfectly in the *'News on the March'* sequence near the beginning of *Citizen Kane*). *March of Time* acknowledged the practice of dramatic reconstruction when it did not have sufficient film material or sound recordings to present a continuous narrative. In this way, it has been suggested, *March of Time* 'actively promoted the notion that even authentic news footage was only symbolic of reality'.[30]

The extent to which the newsreels were heavily mediated sources is demonstrated by research into the history of British newsreels. While newsreel producers clung to the mantra of editorial independence, it is abundantly clear that the institutional links between the five major newsreel companies – British Movietone, British Pathé, Gaumont-British News, British Paramount and Universal – and the National Government determined the content and policy of the newsreels. Thus British newsreels endorsed the policies of the National Government in relation to industrial relations, appeasement and rearmament.[31] Anthony Aldgate concludes his study of British newsreels' representation of the Spanish Civil War – in which he shows that they supported the British government's policy of neutrality and its tacit endorsement of Franco, while at the same time managing to avoid any serious discussion of the causes and politics of the war – that the newsreel companies 'knew that film was a medium which could easily be manipulated and they knew how to manipulate the medium to best advantage'.[32]

One example must suffice to illustrate how the newsreels manipulated public opinion. British Movietone's *Epic of Dunkirk* (6 June 1940) is far from being an objective account of the withdrawal of the British Expeditionary Force from the

French coast. It clearly sets out to place a positive 'spin' on events through its up-tempo music and jaunty commentary. The evacuation itself is presented as an unqualified success: commentary refers to 'the success of this amazing military exploit' and asserts that 'the story of that epic withdrawal will live in history both as a glorious example of discipline and as a monument to seapower.' There is no mention of casualties, and all the shots of British and French troops show them smiling and in good spirits. It can be seen as nothing less than an attempt to position Dunkirk as a victory rather than a defeat. And it makes clear where the blame lies: the 'gallant British and French troops [were] betrayed by the desertion of the Belgian king'. This is not to say that *Epic of Dunkirk* has no value as a historical record of the evacuation: merely that we must be alert to the fact that it presents a highly partial version of events.

The same is true of documentary film. This is not the place for a survey history of documentary practice: rival claimants for the 'father' of documentary include the American Robert Flaherty, the Scot John Grierson and the Lumière brothers of France. The differences between the documentary movement and the newsreels have generally been characterized in terms that see the documentarists as progressive (politically, socially, aesthetically) and the newsreels as conservative. Grierson, for example, derided newsreels for their trivial content: they were 'dim records...of only the evanescent and the essentially unreal, reflecting hardly anything worth preserving of the times they recorded'.[33] The claims of the documentarists to represent reality do not, however, stand up to close scrutiny. British documentary films of the 1930s made use of studio reconstructions and were prone to 'artistic' effects: Grierson spoke of 'the creative treatment of actuality' and admired the Soviet montage cinema of the 1920s. Later documentarists, such as the **Cinéma Vérité** movement in France, claimed to represent 'cinematic truth' by shooting on location without scripts or directorial intervention.[34]

Again, one example must suffice to illustrate a general point. *Triumph of the Will* (1935) was a record of the 1934 Nazi Party rally in Nuremberg compiled from 61 hours of film shot by 16 cameramen under the direction of Leni Riefenstahl. On one level, of course, *Triumph of the Will* acts as a historical record of the rally, documenting Hitler's arrival in Nuremberg and his speech to the party faithful. The ideological project of the flim is to create an impression of a united party following the 'Night of the Long Knives' that had seen the assassination of Ernst Rohm and other members of the SA (Sturm Abteilung). On another level, however, *Triumph of the Will* is clearly a highly crafted piece of propaganda that uses film technique (camera angles, lighting, editing) to promote the notion of *Führerprinzip* (leadership) and to create an impression of mass support for the regime. Richard Taylor, in his study of the film propaganda of Nazi Germany and the Soviet Union, sees no tension between describing it as 'a superb example of documentary cinema art – and a master-piece of film propaganda'.[35]

It is the commercial feature film, however, that is the most problematic as a source of historical evidence. Some historians avoid feature films altogether, while others understand them solely in terms of 'escapism' and 'entertainment' rather than as historical sources. And when feature film has been analysed as a historical source it has generally been in one of two distinct ways. On the one hand films with a realist import, such as *The Grapes of Wrath* (1940) in America or *Love on the Dole* (1941) in Britain, have been understood in relation to the social problems they describe. A consequence of the 'strikingly realist style' of such films is that 'many observers ... see a direct connection between the images on the screen and the real world'.[36] Here the evidential value of the films again relate to their empirical content, in this case their representation of social and economic hardship during the Depression. More problematic in this context are non-realist films which do not obviously relate to social and historical con-ditions. So films such as *The Wizard of Oz* (1939), *The Thief of Bagdad* (1940) or *A Matter of Life and Death* (1946) tend not to feature in this discussion.

On the other hand films purportedly recreating characters and episodes from history 'reflect [the] general attitudes of the period in which they were made'.[37] So films such as *Lady Hamilton* (1941) and *The Young Mr Pitt* (1942) are understood not in terms of what they say about the Napoleonic Wars but rather as reflecting the concerns of Britain at war with Nazi Germany. Here the evidential value of the films is detached from their empirical content: these films mobilize historical events and characters in order to serve the needs of wartime propaganda. Again some films are more readily assimilated into this discourse than others. Sometimes – especially in propaganda films such as the Soviet Union's *Alexander Nevsky* (1938), Britain's *Henry V* (1944) and Germany's *Kolberg* (1945) – the ideological parallels between past and present are quite explicit. *Henry V*, for example, includes a dedication 'to the Commandos and Airborne Troops of Great Britain – the spirit of whose ancestors it has humbly been attempted to recapture in some ensuing scenes'. Here the propagandist intent of the film is inscribed in the text to such an extent that it becomes the preferred reading. Other films, however, are less didactic in their insistence on present-day concerns. On the face of it there would seem little ideological import in a historical biopic such as Korda's *Rembrandt* (1936) or a Biblical epic such as Cecil B. De Mille's *Samson and Delilah* (1949).

It was the work of two French historians in the 1970s, Marc Ferro and Pierre Sorlin, that did most to open up the idea of the historical feature film as a historical source. Ferro – whose examples include both historical features (*Alexander Nevsky*, *Jud Süss*, *La Grande Illusion*) and others contemporaneous with the events they represented (*M*, *Bicycle Thieves*, *The Third Man*) – argues that film was not just a 'source' but also an 'agent' of history. He suggests that the real distinction was not between historical and non-historical films but 'rather between films inscribed in the flow of dominant (or oppositional) currents of thought and those that propose an independent or innovative view of societies'.[38] He concludes that most films fall into the former category – even films as different as *Napoléon* and *Alexander Nevsky* both represent 'official histories' – but identifies some, including *Bicycle Thieves* and Herbert J. Biberman's documentary *Salt of the Earth* (1953), as films that question official histories from outside and below (*Salt of the Earth* focuses on Native American women – a doubly marginalized group in standard accounts of the American West).

Sorlin, in contrast, considers how particular historical periods and events – including the French Revolution, Italian Risorgimento, American Civil War, Russian Revolution and Second World War – have been represented in feature films. He argues that 'historical films are all fictional' (even those based on recorded events) and that they tend to 'reconstruct in a purely imaginary way the greater part of what they show'.[39] Sorlin makes the crucial point that historical films should be judged against the state of historical knowledge that prevailed at the time they were made rather than held up short against more recent historiographical developments. And he also reinforces the point that historical films have provided a space where film-makers could address social and political issues that might otherwise have been proscribed. Jean Renoir's *La Grande Illusion* is again one of his examples:

> *La Grande Illusion* is an answer to the difficulties of French national life. France in 1937 was strongly divided between right and left, Communists and Nationalists: a civil war seemed imminent, especially as Spain was already a battlefield between fascists and the popular front. In that context, a return to the First World War was a means of rediscovering the days when the French were united. France was also surrounded by hostile countries and threatened by the possible outbreak of the Second World War, a prospect that many Frenchmen wanted to avoid...As we said after looking at the film, the most interesting theme is the prophetic vision included in the film: France seen as a prison camp, kept out of the battle; here, the dream is more than the mere denial of reality: it is an anticipation, a rehearsal of the future.[40]

It should be pointed out, however, that Jean Renoir himself denied any such prophetic vision. Later he said: 'In 1936 I made a picture named *La Grande Illusion* in which I tried to express all my deep feelings for the cause of peace. This film was very successful. Three years later the war broke out.'[41] This is not to suggest that Sorlin's reading is wrong: rather it illustrates a point he makes that a film can be understood independently of the intentions of its director.

▶ Robert Rosenstone and the 'New History film'

At this point we must pause to consider a radical intervention in the debate over the nature of film as a historical source. The work of US historian Robert A. Rosenstone suggests an entirely different way of understanding the evidential value of film. Rosenstone came to the subject of film and history following his experiences as a historical adviser on two very different films: Warren Beatty's Academy Award-winning *Reds* (1981), partly based on his biography of John Reed, and a low-budget documentary, *The Good Fight* (1983), about the Lincoln Battalion during the Spanish Civil War. His ideas can be traced through several books, including *Revisioning History* (1995), *Visions of the Past* (1995) and his summative work *History on Film/Film on History* (2006). Rosenstone describes himself as 'a person who has been labelled a "post-modern" historian'.[42] This may or may not be a postmodern way of identifying oneself as a postmodernist: but in any event the influence on Rosenstone's work of Hayden White and Alun Munslow would suggest that the cap fits. In any event Rosenstone's discussion of historical 'texts' and 'discourses' rather than 'sources' and 'evidence' is the language of postmodernism even if he does not accept the label.

Rosenstone has two major ideas. The first is what he calls the 'New History film' – as distinct from the New Film History – which is a film that 'finds the space to *contest* history, to interrogate either the meta-narratives that structure historical knowledge, or smaller historical truths, received wisdoms, conventional images'.[43] Examples of this **genre** include Alain Resnais's *Hiroshima, mon amour* (1959), Tomás Guttiérrez Alea's *Memories of Underdevelopment* (1968), Hans-Jürgen Syderbeg's *Hitler: A Film from Germany* (1977) and Alex Cox's *Walker* (1987). These films are outside the mainstream and tend to be the work of directors with a highly self-conscious style who use historical signifiers and motifs in a symbolic rather than a literal way. *Hiroshima, mon amour*, for example, explores subjectivity and the role of memory by collapsing distinctions between past and present, while *Walker* is an account of the career of a little-known American soldier of fortune who led a revolution in Nicargua in 1895 that is complete with anachronisms such as motor vehicles and computers. These films demonstrate different narrative and formal strategies for representing history: the 'New History film' is characterized by its modernist (and in *Walker*'s case postmodernist) style and its foregrounding of the techniques employed to create a historical world on screen. To this extent it offers an alternative to the **verisimilutude** of the **classical narrative film**, which typically represents the past according to accepted representational codes.

Rosenstone's other major argument is that film should be regarded as a form of history in its own right that is different from but not inferior to academic history. He avers that 'film makers can be and already are historians (some of them) but *of necessity the rules of engagement of their works with the stuff of the past are and must be different from those that govern written history'*.[44] Again he offers examples from outside the mainstream, such as the Spanish documentary *El Perro Negro* (2004), which uses amateur film (home movies) to reconstruct experiences of the Spanish Civil War 'from below', and therefore provides a different account than the 'official' archive sources used in *Mourir à Madrid* (1963). He also considers feature films such as *Glory* (1989), focusing on the experiences of an African American regiment during the American Civil War, which he considers representative of 'mainstream drama', and *October* (1927) as an example of 'innovative drama'. Rosenstone summarizes his position thus: 'My argument is that history films can indeed raise the kinds of questions about moments, movements, individuals and eras that historians raise, and though films deliver answers in their own medium, at their best they engage with, comment upon, add to and contest the larger discourse of a given field.'[45]

Rosenstone's intervention in the debate about film and history is challenging but in the end raises more questions than it answers. It is to be welcomed for casting the net wider than the narrow focus of many film histories to include films from Latin America, Europe, the former Soviet Union and US independent cinema as well as the commercial mainstream. However, his approach is flawed in several ways. For one thing it pays no attention to the historical contexts in which films were made: Rosenstone is content to analyse what films say and how they say it rather than exploring how their representations of the past may have been shaped by external factors. His extended discussion of *October*, for example, entirely neglects the ideological tensions that informed the production of the film: thus Trotsky's role in the October Revolution of 1917 was marginalized in the film at Stalin's insistence.[46] More fundamentally Rosenstone displays the typical postmodern conceit that all forms of historical communication are equal: that a film is as legitimate a source for illuminating the past as a piece of academic history. This returns us to the traditional critique of the historical film: that the blatant historical errors in films such as *Braveheart* (1995) or *Gladiator* (2000) mean it is difficult to accept them as historical sources equivalent to a scholarly biography of William Wallace or a study of the political culture of second-century Rome regardless of the many other points of cultural and ideological interest in the films.

▶ Case study: *Winstanley* (1975)

The issues discussed in this chapter can be demonstrated through a case study of *Winstanley*, an independently produced British film of 1975. Produced and directed by Kevin Brownlow and Andrew Mollo, *Winstanley* is an account of the seventeenth-century English radical Gerrard Winstanley who argued for the common ownership of land and who founded a commune, known as the Diggers, at St George's Hill, near Weybridge in Surrey. It was based on David Caute's historical novel *Comrade Jacob* (1961) and was backed by the British Film Institute Production Board which had a remit to support films that 'reveal some kind of originality'.[47] It was shot over the course of a year, using a largely non-professional cast which necessitated filming mostly at weekends. *Winstanley* had only a limited release, restricted for the most part to festivals and screenings at the National Film Theatre, but it attracted considerable critical interest and was admired for its refreshingly different subject matter in contrast to big-budget films such as Ken Annakin's *Cromwell* (1970).

With its non-linear narrative, its non-professional cast and its use of Winstanley's own writings as authenticating devices rather than the more usual voice-over commentary or rolling captions, *Winstanley* would fit Rosenstone's idea of the 'New History film' (though it is not one of his examples) as one that 'finds the space to *contest* history'. However, it was also a rare example of a film that met the exacting standards of the historical profession. As Christopher Hill, Master of Balliol College, Oxford, and a renowned social historian of the seventeenth century, told readers of the scholarly history journal *Past and Present*:

> Good historical films are sufficiently rare for it to be worth drawing attention to *Winstanley*, directed by Kevin Brownlow and Andrew Mollo. Although made on a shoe-string budget, the film's detail is meticulously accurate, down to the shoes which the Diggers wear, the agricultural implements they use, the breed of animals they farm...But more important than this convincing background is the imaginative reconstruction of the world in which the Diggers lived – still torn by social conflict, but one in which fundamental reform still seemed possible. This film can tell us more about ordinary people in seventeenth-century England than a score of textbooks.[48]

It is rare for a professional historian to offer such a glowing testimonial to a historical film: usually they are only too eager to demonstrate their superior knowledge and to catalogue all the myriad historical errors they can identify. What is even more interesting here, however, is that Hill, who could never be described as a postmodernist, actually anticipates Rosenstone in his suggestion that *Winstanley* could be seen as a historical source in its own right.

A more conventional kind of historical critique – that a historical film is also in some way about the present – has been offered by John C. Tibbetts, who avers that *Winstanley* is 'a presentist view of history. Brownlow and Mollo project contemporary concerns and considerations onto the screen of a meticulously constructed past.'[49] The Diggers had been largely written out of history until Winstanley's writings were rediscovered and published in the 1940s. The communal values and opposition to property ownership that he espoused had found new cultural resonance during the 1960s when hippie communes were established on university campuses in Paris and Berkeley. The cast of *Winstanley* included members of a group who called themselves New Diggers and whose spokesman, Sid Rawle, had set up his own commune in Ireland. The parallels between *Winstanley* and counter-cultural movements of the 1960s extend further. *Winstanley* is a study in failure: the failure of a revolutionary movement. The social experiment of the Diggers is beset by the hardships of communal life (Winstanley, played by Miles Halliwell, learns that his idealism is insufficient to cope with economic reality) and by external opposition (the landowners who resent their presence and who eventually destroy the commune by burning it). The late 1960s, particularly the events of May 1968 in France, had seemed to promise the possibility of both a social and a political revolution in which the catalyst was direct action by students and workers. While this did not materialize, a myth persists among a certain breed of Marxist intellectuals about the 'failure' of the 'revolution' of 1968. Brownlow, however, distanced himself from this reading: 'It isn't really a political film...The film has resonances for today, but we tried not to make obvious parallels. We even dropped the reference to Cromwell's troops fighting in Ireland.'[50]

It will now be clear that the debate over film as a historical source has come a long way since Matuszewski asserted his faith in the 'absolute truth' of the medium as a historical record. Historians have gradually come to acknowledge that, albeit with certain caveats, film can be a useful source for the study of contemporary history, while some have accepted that even a feature film may have some evidential value as a historical source. At the same time there has arisen a more sophisticated understanding of filmic evidence and, especially, the extent to which it has been mediated – by the commercial and ideological imperatives of the film industry, through the interventions of censors, and not least as a consequence of the nature of the medium itself. These considerations have also informed the history of film as a social practice – a subject that rehearses similar issues to film as a historical source but which focuses more directly on the fictional feature film and its relationship to society.

5 Film as a Social Practice

Grasping film in relation to history requires more than just better chronicles of the works or a description of how the various genres evolved. It must look at the historical function of film, at its relationship with the societies that produce and consume it, at the social processes involved in the making of the works, at cinema as a source of history.

Marc Ferro[1]

Since the 1970s there has been an increasing awareness and understanding of the role of film as a social practice. This means exploring the relationship between films and the societies in which they are produced and consumed. To some extent this can be seen as an outgrowth of the 'film and history' movement with its focus on film as a historical source – indeed some of the same players are involved as the above quotation from Ferro attests – but the net is cast wider to include all fiction films regardless of their empirical content. Social film history, as Allen and Gomery call it, involves 'relating the social structure of a given time and place to the representation of that structure in a film'.[2] This may be done in relation to realist films such as *The Grapes of Wrath* or the films of the British new wave; but it can equally be applied to non-realist and fantasy films such as *The Wizard of Oz* or the Hammer horror films. At its most basic level the relating of films to their social contexts is expressed through the idea of film as a 'reflection' or 'mirror' of society. This is one of the most pervasive but also one of the most contested ideas in film history. Social film history is generally concerned less with the individual film, as in aesthetic film history, but rather with popular genres and cycles. As one historian puts it: 'Routine circuit fodder may have little artistic merit but can prove richly rewarding as a reflection of certain ideas and preoccupations.'[3] Therefore this chapter will also consider how genre theory and criticism have informed our understanding of film as a social practice: this involves analysing films not in terms of their unique properties and features but rather in relation to recurring themes and motifs. The chapter concludes, again, with a case study, not this time of an individual film but rather of a cycle (***film noir***) that demonstrates all these issues.

▶ Feature films as a reflection of society

The idea that films reflect the societies in which they are produced and consumed is not a new one. In 1939, for example, Lewis Jacobs wrote about what
he termed the 'social agency' of American cinema in these terms: 'The movies
produced between 1919 and 1929 are eloquent social documents of a lively era
in American life. So thoroughly does the spirit of the decade saturate the films
that they are distinguished perhaps more for their innocent reflection of contemporary life than for their technical advances.'[4] And we saw in Chapter 1 how
Siegfried Kracauer understood the cinema of Weimar Germany as a reflection of
social dislocation and psychological anxiety. It was in the 1970s, however, that
the reflectionist discourse entered into the mainstream of film history. Three
books in particular – Raymond Durgnat's *A Mirror for England* (1970), Jeffrey
Richards's *Visions of Yesterday* (1973) and Robert Sklar's *Movie-Made America*
(1975) – came to define this approach. Durgnat was a practising film critic,
while Richards and Sklar were both professional historians, but what they had in
common was the idea that film, especially popular film, provided insights into
the values of the societies in which it was produced and consumed. Durgnat,
whose book is a survey of British cinema between the Second World War and
the 1960s, avers that popular film 'must echo widespread ideas and experiences'.[5] For Richards, whose book maps three genres across different national cinemas – what he terms 'the Cinema of Empire' (Britain and America), 'the Cinema
of Populism' (America in the 1930s) and 'the Cinema of National Socialism'
(Germany) – 'films are a still largely untapped source of social history'.[6] Sklar,
who covers American cinema from its origins to the 1960s, elaborates thus:

> Throughout their history the movies have served as a primary source of informa-
> tion about society and human behaviour for large masses of people. So significant
> a medium of communication should naturally reflect dominant ideologies and
> interests, and the American movies have often done so. But what is remarkable is
> the way that American movies, through much of their span, have altered or chal-
> lenged many of the values and doctrines of powerful social and cultural forces in
> American society, providing alternative ways of understanding the world.[7]

While covering different subjects, Durgnat, Richards and Sklar all understand
feature films as 'sources' that shed light on wider social attitudes and values.
For Durgnat British films of the 1950s reflect the transition in British society,
as conventionally described, from austerity to affluence. And for Richards the
popularity of films about the British Empire – a cycle that includes both British
and American films – is seen as evidence of broad popular support for the ideology and institutions of British imperialism. It is no coincidence that the end

of the 'Cinema of Empire' as a major genre in the early 1960s coincided with the acceleration of the process of decolonization as Britain withdrew from most of her overseas territories.

The reflectionist idea was also embraced by social historians who, while not focusing solely on cinema, looked to use films as evidence of popular attitudes alongside other sources such as social surveys, diaries, letters and novels. Perhaps the arch exponent of this approach was Arthur Marwick, who employed feature films as evidence in his comparative study of changing attitudes towards social class in Britain, France and America:

> The more one makes a comparative study of films, the more one becomes aware that, however exceptional within the context of its own country, every film is in fact a product of its own culture...Thus a comparison across different countries of different films brings out very striking contrasts in basic perceptions about the nature of class in the three countries.[8]

In this context Marwick made an informative comparison between the films of the French **Nouvelle Vague** in the late 1950s and early 1960s, where he felt that the real innovation was in matters of film style rather than their content, and the contemporaneous British new wave, where, in contrast, social realism was the prevailing style and class the dominant theme. 'In the end we learn little about the Cultural Revolution and its relationship to class,' he wrote, 'but we learn a lot about the contrasting obsessions of the British and the French.'[9]

However, the notion of film as a mirror or reflection of society was contested by more theoretically-inclined scholars who found it wanting as a methodology. For one thing much of the social history of film, especially in the 1970s, seemed to focus on the representation of class at the expense of other subjects such as gender and race. As late as 2000, for example, the editors of a collection on British cinema wrote that 'we were disappointed by the scarcity of scholarship discussing British cinema in terms of race, ethnicity and multiculturalism.'[10] Another criticism of the reflectionist approach is on methodological grounds: that in seeing films as a mirror of social reality it does not properly take account of the ways in which films are complex cultural artefacts that express meaning through their own formal properties and representational conventions. 'Film does not reflect or even record reality,' writes Graeme Turner; 'like any other medium of representation it constructs and "re-presents" its pictures of reality by way of the codes, conventions, myths and ideologies of its culture as well as by way of the specific signifying practices of the medium.'[11] In this view film is not a reflection of society but a representation of it: it does not act as a mirror of the world but rather creates its own image of the world. Thus a film bears no more relation to social reality than, say, the novels of Charles Dickens do to the social conditions of Victorian England.

This is the point made, often quite trenchantly, in critical responses to the work of the reflectionists. John Hill, for example, replied that 'the difficulty of such a well known book as Raymond Durgnat's *A Mirror for England* is that it simply assumes that conclusions about British society can be arrived at on the evidence of the films alone'. 'But, of course,' he expands, 'films do much more than just "reflect"; they also actively explain and interpret the way in which the world is to be perceived and understood.'[12] Jacques Segond, similarly, criticized the 'reductionist historical determinism' of *Visions of Yesterday*, asserting that 'the explicit content of a film (and in particular its plot and dialogue) is only part of the form that expresses the implicit meaning'.[13] Segond argued instead for a close 'textual reading' of the films that would highlight their formal properties such as editing and *mise-en-scène*. Andy Medhurst echoed this point when he attacked Marwick for using 'film texts as pieces of bald, simple "evidence" of particular social trends' – an approach which he felt was 'absurdly reductive, displaying a total disregard for textual complexity and contradiction'.[14]

These contrasting methodological positions – films as a reflection of society versus films as social or cultural constructs – might seem to be fundamentally irreconcilable. In fact they are not. It merely requires the historian to consider also the formal properties and visual style of film texts as well as analysing their conditions of production and reception. Elizabeth Grottle Strebel, for example, in her study of the 1930s films of Jean Renoir, contends that while 'the historian must still look to the films themselves as the central documents', it also becomes necessary 'to examine cinematic form and content as an expression of the times'.[15] To be fair to the reflectionists, their approach had never been quite as reductive as their critics claimed. Elsewhere, for instance, Marwick wrote that 'very loud warnings have to be sounded against any simplistic reading of cultural artefacts as "a mirror of their times" or as expressing "the spirit of the age"'.[16] Furthermore, the notion of film purely as a social or cultural construct is just as reductive in its own way as reflectionism: taken to its extreme it detaches films from any historical context whatsoever.

The dominant metaphor now in understanding the relationship between cinema and society is not 'reflection' but 'mediation'. John Belton, for example, contends that 'the relationship between American film and American social and historical reality is highly mediated and extremely complex'. He elaborates thus:

> Films, quite clearly, cannot be viewed as simple mirrors of cultural reality. As fictional works, they do, however, have a 'use-value'. They can be analyzed – even psychoanalyzed – to reveal something about the cultural conditions that produced them and attracted audiences to them…In other words, the films do reflect American reality but in a distorted and displaced way.[17]

This model allows for a more dynamic relationship between films and the social processes that produce them. It accepts that films do not necessarily speak for the whole of society, especially regarding marginalized groups (Native Americans, African Americans, women, homosexuals) whose film images often 'have only an indirect relationship to the real status of these individuals [sic] within American society'. If film is a mirror of society, then in this model it is 'a two-sided mirror' through which 'we can see how American identity is shaped in the movies and, at the same time, how the movies are shaped by it'.[18] This is echoed by John Hill, who similarly suggests that 'it is not only what films tell us about society that is important but also what an understanding of the society can tell us about the films and the nature of their representations'.[19]

Nevertheless the reflectionist idea remains pervasive. Evidence that the metaphor is not confined solely to Anglo-American intellectual culture is provided by the Indian scholar Prem Chowdhry in her study of the cinema of Colonial India:

> Films, as popular culture, need to be considered as one of the repositories of twentieth-century consciousness in that they reflect and articulate, as well as shape, much of the awareness of the men and women who form that consciousness. Films are both part of and reflect their historical contexts. Cinema therefore needs to be recognised as a valid historical archive for the writing of political, social and cultural history, in addition to being a primary object of study in its own right.[20]

Chowdhry thus echoes both Kracauer, through her reference to films as repositories of social consciousness, and historians such as Richards and Sklar, with their insistence upon the value of films as primary sources. Her study is a useful counterweight to Richards's discussion of the 'Cinema of Empire' in that she shows that 1930s Northwest Frontier films such as *The Drum* and *Gunga Din* provoked a critical backlash in India for their negative representations and racist stereotypes of Indian people. It seems more than a little ironic that films produced with the aim of promoting the ideology of imperialism may have played a role in undermining that ideology in the eyes of the colonized subjects.

▶ Beyond reflectionism: contextual film histories

The late 1970s and 1980s saw the emergence of a new approach to understanding film as a social practice that not only took account of the criticisms of the reflectionist model but also highlighted what Marc Ferro had called 'the social processes involved in the making of the works'. In a sense this approach might be seen as a modified version of reflectionism – the primary focus of the research remained the relationship between films and their historical contexts – but it was now accompanied by an emphasis on finding the primary sources to document the processes and external contextual factors that shaped the content of the films. The emergence of what came to be known as contextual film history was exemplified by three edited collections – John O'Connor and Martin Jackson's *American History/American Film* (1979), K. R. M. Short's *Feature Films as History* (1981) and Peter Rollins's *Hollywood as Historian* (1983) – and two books co-authored by British historians Jeffrey Richards and Anthony Aldgate, *Best of British* (1983) and *Britain Can Take It* (1986),[21] as well as by articles in journals such as the *Historical Journal of Film, Radio and Television*.[22] In contrast to the broad surveys of genres and periods that characterized books such as Richards's *Visions of Yesterday* and Sklar's *Movie-Made America*, the preferred form of contextual film histories was the case study. Richards outlined the approach thus:

> In examining each of them in turn we have borne in mind three main concerns. The first is the need to analyse what the film is saying, and that involves looking at the structure and meaning of the film, as conveyed by script, visuals, acting, direction, photography and music. Second, we attempt to put it in context with respect to both the film industry itself and the political and social situation which produced it. Third, we try to find out how the films were received and what audience reaction to them was.[23]

This approach necessitated detailed case studies rather than broad-brush generalizations. To this extent contextual film history (or as Richards preferred 'contextual cinematic history') is a form of micro-history based on the specific circumstances and histories of individual films. This is no bad thing of course – all films are unique and therefore all production histories are unique – though the prevalence of case studies has meant that, unlike aesthetic film histories, the approach does not easily lend itself to general works of synthesis and synopsis.

What are the characteristics of contextual film history? One is that it recognizes the criticism made of the reflectionist approach that it paid insufficient heed to the formal properties of film, particularly *mise-en-scène*, in accounting for how films create meaning. While some of the more trenchant critics may argue that the contextual approach is still too under-theorized, it nevertheless demonstrates that historians have taken on board some of the criticisms made of their work. Another characteristic is that in moving beyond reflectionism it focuses attention on how the film industry has not only responded to what it believes its audiences want but how at times it has deliberately and consciously set out to influence public opinion. To this extent contextual film history can be understood in parallel to Gramscian cultural studies and its concept of hegemony. What differentiates the historical approach, however, is the search for primary sources to provide evidence of the points of 'negotiation' and 'transaction' in the relationship between film and society.

It is no coincidence that much contextual film history concerns the role of film as an instrument of propaganda in the mid-twentieth century, especially during the Second World War. Histories of film propaganada initially focused on totalitarian regimes such as Soviet Russia and Nazi Germany. These were, as Richard Taylor puts it, 'the best known and best documented examples of highly politicised societies that the world has ever seen'.[24] And their films 'are given added interest by their importance as works of art and by the fact that they have helped to shape the histories of their respective countries and to carry the images of those countries abroad'.[25] It used to be held that the films of, say, the Third Reich could be read as straightforward expressions of an officially sanctioned ideology. However, this view has been nuanced by studies of the organization and policies of the Ministry for Popular Enlightenment and Propaganda. David Welch, for example, has shown not only that the majority of feature films produced in Germany between 1933 and 1945 were essentially popular entertainments that often contain little or no propaganda content, but that German audiences sometimes proved resistant to some of the more didactically propagandistic films. Shortly after the Nazi accession to power in 1933, for example, three feature films made with the aim of glorifying the NSDAP and its early martyrs – *SA-Mann Brand*, *Hitlerjunge Quex* and *Hans Westmar* – met with a decidedly mixed reception from both critics and audiences.[26] Similarly, in 1940, when two anti-Semitic films were released as part of a campaign to stir up even further hatred of Jews, it was found that *Jud Süss*, which veiled its anti-Semitism within the familiar genre of costume melodrama, was better received than the 'hate' documentary *Der Ewige Jude* (*The Eternal Jew*), which alienated some cinema-goers who found it too didactically anti-Semitic for their tastes.[27] Welch concludes that German cinema during the Third Reich was no less subject to the laws of the box office than in liberal democracies: while the state could direct film production, it could not dictate how films were received.

As an example of how contextual film histories differ from ideological criticism, we can compare Welch's study of *Jud Süss* and *Der Ewige Jude* to Steve Neale's analysis of the same two films in *Screen*. Neale focuses not on the reception of the films but rather on their 'modes of address' and their 'ideological apparatuses'. He argues that propaganda is present in films only when they break with the conventions of the classic realist film and invoke a specific mode of address to the spectator. Hence, while the two films are 'closely related in producing an anti-Semitic position', *Der Ewige Jude*, by dint of its didactic style and direct mode of address, is propaganda, whereas *Jud Süss*, because it conforms to the conventions of the classic realist film, cannot be described as propaganda but rather is a film that serves a 'propagandistic function'.[28] While this distinction may strike some as unduly semantic, it does perhaps help to explain the contrasting reception of the two films.

It was not only in totalitarian states, however, that film was recognized as a medium of mass persuasion. British documentary film-makers such as John Grierson disliked the term 'propaganda' and preferred to characterize their efforts as 'information' or 'education': but at the same time their ideas were informed by mass communications theory and their practice by the example of **Soviet montage** cinema of the 1920s.[29] British cinema in general provides a particularly good example of how, even in a supposedly liberal and democratic society, the cinema can function as an agency of social control. (Again there is a parallel here with film theory: cinema as an **ideological apparatus**.) It has been argued, chiefly by Richards and Aldgate in both their joint and separate endeavours, that the ideological project of British cinema, especially during the 1930s, was the promotion of consensus. This was achieved in two ways. On the one hand the British Board of Film Censors (BBFC) – a trade rather than a state body, though its president was appointed by the Home Secretary – exercised rigorous control over film content through scrutinizing scripts (a voluntary process to which, however, most producers acceded) and through refusing to certificate for general release any films that were overtly critical of the social and political status quo. Hence the censors would permit no criticism of institutions such as the monarchy, parliament, church, army, police or judiciary. This meant that controversial subjects such as a proposed film of Walter Greenwood's novel *Love on the Dole* were kept off the screen.[30] On the other hand the major British producers were, by and large, conservative in outlook and naturally tended towards the preservation of what Aldgate describes as an 'ideological consensus' in British society: hence 'the ideological role of the British cinema in fostering harmony and social integration' during the 1930s.[31]

American cinema has also been understood as an instrument of consensus and social control. The professional ideology of Hollywood film-makers was that they were producers of 'harmless entertainment' that would appeal to 'the largest possible audience'.[32] (This idea is satirized brilliantly in Preston Sturges's 1941 film *Sullivan's Travels* in which an idealistic screenwriter with a social conscience wants to make a film about 'the problems that confront the modern man' entitled *Oh Brother Where Art Thou?* A series of misadventures both comic and tragic ends with Sullivan attending a church service where the audience comprises social outcasts such as prisoners and African Americans: the ecstatic reaction to a Mickey Mouse cartoon brings home to him the need for 'harmless entertainment'.) Some historians point to a cycle of 'social conscience' films in the early 1930s such as *I Am a Fugitive from a Chain Gang* as evidence that Hollywood did seek to address social problems. Ed Buscombe is one who identifies 'the vaguely and uncertainly radical leanings' of Warner Bros. in the 1930s.[33] Even so, however, such films were not representative of Hollywood's total output at the time, which tended towards romantic dramas, sophisticated comedies and Art Deco musicals.

There were in fact two agencies of social control in Hollywood during the heyday of the **studio system**. One was the Production Code Administration (PCA) which, like the BBFC, vetted scripts before production and adhered to a strict code which forbade any suggestion of immorality, obscenity, blasphemy or profanity. Historians of the PCA such as Ruth Vasey have argued that its control of content extended beyond the familiar objections to sexuality and violence and took into account political and economic affairs. Like the BBFC it sought to regulate the representation of strikes and industrial unrest and policed the images of foreign nationalities: the latter was as much a commercial as a political strategy as the PCA was part of the Motion Picture Producers and Distributors Association and was concerned to protect foreign markets.[34] The other agency of social control was the Legion of Decency, founded in 1933, which bound millions of Roman Catholics to a pledge to boycott any film it deemed immoral. Gregory Black concludes his history of the censorship of American cinema by asserting that the combined efforts of the PCA and the Roman Catholic Church 'prevented Hollywood from interpreting the morals and manners, the economics and politics, and the social and ethical issues facing American society in direct and honest terms'.[35] In this reading it was the industry's own regulation that prevented films from acting as a true mirror or reflection of society. Indeed one of the major outcomes of contextual histories of cinema has been to show just how heavily regulated most film industries were at the height of their popularity in the mid-twentieth century. Again this is as true for the film industries of liberal democracies as for dictator states such as Hitler's Germany and Stalin's Russia.

Finally the contextual approach has also demonstrated how changes in film style and content that had previously been attributed to them reflecting social change might also be understood, at least in part, as consequences of changing regulatory institutions and regimes. Nowhere is this better illustrated than in Anthony Aldgate's study of the response of the British Board of Film Censors to the British new wave films of the late 1950s and early 1960s. Most accounts of films such as *Room at the Top*, *Saturday Night and Sunday Morning* and *The Loneliness of the Long Distance Runner* have seen them as an outcome of social change at the onset of the 1960s. Arthur Marwick, for example, argues that these films were 'both new cultural artefacts born of change, and themselves productive of more rapid change'.[36] Aldgate's research into the correspondence files of the BBFC advances another explanation for the emergence of these films – generally seen as challenging the prevailing social consensus – at this time. He marshals a wealth of primary source evidence to suggest that the new wave films were tacitly encouraged by the BBFC, and particularly by its new secretary, John Trevelyan, as a means of legitimating the 'X' certificate, hitherto mostly the preserve of sensational horror and exploitation films, as a form of serious 'adult' cinema. The much-vaunted social realism of these so-called 'kitchen sink' films was, Aldgate shows, at least in part mandated by the BBFC which was prepared to be more permissive in allowing 'frank' subject matter, including sexual relations, abortion and homosexuality, provided that it was treated in a 'realistic' rather than a 'sensational' manner.[37]

▶ Genre theory and criticism

Genre theory and criticism offer another avenue to understanding film as a social practice. 'Stated simply,' writes Barry Keith Grant, 'genre movies are those commercial feature films which, through repetition and variation, tell familiar stories with familiar characters in familiar situations.'[38] Genres have been the lifeblood of the film industry since it organized on mass-production lines. For the industry genres represent a form of product standardization and differentiation: each genre film is similar to others of the same type (for example every Western shares common features with other Westerns), while each film genre is distinct from other genres (a Western is different from a musical which is different from a horror film). Genres are therefore a means of regulating production and minimizing the economic risks inherent in film-making. The genres that have endured for long periods have done so because they have provided an entertainment pattern that meets the demands of their audiences. As the US critic Robert Warshaw put it: 'For a type to be successful means that its conventions have imposed themselves upon the general consciousness and become the accepted vehicles of a particular set of attitudes and a particular aesthetic effect.'[39]

The adoption of genre theory and criticism onto the agenda of film studies in the late 1960s and 1970s – the foundational texts included Jim Kitses's *Horizons West* (1969), Colin McArthur's *Underworld USA* (1972) and Will Wright's *Sixguns and Society* (1975)[40] – was to some extent a reaction against the prevalence of the ***auteur* theory** and its privileging of the idea of the film-maker as an artist. Genre criticism instead offered a way of analysing films that did not automatically assign creative agency to the director and which enabled the critic to examine the social and ideological processes at work in popular cinema. For example, in *Signs and Meaning in the Cinema* Peter Wollen had analysed the Westerns of John Ford in terms of the thematic and structural patterns that were repeated throughout his *œuvre*. Wollen averred that Ford's Westerns are 'governed by a set of oppositions…The most relevant are garden versus wilderness, ploughshare versus sabre, settler versus nomad, European versus Indian, civilised versus savage, book versus gun, married versus unmarried, East versus West.'[41] However, Jim Kitses recognized that, rather than being unique to Ford, these structural patterns were a characteristic of the Western as a whole. Kitses argues that the Western revolves around 'a series of antinomies' – wilderness/civilization, nature/culture, Garden/Desert, individual/community, West/East – which are rehearsed in different ways in each Western film. Just as 'the West' was not a fixed geographical space, but a constantly shifting and expanding frontier, so too the Western is not a fixed pattern but rather 'a varied and flexible structure, a thematically fertile and ambiguous world of historical material shot through with archetypal elements which are themselves ever in flux'.[42]

Early genre criticism focused on American cinema and, especially, on genres such as the Western and the gangster film which were identified through their **iconography**. A Western, for example, typically features a particular kind of landscape and characters whose appearance identifies the kind of types they represent (cowboy, gunslinger, sheriff, gambler, schoolteacher, saloon girl, and so on). The Western and the gangster film remained at the forefront of genre studies as critical attention shifted from iconography to the ideological and thematic concerns of genre. Colin McArthur, for example, suggests that 'the western and the gangster film have a special relationship with American society…It could be said that they represent America talking to itself about, in the case of the western, its agrarian past, and in the case of the gangster film/thriller, its urban technological present.'[43] Other genres with a less clearly defined iconography could also be analysed in relation to their social contexts. Accordingly the musical has been seen as a vehicle for the promotion of a utopian fantasy of America as a perfectible society, while the melodrama has been understood as a means of exploring changing family values and attitudes towards gender. Film historians see genres as means of examining the ideological values prevalent in society. Thomas Schatz, for example, argues that 'genres can be seen as a form of social ritual' and draws upon Gramscian terminology when he writes that American film genres are 'formal strategies for renegotiating and reinforcing American ideology'.[44] John Belton, similarly, suggests that 'by looking at the large body of individual films within individual genres, we can see how those genres help to shape and are shaped by our understanding of American culture, character, and identity.'[45]

A few examples must suffice to illustrate the social agency of genres. The Western is a genre that enjoys a particular relationship with American history and society: André Bazin described the Western as 'the American film *par excellence*'.[46] Westerns range from nation-building epics (*The Iron Horse, Union*

Pacific, How the West Was Won) to films lamenting the closure of the frontier (*Ride the High Country, Butch Cassidy and the Sundance Kid, The Shootist*). Recurring themes include the pacification of Native Americans (*Fort Apache, She Wore a Yellow Ribbon, Soldier Blue*) and the taming of lawless frontier towns (*Dodge City, My Darling Clementine, High Plains Drifter*). The Western has been a vehicle for addressing the place of racial minorities in American society (*Broken Arrow, Sergeant Rutledge*) and for political allegory (*High Noon, Warlock*). It has explored codes of masculinity (*Rio Bravo, The Big Country*) and has even been a vehicle for proto-feminist cultural politics (*Johnny Guitar, Forty Guns*). It will be clear even from this short list that the ideological work of the Western has often been in responding to issues in American society and politics. In his study of national identity in the Western, Michael Coyne argues that the genre 'had roots in a once dominant ideology predicated on belief in exceptional national destiny'.[47] He further argues that the Western has lost its cultural and ideological currency since the 1970s when the notion of American exceptionalism was dented by Vietnam and Watergate.

The musical might seem, on the face of it, an unlikely site for the projection of ideology. The joyous non-naturalism of the musical whereby characters break into song and dance on the slightest of pretexts would seem to suggest this is not a genre to be taken seriously. Or, as Jane Feuer puts it: 'Westerns might now be seen as a conflict between chaos and civilization, but Fred Astaire remained ineffable.'[48] However, the musical is one of the most ideological of all genres: it projects America as a land of material wealth and as a heterosexual utopia. It is through the musical that Hollywood offers visions of social optimism during the Great Depression (*Gold Diggers of 1933*) and promotes the attraction of capitalism to a Soviet lady commissar (*Silk Stockings*). The musical projects a stable and harmonious society: it resolves generational conflict (*The Jazz Singer*), reconciles separated couples (*The Barkleys of Broadway*), overcomes racial prejudice (*South Pacific*) and brings an end to factional strife (*West Side Story*). It is also the most self-reflexive of all genres: the musical is how Hollywood mythologizes its own past (*The Jolson Story, Singin' in the Rain*). Anyone who doubts the cultural significance of the musical need only be reminded that *The Sound of Music* and *Grease* rank among Hollywood's biggest box-office hits.

This is not to say that genre theory and criticism are without their problems. There is a tendency in some work to see genres as fixed and static. Will Wright's structuralist study of the Western, for instance, sees all Westerns as variations on what he terms the 'classical plot'. This is 'the story of the lone stranger who rides into a troubled town and cleans it up, winning the respect of the townsfolk and the love of the schoolmarm'. 'The classical plot defines the genre,' Wright adds, '...the other plots – vengeance, transition, professional – are all built upon the symbolic foundation and depend upon the foundation for their meaning.'[49] Not only is this a reductive view of genre, however, it can also be challenged on empirical grounds. There are in fact very few Westerns which conform to Wright's classical model: *My Darling Clementine* (1946) is perhaps the closest fit. This also demonstrates one of the theoretical problems with using genre as a critical tool: the question of definition. As Andrew Tudor explains: 'To take a genre such as the "western", analyse it, and list its principal characteristics, is to beg the question that we must first isolate the body of films which are "westerns". But they can only be isolated on the basis of the "principal characteristics" which can only be discovered from the films themselves after they have been isolated.'[50]

Another problem with genre theory is the tendency, in some work at least, to detach genres from their industrial contexts of production. Tino Balio has argued that the history of film production in Hollywood during the 1930s is best understood in terms of production trends and cycles rather than working within genres. He suggests that the 'prestige picture' was 'the most popular production trend of the decade' but points out that this category does not correspond to critical ideas of genre film-making: 'The prestige picture is not a genre; rather, the term designates production values and promotion treatment.'[51] Examples of the Hollywood 'prestige picture' in the 1930s include *Grand Hotel* (melodrama), *A Midsummer Night's Dream* (Shakespearean adaptation), *The Great Ziegfeld* (musical biopic) and *Gone With the Wind* (historical-costume film). 'On occasion,' points out Richard Maltby, 'critics have elevated what the production industry understood as a cycle to the status of a genre.'[52] He cites the example of the gangster film, which emerged in the production season of 1930–1 with films such as *Little Ceasar*, *The Public Enemy* and *Scarface*. And Jeanine Basinger has shown how the genre commonly known as the war movie – which, in any case, she avers, was known in the film industry as the combat movie – was the product of the ideological context of the Second World War when the Office of War Information mandated the production of films dealing with the American armed forces: *Bataan, Guadalcanal Diary, Air Force, They Were Expendable, Objective, Burma!, The Story of G.I. Joe.*[53]

A further issue with genre criticism – which will already have become evident from the examples cited hitherto – is that it has focused overwhelmingly on American cinema. It is only quite recently that studies of non-American genres have appeared. Partly this is due to the prevalence of aesthetic histories of film which equate American cinema with populism (hence genres such as the Western and the musical figure prominently) but identify European cinema with 'art' (meaning that *auteurs* are privileged over genres). As Richard Dyer and Ginette Vincendeau have remarked: 'The popular cinema of any given European country is not always acknowledged even in the general national histories of film in that country. When it is, it is generally marginalized in favour of the often little-seen but critically-acclaimed art film traditions.'[54] Hence whole cycles of popular cinema – such as Nazi and Soviet musicals, Italian 'peplums' and 'Spaghetti Westerns', Scandinavian crime thrillers, French erotic dramas and British sex comedies – have been largely written out of film history.

Another reason for the dearth of critical work on European popular cinema is that for many years European genres were regarded – quite unfairly – as pale imitations of Hollywood. Nowhere has this been more evident than in the case of British cinema. Jacques Rivette once infamously dismissed an entire national cinema thus: 'British cinema is a genre cinema, but one where the genres have no genuine roots...There are just false, in the sense of imitative, genres.'[55] Fortunately this attitude no longer persists. In 1998 the editors of the first issue of the *Journal of Popular British Cinema* detected evidence of 'a welcome trend to treat British film genres in relation to their cultural and historical conditions, as well as dealing with them as particular stylistic and thematic configurations'.[56] The chief beneficiaries of this historical revisionism have been once critically-despised but nevertheless enormously popular cycles of films such as the Gainsborough costume melodramas of the 1940s (*The Man in Grey, Fanny by Gaslight, Madonna of the Seven Moons, The Wicked Lady, Jassy*) and the Gothic horrors associated with Hammer Films (*The Curse of Frankenstein, Dracula, The Mummy, Curse of the Werewolf, The Two Faces of Dr Jekyll*) that have been analysed in terms of their class and gender politics as well as for their extravagant and excessive visual styles in contrast to the sober realism of much British cinema.[57] In contrast to Rivette's assertion that British genres have 'no genuine roots', David Pirie sees what he terms 'English Gothic cinema' as 'the only staple cinematic myth which Britain can properly claim as its own, and which relates to it in the same way as the western relates to America'.[58]

▶ Case study: *film noir* – 'a dark mirror to post-war America'

The issues discussed in this chapter are highlighted by the example of *film noir* – a cycle of films that not only problematize the idea of film as a reflection or mirror of society but also provide a useful introduction to genre theory and criticism. It is important to recognize in the first instance that *film noir* is a critical label – originally coined by French critics to describe a style of American movies shown in France following the end of the Second World War – and not, like other genres such as the Western or the musical, a category used by the film industry itself. It meant, literally, 'dark film', and it was used to describe films that stood out by dint of their low-key, expressionist, black-and-white cinematography and their pervading mood of disillusionment, cynicism and

despair. The canon of *film noir* has expanded over the years. In 1955 Raymond
Borde and Etienne Chaumeton identifed 22 '*films noirs*' in the appendix to their
book *Panorama du Film Noir Américain*.[59] In the third edition (1992) of their
book *Film Noir: An Encyclopedic Reference Guide to the American Style*, however,
Alain Silver and Elizabeth Ward list 312 films between 1941 and 1958 – dates
which most film historians agree represent the parameters of the *noir* cycle.[60]
Among the films usually included within the *noir* cycle are *Double Indemnity*,
Laura, *Murder My Sweet*, *The Killers*, *Detour*, *The Big Sleep*, *The Blue Dahlia*, *Gilda*,
The Postman Always Rings Twice, *Somewhere in the Night*, *Out of the Past*, *Crossfire*,
Gun Crazy, *In a Lonely Place*, *The Asphalt Jungle*, *They Live by Night*, *The Big Heat*,
The Big Combo, *Kiss Me Deadly* and *Touch of Evil*.

The response to these films from contemporary critics was to understand
them as a reflection of the **Zeitgeist**. This is exemplified by the producer
John Houseman, who, while reviewing *The Big Sleep* for the journal *Hollywood
Quarterly*, lamented the rise of what he called the 'tough movie' which, he felt,
'presents a fairly accurate reflection of the neurotic personality of the United
States of America in the year 1947'. Houseman found such films 'repugnant'
due to 'their lack of moral energy, [and] their listless fatalistic despair'.[61] It was
not only in America that the films were seen in this way. British critic Richard
Winnington, reviewing *Out of the Past* (released in Britain as *Build My Gallows
High*), asked rhetorically: 'Is this not an outcrop of the national masochism
induced by a quite aimless and heavily industrialized society proceeding rapidly on its way to nowhere?'[62]

The metaphor here is the familiar one that films reflect the societies in which
they are produced and consumed. And the idea of *film noir* as a reflection of
ideological currents in post-war American society has persisted in many general
histories of American cinema. In these readings the emergence of *film noir* is
related to a range of historical factors, including the social dislocation expe-
rienced during and after the Second World War, the psychological problems
faced by returning servicemen in readjusting to civilian life, and the paranoia of
the early Cold War that found its most extreme expression in the witch hunts
orchestrated by Senator Joseph McCarthy and the House UnAmerican Activities
Committee. It is no accident that the protagonists of *film noir* are often returning ex-servicemen (for example in *The Blue Dahlia*, *Somewhere in the Night* and
Crossfire) or that one of the recurring character types is the *femme fatale* whose
social and sexual empowerment challenges or perhaps even subverts accepted
gender roles (as in *Double Indemnity*, *The Postman Always Rings Twice*, *Gilda* and
The Lady from Shanghai). Later entries in the *noir* cycle, such as *The House on
92nd Street*, *Pickup on South Street* and *Kiss Me Deadly* are typically understood as
expressions of Cold War anxiety and paranoia. So, for example, Thomas Schatz
writes that *film noir* 'reflected the progressively darkening cultural attitudes

during and after the war' and 'documented the growing disillusionment with certain traditional American values in the face of complex and often contradictory social, political, scientific, and economic developments'.[63] And David A. Cook similarly contends that '*film noir* held up a dark mirror to post-war America and reflected its moral anarchy'.[64]

However, there are several caveats that must be lodged against the argument that *film noir* was a reflection of the *Zeitgeist*. The first is that *Zeitgeist* criticism tends to be highly selective: it often picks out examples that are not necessarily representative of cultural production across the board. This point was recognized at the time by critic Lester Asheim, who responded to Houseman's gloomy prognosis by pointing out that the most popular films at the US box office in the year of *The Big Sleep* included the sentimental drama *The Bells of St Mary's*, the musical *Blue Skies* and the zany comedy *Road to Utopia*. These films, Asheim observed, were 'pure entertainment, light and gay, preferably with music; yet no claim is made that postwar America is a lighthearted, song-in-its-heart haven of romance and the joys of youth'.[65] Any attempt to read films as an expression of the *Zeitgeist* should take account of the entirety of film production rather than selecting just one genre. In this sense the critical and historical interest in *film noir* is disproportionate in relation to the film industry at large. If we accept Silver and Ward's figure of 312 *noir* films between 1941 and 1958, it still represents only 5 per cent of the approximately 6,300 films released over that period.[66] Nor were *noir*s necessarily the most popular films: in 1946–7, when *noir* first became a significant production trend, the top-grossing films were an affirmative drama (*The Best Years of Our Lives*), a Western (*Duel in the Sun*) and a nostalgic musical biopic (*The Jolson Story*). Robert B. Ray has drawn attention to the fact that no *noir*s figured in the annual top three box-office attractions between 1947 and 1958. 'In no other period in the history of the American popular film,' he writes, 'had there existed such an enormous discrepancy between the most commercially successful movies and those that have ultimately been seen as significant.'[67]

The visual style of *film noir* – with its fragmented *mise-en-scène*, acute camera angles, deep shadows and **chiaroscuro** lighting – represents a form of extreme stylization that is not only different from the prevailing norms of **classical Hollywood** but is also the antithesis of conventional notions of **realism**. In this context it should be noted that many of the creative personnel involved in the *noir* cycle – including directors Fritz Lang, Robert Siodmak, Billy Wilder and Otto Preminger, and cinematographers Karl Freund and Rudolph Maté – were European *émigrés* whose formative influences came from **German Expressionism**. Added to this is the formal complexity of *film noir*, employing devices such as non-linear narrative and flashbacks to a much greater extent than usual in classical Hollywood. A characteristic of *film noir* is its extreme subjectivity: *The Lady in the Lake* (1946) even went so far as to adopt the technique of the 'camera-eye' throughout in an attempt to replicate the first-person narration of the Raymond Chandler novel on which it was based. Hence the face of private eye Philip Marlowe (played by actor-director Robert Montgomery) is only seen when the character looks in a mirror. Billy Wilder's *Sunset Boulevard* (1950) – a melodrama that some critics identify as *noir* – is narrated by a character who turns out to be the man whose body has been seen floating in a swimming pool at the start of the film.

There is something of a tension here, therefore, in the fact that a type of film which is seen as holding a mirror to society is in fact so highly stylized. *Film noir* does not exhibit the realist style of films like, say, *The Grapes of Wrath* or *The Best Years of Our Lives*. So if *film noir* is a reflection of social reality then it is one seen through a heavily distorting mirror. Other commentators have argued that *film noir* should be understood not as a reflection of society but as a highly stylized construction or representation of society. J. A. Place and L. S. Pearson, for example, suggest that the *mise-en-scène* of *film noir* is 'designed to unsettle, jar, and disorient the viewer in correlation with the disorientation felt by the noir heroes'.[68] Others have argued even further that the visual style of *film noir* is so highly aestheticized that it should be seen as a representation of a fictional rather than a real world. Paul Schrader – a film critic who later turned screenwriter, most notably with Martin Scorsese's *Taxi Driver* (1976) – argues that '*film noir* attacked and interpreted its sociological conditions, and, by the close of the *noir* period, created a new artistic world that went beyond a simply sociological reflection, a nightmarish world of American mannerism which was by far more a creation than a reflection'.[69] This is echoed by Robert B. Ray in his discussion *Touch of Evil* (1958), often seen as marking the end of the *noir* cycle. Ray argues that Orson Welles 'used a tawdry melodrama…as an occasion to create a stylistic universe whose deep shadows, looming **close-ups**, oblique camera angles, prowling camera, and crowded compositions intimated a sense of entrapment and loss that went far beyond the mere events of the plot'.[70]

These different historical and critical perspectives on *film noir* – *noir* as a reflection of sociological conditions versus *noir* as a cultural and aesthetic construct – rehearse once again the debate between historians and film theorists over the relationship between film and its social contexts. Can these theoretically opposed interpretations be reconciled? To do so requires a method that recognizes the historical specificity of *film noir* while also taking cognizance of its formal and stylistic properties. Paul Kerr has argued that the period of *film noir* was defined by a combination of industrial and aesthetic determinants. Most *noir*s were produced relatively cheaply: their minimal sets and low-key lighting were perfectly suited to economical production practices. It is no coincidence that studios such as Warner Bros., RKO and Columbia, who all had a reputation for cost-conscious film-making, were more prolific in the production of *noirs* than traditionally more lavish studios like MGM and Paramount. Kerr further argues that the period of *film noir* coincided with a major shift in aesthetic and industrial practices:

> The period of this transition, the period in which the equation between black and white on the one hand and realism on the other was it its most fragile, was thus the period from the late 1930s – when television, Technicolor and the double bill were first operating – to the late 1950s, when television and colour had established themselves, both economically and ideologically, as powerful lobbies in the industry, and the double bill had virtually disappeared. That period, of something less than twenty years, saw the conjunction of a primarily economically determined mode of production, known as B film-making, with what were primarily ideologically defined modes of 'difference', known as the *film noir*.[71]

At the beginning of the *noir* period, colour was a novelty reserved for spectacular fantasy genres like the musical and the swashbuckler, and monochrome was the preferred mode for realist film-making, whereas by the end of the 1950s colour, which had become cheaper, was now the norm while monochrome was on the way out. It is no coincidence that the end of the *noir* cycle in the late 1950s coincided with the ascendancy of colour. What this demonstrates is the need to understand genres or cycles like *film noir* not only as a set of visual motifs and thematic structures but also as the products of historically specific industrial and economic circumstances.

6 A Historical Sociology of Film

It would be difficult to underestimate the social and psychological significance of movies. Like all institutions, they both reflect and influence society. It is hoped that a future project will be concerned with learning about this two-way process, including both an analysis of culture patterns in movies and detailed field studies of audience reactions. The present study of Hollywood and the system in which movies are made is the first step in the larger project.

Hortense Powdermaker[1]

Hortense Powdermaker's *Hollywood the Dream Factory* (1950) is a pioneering study of the film industry. Powdermaker, a social anthropologist, spent a year in Hollywood conducting interviews with studio executives, producers, writers and actors in order 'to understand better the nature of our movies'.[2] Her work marked the first academic study of the film industry, as seen through the outlook and values of those who worked in it, rather than the more familiar biographical or autobiographical accounts that are rich in anecdote but reveal little or nothing about the actual working practices and professional ideologies of the industry. Powdermaker saw beneath the tinsel of Hollywood to identify a system of social organization where 'most of the men who enjoy power have it simply because they got there first and were able to form the social structure of movie making as they desired', whereas creative artists 'fight openly to gain power, that is, to get into positions in which they can make important decisions and influence the movies'.[3] In this regard little changes: Powdermaker's account of the industry in terms of social networks and power relations is much the same picture of Hollywood as that put forward 40 years later in Robert Altman's film *The Player* (1992).

The 'larger project' which Powdermaker anticipated has since emerged in what Ian Jarvie has called a 'sociology of film'. Jarvie identifies four questions that inform a sociology of film: Who makes films and why? Who sees films, how and why? What is seen, how and why? And how do films get evaluated, by whom and why?[4] Allen and Gomery suggest that framing these questions in the past tense leads to what they term 'social film history'. Social film history therefore includes histories of film-making (who made films and how?), histories of cinema-going (who saw films?), histories of exhibition (what was seen?) and histories of film criticism and culture (how have films been evaluated?).[5] Rather than being separate histories, however, Allen and Gomery suggest that these questions are linked through the 'film viewing situation' – the point at which films and audiences converge – and which 'has represented the point of convergence for three distinct social processes: that which pro-duced the film on the screen, that which brought the audience to the theater, and the process of social representation occurring on the screen within the filmic text'.[6] For the purpose of this chapter it will be useful to delineate spe-cific approaches and methodologies within what I will call (as a combination of Jarvie and Allen-Gomery) a historical sociology of film. Histories of pro-duction examine the conditions under which films were made, the working practices of the film industry, and the role of individuals in the film-making process. Histories of reception explore how contemporary audiences and critics responded to particular films, while histories of cinema-going analyse the social composition of cinema audiences, their film preferences and cultural tastes.

▶ Histories of production

Histories of production offer an alternative to the idea of film as a reflection or mirror of society: instead the emphasis is on understanding the actual his-torical conditions in which films are made and the various determinants that shape their content and form. These include – but are not limited to – the com-mercial and aesthetic strategies of the studio or producer, relations between the various creative personnel involved (directors, writers, art directors, costume designers, cinematographers, actors, etc), economic and technological determi-nants, and the interventions of external bodies such as censors, trade organiza-tions and lobby groups. Histories of production foreground questions of agency and process: who makes films and how they are made. There are broadly two kinds of production histories: histories of particular film companies and their production strategies, usually focusing on Hollywood during the **studio sys-tem**, and case studies of the making of particular films.

What is the value of histories of production? On the most basic level research into the structure and organization of the film industry is a means of debunk-ing some of the popular myths that have accrued around the 'dream factory'. One of these is the power of the movie moguls – the charismatic heads of production at the major studios such as Louis B. Mayer (MGM), Jack Warner (Warner Bros), Darryl F. Zanuck (Twentieth Century-Fox) and Adolph Zukor (Paramount) and independent producers such as Sam Goldwyn and David O. Selznick. Most of the moguls were first- or second-generation European Jewish immigrants, and much has been made of their ethnic and cultural origins in sociological histories of Hollywood. Neal Gabler, for example, is in no doubt that their Jewishness was a crucial factor:

> The Jews also had a special compatibility with the industry, one that gave them certain advantages over their competitors. For one thing, having come primarily from fashion and retail, they understood public taste and were masters at gauging market swings... For another, as immigrants themselves, they had a peculiar sensitivity to the dreams and aspirations of other immigrants and working-class families, two overlapping categories that made up a significant proportion of the early moviegoing audience.[7]

Other historians, such as Richard Maltby, have downplayed the Jewishness of the moguls, however, pointing out that they were passionate supporters of WASPish American culture, and that their special standing in the industry was due more to their ability to create their own myths than to their ethnicity: 'They more or less deliberately set out to create in Hollywood a separate, enclosed world, whose image to the rest of America was as important an ingredient in the product they sold as were the stars or plots of individual films.'[8] And, while the studio heads revelled in their images as all-powerful autocrats who could make or break the careers of actors and directors, the real power in the film industry resided with the head offices on the East Coast. When Louis B. Mayer clashed with Nicholas Schenck, president of MGM's parent company Loew's Incorporated, in 1951, he found himself unceremoniously dumped as chief executive of the studio that still bore his name.[9]

   There are different levels of production histories ranging from, at one level, popular 'tie-in' books for the mass market published to coincide with the release of the latest studio blockbuster and often written by a journalist with privileged access to cast and crew on set, to, at the other, highly detailed case studies packed with footnotes and usually published as articles in scholarly journals such as the *Historical Journal of Film, Radio and Television*. In between these extremes, somewhere, are journalistic-style histories of the making of popular classics, often drawing on archive sources but presented essentially as stories and without the scholarly baggage of notions of context and process: Aljean Harmetz's books on the making of *The Wizard of Oz* and *Casablanca* are good examples of this type.[10] In reading production histories we should always take account of the nature of the sources on which they are based. In particular we should treat with caution interviews with directors and actors years after the films were made: human memory is fallible and there is an inevitable tendency to see events through the rosy tint of nostalgia. Accounts based solely on the trade press and studio publicity are also problematic: these sources need to be used with care as they often represent attempts by the studios to 'position' their films in order to maximize their box-office returns. The most useful production histories are generally those based on studio archives and/or the papers of key production personnel. Even here it must be borne in mind that the personal papers of one individual (say the director) may tell a different story to those of another (for example the star). The role of the historian is to assess and interpret the sources in order to arrive at the most likely sequence of events and explanations for the decisions taken.

The best production histories provide us with insights into the nature of film-making as a social and industrial process. This can be a useful corrective to histories of film-making posited on the *auteur* **theory**. Often production histories highlight the agency of the producer rather than the director. To take one example: Rudy Behlmer's account of the production of the 1940 Warner Bros. film *The Sea Hawk* demonstrates that despite no fewer than three screenplays (by Delmer Daves, Seton I. Miller and Howard Koch) and the studio's foremost director Michael Curtiz at the helm, it was producer Hal B. Wallis who really held the upper hand. Wallis intervened at every stage of the production process, commenting on the various drafts of the screenplay, supervising the casting, instructing Curtiz to stick to the shooting script, reigning in the director's penchant for introducing excessive brutality into the action sequences in order to appease the censors, and even instructing him how to stage and light particular scenes including the climactic duel between Errol Flynn and Henry Daniell (who had to be extensively doubled).[11] Behlmer's study is one of an excellent series of annotated screenplays of Warner Bros. films published by the University of Wisconsin Press based on the Warner Bros. archives. According to general editor Tino Balio the aim of the series – which also includes *Little Caesar, The Public Enemy, 42nd Street, Gold Diggers of 1933, The Mystery of the Wax Museum, I Am a Fugitive from a Chain Gang, The Adventures of Robin Hood, Dark Victory, Yankee Doodle Dandy, Mildred Pierce* and *Mission to Moscow* – is chiefly 'to explicate the art of screenwriting during the thirties and forties' but in addition 'to incorporate supplemental information concerning the studio system of motion picture production'.[12] The particular value of the series is that it builds a series of case studies into a detailed and systematic account of the working practices of the studio.

As Bordwell and Thompson have written: 'Among students of film, no question starts an argument faster than "Who is the author of a studio-made film?"'[13] Histories of production can help us to answer this question. As a case study, let us turn again to one of the most famous films ever made: *Citizen Kane*. We have seen in Chapter 2 how *Citizen Kane* has been accorded a privileged status in aesthetic histories of film. But it also demonstrates how archival research can shed light on one of the major controversies of film history. For many years the 'known' facts about *Citizen Kane* were as follows. In 1939 the young theatre *impressario* Orson Welles was recruited by RKO Radio Pictures on a two-picture contract as producer, writer, director and actor. Welles worked initially on an adaptation of Joseph Conrad's *Heart of Darkness* but abandoned this in favour of an original film story known variously as *The American* and *Citizen John USA* before it became *Citizen Kane*. Welles wrote the screenplay in collaboration with Herman J. Mankiewicz, a former journalist who turned screenwriter in the 1930s. *Citizen Kane* was a loosely disguised biopic (industry short hand for 'biographical picture') of newspaper magnate William Randolph Hearst, who was so incensed that he tried to pressure RKO into not releasing the film. *Citizen Kane* was released in May 1941: it was a critical success (voted best film of the year by the New York Critics and by the National Board of Review) but a box-office failure.

Citizen Kane soon acquired a special reputation as a landmark of film art, and by the 1960s had started to top 'best film' polls. Its growing critical status was in inverse proportion to Welles's career, which never fully recovered from the critical mauling of his next film for RKO, *The Magnificent Ambersons*, or from the reputation he acquired for being 'difficult'. A 'biographical legend' emerged – propagated largely by Welles himself – which cast Welles as the boy genius whose talent was never fully recognized by the philistine world of Hollywood and who was condemned to spend the rest of his career picking up work as a peripatetic director and jobbing actor. The decline of Welles's career only served to enhance the status of *Citizen Kane*: what he might otherwise have achieved 'if only…'

In 1971, however, Welles's claim to be the 'author' of *Citizen Kane* was challenged by Pauline Kael, the film critic of the *New Yorker*. Kael's essay 'Raising Kane' – written as an introduction to a published version of the screenplay – is a long (50,000 words), rambling polemic which sets out to debunk Welles's claim that he alone was responsible for the script of *Citizen Kane*. Basing her account on interviews with friends and colleagues of Herman J. Mankiewicz (who had died in 1953) and on reports about the making of the film in the trade press, Kael claims that Mankiewicz alone wrote the screenplay, with little or no input from Welles. She further asserts that Welles then tried to deny Mankiewicz a scriptwriting credit. In the event, and only following intervention from the Screen Writers' Guild, Mankiewicz and Welles shared the writing credit. Kael's argument is as much inductive as deductive. The subsequent decline of Welles's career, she feels, was evidence that *Citizen Kane* cannot have been his vision alone: 'He has never again worked on a subject with the immediacy and impact of *Kane*. His later films…haven't been *conceived* in terms of daring modern subjects that excite us, as the very idea of *Kane* excites us.'[14] And she avers that Welles tried to deny credit to Mankiewicz because he had started to believe in his own biographical legend: 'Welles seems to have fallen into the trap that has caught so many lesser men – believing his own publicity, believing that he really was the whole creative works, producer-director-writer-actor. Because he *could* do all these things, he imagined that he *did* do them.'[15]

Robert Carringer's book on the making of *Citizen Kane* has in turn debunked many of Kael's claims while at the same time adding to and nuancing the known facts about the film. Carringer had access to the RKO studio archives as well as to the personal papers of Welles and his theatre partner John Houseman. He was also able to draw upon several PhD theses, including Richard Jewell's important study of the economic history of RKO.[16] Several important points emerged from this research. For one thing Carringer finds that the popular reception of *Citizen Kane* was more varied than often assumed. It seems to have done well in large metropolitan centres but 'did not play' (in the industry's parlance) in provincial movie theatres. RKO eventually recorded a loss of *c.*$150,000 on the film. Its negative cost had been *c.*$840,000, which was not extravagantly expensive by the standards of an industry where by the early 1940s a major studio 'prestige' film often cost over $1 million.[17]

The most significant point to emerge from Carringer's research, however, was that he was able to substantiate, once and for all, the disputed authorship of *Citizen Kane*. He shows that the preparation of the screenplay was a collaborative process in which Mankiewicz's role was to impose a structure onto Welles's story ideas and to flesh out the characters. It was Mankiewicz who wrote the early drafts, working at Victorville (a desert ranch in California), which were then revised by Welles in Hollywood. Carringer makes the important point (one entirely overlooked by other historians) that some of the changes Welles introduced were not for artistic reasons but rather to reduce the projected budget which in the early stages was costed at over $1 million.[18] Carringer concludes that the final shooting script incorporated elements that can be attributed to both Mankiewicz and Welles, with the former providing the story and structure and the latter most of the virtuoso scenes and moments:

> To summarize: Mankiewicz (with assistance from Houseman and Welles) wrote the first two drafts. His principal contributions were the story frame, a cast of characters, various individual scenes, and a good share of the dialogue. Certain parts were already in close to final form in the Victorville script, in particular the beginning and end, the newsreel, the projection room sequence, the first visit to Susan, and Colorado. Welles added the narrative brilliance – the visual and verbal wit, the stylistic fluidity, and such stunningly original strokes as the newspaper montages and the breakfast table sequence. He also transformed Kane from a cardboard characterization of Hearst into a figure of mystery and epic magnificence.[19]

Carringer attributes to Welles the qualities of 'brilliance' and 'genius', in comparison to the 'plodding' Mankiewicz. Whereas Kael had contended that it was Mankiewicz who had the journalistic skill to translate a loosely disguised biopic of William Randolph Hearst into a satire of American political life, Carringer considers that it was Welles who transformed the film from a conventional biopic into something more ambitious.

▶ Histories of reception

The emergence of reception studies in the 1990s marked a fundamental shift in film history. Hitherto film analysis had been geared towards investigating meanings within the text itself, whether through the creative role of an *auteur* or through the ideological structures embedded within the text. Scholars and critics would therefore seek to persuade their readers that their interpretation of a film was, if not definitive, then at least a preferred reading. This faith in the interpretational skills of the critic was challenged, however, first from a theoretical perspective by scholars from literary and cultural studies who pointed out that any critical interpretation is just one of a range of possible meanings that may be attached to a film, and then from a historical perspective by scholars who sought to identify how actual audiences in real historical situations have understood the meanings of films. The landmark texts in the emergence of historically-based reception studies were Janet Staiger's *Interpreting Films* (1992), Miriam Hansen's *Babel and Babylon* (1991), Barbara Klinger's *Melodrama and Meaning* (1994) and Jackie Stacey's *Star Gazing* (1994).[20] While they adopted different methodologies, collectively these studies marked a shift away from the assumption evident within much '**Screen theory**' that the film text itself constructs the spectator. Instead they sought to show how a film was understood within specific historical, social and cultural contexts. This involves analysing what has been called the 'discursive surround' of a film by examining the contemporary discourses circulating around it: these include reviews, publicity materials and (where available) studies of the audiences themselves.

There are several distinct methodological approaches within reception studies. Janet Staiger argues for what she calls a 'historical-materialist' approach that involves 'tracing as far as possible dominant and marginalized interpretative strategies as mediated by language and context'.[21] Among her case studies are *The Birth of a Nation*, where she maps changing perspectives towards its racist overtones, showing, for example, that a reissue of the film in the 1930s prompted a reformulation of ideological critiques of the film away from race and towards class, so that it became 'a nodal point for their [the American Communist Party's] argument that connections exist between racism and class exploitation'.[22] Similarly, Barbara Klinger's study of the films of Douglas

Sirk – already an important point of reference for film studies – shows how a film like *Written on the Wind* (1956) could in the 1950s be interpreted as an adult melodrama, becoming in the 1970s a critique of American capitalism and then in the 1990s transforming into a camp classic.[23] What Staiger and Klinger demonstrate is that the meanings attached to a film are both histori- cally specific and may change over time: the meanings of a film are not fixed but change in response to the ideological and cultural climate. Staiger's point that reception studies 'is not textual interpretation but a historical explanation of the activities of interpretation' cannot be over-emphasized.[24]

Another approach to reception studies has been to apply theories of specta- torship to a specific historical and cultural context rather than treating them in the abstract. Miriam Hansen's study of spectatorship in American silent cin- ema is a case in point. Hansen argues that, in its early period, cinema depended for its appeal on marginalized social groups, particularly women and immi- grants, and that therefore it set out to cater for those audiences through the construction of what she terms an 'alternative public sphere'. Her case study of D. W. Griffith's epic *Intolerance* (1916) considers its 'curious pattern of recep- tion' – critically acclaimed but after a strong opening losing momentum dur- ing its general release only to be reclaimed as a masterpiece of film art in the 1930s – and shows how 'the film throws into relief diverging concepts of rep- resentation and spectatorship at a historically crucial juncture, the threshold of Hollywood's classical period'.[25] Another case study, on the female fans of romantic matinée idol Rudolph Valentino, draws upon both textual analysis of his films and a consideration of their publicity and marketing strategies. Hansen argues that Valentino's ambiguous star image – an image that repre- sented both a certain archetype of masculinity and a feminized alter ego – was only partly constructed through his films. She highlights 'a considerable ten- sion...between the textually constructed spectator-subject of classical cin- ema and empirical audiences that were defined by particular and multiple social affiliations and capable of sharing culturally and historically specific readings'.[26]

Jackie Stacey's research into British cinema audiences of the 1940s also focuses on the female spectator, but from a very different perspective. Stacey draws upon a tradition of **ethnographic** research – involving questionnaires sent to women who had been active film-goers and who responded to a let- ter published in a women's magazine – to explore the meanings that British women attached to Hollywood's female stars of the 1940s and 1950s. Stacey identifies three 'discourses of spectatorship' – escapism, identification and consumption – which emerge from her respondents. One of the focal points of her research is the extent to which British women cinema-goers identified with stars such as Bette Davis and Doris Day to the extent of copying their

clothing, make-up and hair styles. Again she emphasizes the historical specificity of spectatorship, as in the 1940s and 1950s 'Hollywood stars signified
unattainable otherness which precisely constituted their appeal in Britain at
this time'.[27] Helen Taylor applies a similar approach but focuses on responses
to one film: *Gone With the Wind*. Her research into the film's female fans highlights 'the varied and contradictory ways in which this one work has accumu-
lated significance in their lives, making the notion of a single *Gone With the
Wind* impossible'.[28]

The recourse to ethnographic methodology based on interviews or questionnaires is acknowledged as problematic by those who have employed it: people's
accounts of their response to films may have been coloured by hindsight and
there is always a danger that the most committed fans (those most likely to par-
ticipate in such research) are not representative of all cinema-goers. But at the
same time it also highlights one of the underlying problems of reception studies: the absence of sources. Unlike production histories, where sources can usually be found for the making of films (even if only in the trade press), there are
fewer sources for the moment of reception and those that exist are more difficult to interpret. Box-office data, for example, even when it is available, offers a
quantitative rather than a qualitative index of popularity: it tells us which films
were successful (and which were not) but not what drew audiences to them.
An important source for historically-based reception studies are contemporary
reviews, but again these are difficult to interpret: the historian must take into
account the political, cultural and aesthetic orientation of the critic, the newspaper or magazine they were writing for, and its readership. Nor are critics necessarily representative of popular taste generally: in particular popular **genre**
films (studio blockbusters, Bollywood spectaculars, James Bond movies) are
often greeted with ill-disguised disdain by 'quality' critics yet are evidently successful at the box office. Where there are some similarities between reception
histories and production histories is that they tend to be case study-focused.
Again the reception of any film is a unique activity: this makes general histories of reception problematic.

As a case study of reception let us consider Alfred Hitchcock's *Rear Window*
(1954), which offers a text-book example of how the meanings attached to a
particular film have been modified over time in response to a changing historical and intellectual climate. *Rear Window* was Hitchcock's first film under
a lucrative contract for Paramount Pictures in the 1950s. It was a critical and
popular success, for many critics marking a return to form for the 'master of
suspense' following a relatively fallow period in the late 1940s and early 1950s.
It was not, however, regarded as a particularly important or deep film, but
rather was admired as a polished romantic thriller whose popular success probably had as much to do with the appeal of its stars (James Stewart and Grace

Kelly) as anything else. Robert Kapsis, in his study of Hitchcock's critical reputation, summarizes the contemporary critical reception thus: 'Virtually all reviewers praised the film for its entertainment values – "exhilerating", "full bodied", "the most roundly enjoyable" Hitchcock film in years. At the same time, practically no one saw it as a significant film or as a deeply personal statement.'[29]

After the fact, however, the reputation and understanding of *Rear Window* changed. Its reputation grew partly because it was one of several Hitchcock films (along with *Vertigo*, *The Trouble With Harry* and the remake of *The Man Who Knew Too Much*) that for various contractual reasons were not reissued and were not sold to television. Robin Wood, writing in the mid-1960s but without the benefit of having seen the film recently, felt that it was 'the first of Hitchcock's films to which the term masterpiece can reasonably be applied' and that 'the morality of the film is far subtler and more profound' than had hitherto been allowed.[30] The reading of *Rear Window* was now influenced by a retrospective critical construction of Hitchcock as an *auteur* – a perspective that had not been available to reviewers at the time of its release in 1954 and was influenced by knowledge of later films such as *Vertigo*, *Psycho* and *Marnie* which could be seen as developing some of the themes of *Rear Window*. *Rear Window* now emerged as a compendium of classic 'Hitchcockian' themes and motifs: as a morality play, as a psychological study of voyeurism, as a 'transference of guilt', and as an exploration of the 'chaos world' lurking beneath the surface of everyday normality.[31]

In the 1970s and 1980s yet another reading of *Rear Window* emerged: that the film is a metaphor for the whole apparatus of cinema itself. François Truffaut, for example, saw the protagonist Jeff, confined to a wheelchair and passing the time spying on his neighbours through binoculars, as analogous to the film director: 'The courtyard is the world, the reporter/photographer is the filmmaker, the binoculars stand for the camera and its lenses.'[32] Other critics have suggested that Jeff is a surrogate for the spectator in the cinema: he sits (often in the dark) and watches a series of miniature dramas seen through the windows of the neighbouring apartments. Robert Stam and Roberta Pearson, writing on the occasion of the film's reissue in 1983, describe *Rear Window* as 'a brilliant essay on the cinema and on the nature of the cinematic experience'.[33] This has now become the dominant reading of *Rear Window*. However, it is a reading that is informed entirely by theoretical developments in film studies rather than by any empirical evidence about the responses of actual audiences. (When I saw *Rear Window* for the first time in 1986, for example, what attracted me was the elegant beauty of Grace Kelly rather than the voyeuristic impulse behind James Stewart's actions or the notion that he somehow represented 'me' in the text: it was only when I read about the film after seeing it that I started to understand it in this way.)

Since the 1990s the emergence and expansion of the World Wide Web and Internet has provided another avenue into researching reception contexts. Online discussion boards, newsgroups and email digests are all sites of audience activity that provide insights into how online consumers respond to films and other cultural media. In particular the Internet has become a means of investigating the nature of fan communities, often those congregated around 'cult' media – including television, comics, popular music and certain types of film. The methodologies of web ethnography are still developing and there are various problems associated with this type of research. Online communities are historical audiences only for contemporary media (for example fan discussion and response to the new *Star Wars* films). For older media they provide evidence not of the historical reception of texts but rather of retrospective views of those texts. Furthermore, the membership and composition of online fan communities is constantly in flux as newcomers join discussion boards and others fade away. And whereas traditional ethnographic research methods emphasize factors such as age, gender and ethnicity in contextualizing responses, the anonymous nature of the Internet means that users may if they wish conceal their real identities. This is not to say that web ethnography has no value for the film historian. Justin Smith's research on the web digest for the cult film *The Wicker Man* (1973), for example, illustrates how this method can reveal some new insights into the nature of the cult film experience and the activities of fandom. Smith finds that fan discourses around this film bring together a range of sub-cultural interests (including paganism, folk music and alternative lifestyles) which provide a shared critical framework for their engagement with the text. He also finds that in this instance the organization of the discussion group itself 'provides the ritualistic framework and structure which complement fans' attachment to the text perfectly'.[34]

▶ **Histories of audiences**

Histories of audiences are related to but are not synonymous with histories of reception. The focus of reception studies is on responses to specific films or stars. Researching audiences, however, shifts attention away from films themselves to examine instead the act of cinema-going as a social practice in its own right. Robert C. Allen, who perhaps more than anyone, certainly in the United States, has pioneered the history of cinema-going has said that he was prompted along this path following his realization that hitherto 'film history had been written as if films had no audiences or were seen by everyone and in the same way'.[35] Furthermore, there has often been a tendency in film studies to consider 'the audience' in the most abstract sense: as an undifferentiated mass whose experience of watching films is uniformly the same. Clearly this assumption will not withstand close scrutiny: no histories of social organization, whether focusing on political parties, religious groups, the English gentry, or whatever, would treat them as an entirely homogenous body. Why should cinema audiences be any different?

The principal obstacle to researching cinema audiences has always been the dearth of sources. One of the main reasons why film history has often been seen as the history of films is simply that it is easier to analyse texts that survive than it is to research social groups which no longer exist: the cinema audience is 'lost' to the historian in a way that films are not. (Even 'lost' films can be partly reconstructed by looking at contemporary reviews and publicity materials: the same is not true for audiences.) The most useful sources for historians of cinema-going are surveys undertaken either by the industry or by social investigators such as Margaret Thorp's *America at the Movies* (1946) and J. P. Mayer's *British Cinemas and their Audiences* (1948) which provide evidence of the social composition and cultural preferences of audiences in particular historical periods.[36] In Britain the work of the social survey organization Mass-Observation between the late 1930s and the early 1950s also yielded valuable data about cinema audiences.[37] Of course the value of these sources depends in large measure upon the methodological rigour of the original studies and the aims of the contemporary researchers. In fact reliable studies of this sort are few and far between, even for the more recent periods, and are virtually non-existent for non-Western countries.

Like reception histories, audience histories have tended to be case-study based: often the focus is on either an individual cinema where attendance records have survived (a matter of chance: the discovery of such records represent 'eureka moments' for film historians) or on the nature of cinema-going in a specific locality. Moving from the local and the specific to the national and the general is problematic, especially given that what local studies often suggest is a diversity of audience composition and taste even within particular cities and neighbourhoods. Much of the historical research into cinema audiences has focused on the **nickelodeon** period in the United States between 1905 and 1910. The 'nickelodeons' were the first cinemas that showed only films rather than incorporating films into vaudeville or fairground shows: they were often converted stores with a small seating capacity (usually fewer than 200) which showed mixed programmes of films running for up to an hour. The number of nickelodeons increased from an estimated 2,500 in 1905 to 10,000 in 1910: the greatest concentrations were in New York and Chicago.[38] The nickelodeons have typically been characterized as dingy, spartan places, whose patrons were the urban proletariat and immigrant workers. However, local studies by historians including Robert C. Allen, Douglas Gomery, Charles Musser and Ben Singer have shown

that there were considerable variations in location and in the type of establishment. In Manhattan, for example, nickelodeons were not evenly distributed:
there were large clusters around working-class and poor immigrant neighbourhoods such as the Lower East Side, but there were also significant numbers in
more affluent areas such as Harlem (then a middle/lower-middle class neigh-
bourhood). Nor were all nickelodeons the dim and dingy places of notorious
legend: those in more prosperous areas were often quite well appointed.[39]

The study of nickelodeons has to some extent challenged the received wisdom that early cinema audiences were composed predominantly of working-
class immigrant workers. There is evidence to suggest that women and children
made up a significant proportion of early film audiences. Kathy Peiss has suggested that the nickelodeon provided an important 'woman's space' in the new
urban environments of the early twentieth century.[40] Therefore the view that
nickelodeons catered principally for the entertainment needs of immigrant
workers needs to be qualified. It seems reasonable to assume, in the big cities at
least, that nickelodeons would have brought about a socially demarcated form
of exhibition: depending upon their location they attracted either predominantly blue-collar or white-collar clientele. In smaller towns, in contrast, 'a
nickelodeon might be the only place showing films, and people from all strata
of society would watch movies together'.[41]

Recently attention has shifted away from the large US cities to consider
the practice of cinema-going in smaller towns and non-metropolitan communities. This is exemplified by the 'Going to the Show' project undertaken
by the University of North Carolina, Wilmington, which is 'an experiment in
re-locating the experience of cinema, of resituating movies and moviegoing
within a few of the hundreds of thousands of places in tens of thousands of
communities where people went to the show'.[42] The project uses fire insurance
maps to identify the location of cinemas in towns and cities in North Carolina
and local newspapers to establish (where possible) what sort of films were
shown. Three particular points emerge from this research that significantly
adds to our understanding of early cinema exhibition and audiences. The first
is the diversity of exhibition practices: films were shown not only in the nickelodeons but also in fairgrounds, amusement parks, social clubs, YMCAs and
seasonal open-air venues. The second is the extent to which film exhibition
was determined largely by local circumstances. In particular North Carolina
was a state that enforced the notorious Jim Crow Laws on racial segregation:
the existence of cinemas designated 'colored' or 'negro' indicates that cinema-
going at this time was demarcated by race as well as by class. The third point
to emerge from the research is that 'going to the show' seems to have been an
ingrained social practice regardless of the content of the film programme. Films
changed so swiftly that 'any particular film was part of that experience for only

a day or two'.[43] In other words it was the cinema (as a social institution) that mattered rather than individual films.

▶ Case study: researching British cinema audiences

Research into the nature of cinema audiences in Britain demonstrates the range of methods available to the film historian, while also illustrating how different methods may give rise to different answers. Until recently little was known about either the social composition or the popular tastes of British cinema-goers. Sources such as the Mass-Observation surveys and the Bernstein Questionnaires (evidence gathered for Sidney Bernstein's Granada cinema chain in the late 1940s) provided snapshots of cinema habits and preferences but the bigger picture was missing. Nor is there reliable evidence, at least until the 1970s, of box-office trends. Unlike the US trade press, which reported box-office data, British trade papers did not reveal the grosses of individual films. Instead the only sources are the somewhat impressionistic annual surveys of 'winners' and 'losers' in the trade paper *Kinematograph Weekly* and the records of the Board of Trade in the National Archives, which, however, include only films released since 1945 and even then are far from being a complete record.

The first thoroughgoing social history of cinema in Britain was Jeffrey Richards's *The Age of the Dream Palace* (1984), which focused on the 1930s. Richards marshals a wealth of evidence – compiled from contemporary social surveys, educational reports and the industry data amassed by statistician Simon Rowson – to provide a comprehensive survey of the nature of the cinema-going audience and its taste in films. The general picture that emerges is that cinema-going was a genuinely widespread activity with up to two thirds of the British population 'going to the pictures' on at least an occasional basis and one-third being regular cinema-goers who went at least once a week and frequently more often. When broken down by class, age and gender, it emerges that the cinema-going habit was most ingrained among the working classes and that under-40s were more regular cinema-goers than older groups. It also emerges that nearly 70 per cent of the most regular cinema-goers were women. Richards concludes 'that while a large proportion of the population at large went to the cinema occasionally, the enthusiasts were young, working-class and more often female than male.'[44]

Richards also examines which films British audiences preferred, drawing not only on the trade press but also on the evidence of fan magazines and newspaper reviews. He defends the use of reviews on the grounds that 'the critics were writing with the tastes and interests of their readers in mind'.[45] He nuances the assumption that British films were not popular with British audiences and suggests that it 'would be misleading to exaggerate the differences…between British and American films'.[46] He pays particular attention to the popularity of film stars: it was stars as much as stories that informed many cinema-goers' choice of films. The most intriguing point to emerge here is that, while the leading Hollywood stars were always popular, there were fluctuations in their appeal, whereas the most popular British stars were, consistently, Gracie Fields and George Formby, both distinctly unglamorous, 'normal' types who represented a specifically northern and working-class Britishness.[47] We might conclude that while the glamour and sophistication of Hollywood stars made them aspirational models, the 'ordinariness' of Fields and Formby meant that British audiences preferred home-grown stars to be more down to earth. Richards concludes: 'The public seem on the whole to have been happy with the films they were given during the 1930s, and those films for the most part played their role in maintaining consensus and the *status quo*.'[48]

John Sedgwick's statistical research into film preferences has confirmed some of Richards's conclusions while challenging others. In the absence of industry data regarding the box-office performance of films, Sedgwick, a business historian, has devised a methodology known as 'POPSTAT' which ranks the popularity of films through an index calculated from exhibition records. He uses local newspapers to ascertain how long films ran in particular cinemas and business directories to establish the seating capacity of those cinemas. The exhaustive evidence-gathering required for this kind of study necessitates local case studies: Sedgwick bases his on the West End of London and two very different provincial towns in Brighton and Bolton. Sedgwick suggests that, while in general Hollywood films held the ascendancy, British films were not only also popular but were often among the most successful. Thus, according to POPSTAT, 96 British films make it into the top fifty releases between 1932 and 1937, with five British films in the top ten in 1932 and 1935, four in 1934, two in 1933 and 1936 and one in 1937 (a year that saw a downturn in British production following an economic crisis in the industry).[49] In his analysis of the most popular stars, however, Sedgwick finds that the leading British stars over the same period were Ronald Colman, George Arliss and Charles Laughton. Gracie Fields creeps into the top hundred (at eighty-six) but George Formby is nowhere to be found.[50] This highlights a discrepancy between the contemporary popularity polls and the data generated through POPSTAT.

Sedgwick acknowledges that his research is quantitative rather than qualitative: what it cannot do is explain the popularity of particular films or stars. And it is based on a narrow data set: a comprehensive POPSTAT analysis would require further research into other towns and cities. To date no-one else has taken on the project. A very different methodology, and one that produces qualitative rather than quantitative responses, has been applied by Annette

Kuhn in her research into memories of cinema-going in the 1930s. Kuhn's research is based on interviews and questionnaires in which respondents were invited to discuss their cinema habits and experiences. Her investigation of the cultural memory of cinema-going confirms the view that 'going to the pictures' as a pastime was as much an activity in itself as going to see a particular film. The research affirms the importance of stars, highlighting that what cinema-goers remember are not specific films (many of which are often mis-remembered) but rather star images. Again this methodology raises some interesting discrepancies between different kinds of evidence. For example, musical stars such as Fred Astaire and Ginger Rogers, Jeanette MacDonald and Nelson Eddy, and Deanna Durbin have retained a stronger hold on the memories of cinema-goers than their relative popularity at the time would suggest. Kuhn's research also highlights significant class differences in the response to particular stars. Ginger Rogers and Deanna Durbin feature prominently, as they 'offer interestingly contrasting modes of feminine identification for the adolescent [female] of the 1930s'.[51] There were marked differences between fans of Ginger Rogers (who were 'overwhelmingly working class or from rural areas') and Deanna Durbin ('middle class and metropolitan'). However, Gracie Fields and George Formby do not seem to feature in the memories of cinema-goers: at least there are no references to them in the published research.

Another approach to the history of cinema-going in Britain is provided by micro-level studies focusing on particular cinemas. These are determined by the historical accident of where records of admissions and/or box-office receipts have survived: there are surprisingly few examples given that in the 1930s and 1940s there were over 4,000 cinemas in Britain.[52] It is only to be expected that local studies will highlight variations from the national picture. Sue Harper's research on Portsmouth's Regent Cinema is an exemplary case study of how local film tastes may be determined by a range of external factors, including the impact of war and consequent changes in the social composition of audiences. The Regent was 'the biggest and most luxurious of Portsmouth cinemas in the 1930s' and its regular clientele was mostly lower-middle class. There was a clear preference for more sophisticated films – *Top Hat*, *Cavalcade* and *Snow White and the Seven Dwarfs* were among the 'runaway hits' – and British films, especially Will Hay's comedies, were disproportionately popular in relation to the national picture. Harper suggests that 'medium successes' – including British costume films such as *Jew Süss*, *Tudor Rose* and *Knight Without Armour* – indicated 'that some stable part of the Regent audience liked more demanding fare'. The least successful were war films (including *All Quiet on the Western Front*) and vulgar comedies.[53] However, the nature of the Regent's audiences changed during the Second World War when it was patronized by transient workers and servicemen stationed in the city. Harper identifies two, related trends during the war: the greater popularity of American films in preference to British among the 'runaway hits' and 'major successes', and the increasing prominence of previously despised low-brow comedies. *Citizen Kane*, a film that might have appealed to the more intellectually imaginative tastes of the cinema's patrons in the 1930s, fared very badly. Harper concludes 'that Regent taste in the war years was much more low-brow, and that the male service audience was in evidence with the thriller and cowboy favourites.'[54]

While local studies of cinema-going highlight significant variations between the local and the national, the study of fan magazines offers another way of mapping popular tastes in film. Mark Glancy's analysis of articles and letters in *Picturegoer* between 1939 and 1945 demonstrates how the fan press 'serves as a reminder of the complexities of the past, and the challenge of rediscovering the disposition, attitudes and opinions of historical audiences'.[55] *Picturegoer* was the leading fan magazine in Britain, with a circulation of around 325,000 by the end of the Second World War, and while there is anecdotal evidence that its readership was biased towards women and the working classes (who, as other studies have shown, made up a larger proportion of the cinema-going audience in any case), what Glancy's research highlights is the extraordinarily broad and catholic interests of that readership. There is less evidence of a clear-cut distinction between the middle-brow and the popular that pervades most other accounts of film culture: *Picturegoer* and its readers were happy to discuss *The Magnificent Ambersons* alongside *Tarzan and the Amazons*. Glancy argues, persuasively, that *Picturegoer* 'walked a fine line between stoking debates and manufacturing a consensus within a popular film culture that was riddled with doubts' – doubts that included the tension between escapism and propaganda – and that, viewed as a historical source, it 'represents a more diverse film culture than most accounts of wartime British cinema suggest'.[56]

It will be clear that the historical sociology of film is a diverse and multifaceted area of enquiry that encompasses a wide range of methods and approaches. These range from the nitty-gritty nuts-and-bolts documentation of the production of individual films to the historical archæology involved in recovering the tastes and preferences of cinema audiences. Where the historical sociology of film differs fundamentally from the history of film as an art form is in its emphasis not solely on the film text itself but rather on the relationships between the text and its producers and between the text and its consumers. The relationships between films and their historical contexts are understood to have been mediated – first through the processes of production (how the content and form of films are determined by industrial and other factors) and then through their reception (how the meanings attached to films arise from interactions between the film and its audiences). In this type of film history, therefore, films themselves are no longer the only, or even the primary, objects of analysis.

Conclusion

There remains...a great deal of ordinary cinema history yet to be written. By now, however, there is an orthodox practice of film history by which an article on authorship in Hollywood can emerge from a trawl of the trade papers and an archive box containing a couple of contracts and a cache of letters...But the larger picture – the understanding of cinema's social agency in the twentieth century once promised by 1970s theories of ideology – continues to evade us.

Richard Maltby[1]

It will be clear that the discipline of film history has come a long way over the last 40 years or so. Since the 1970s the Standard Version of film history as an evolutionary narrative of new technologies and the corresponding formal and aesthetic advances in the medium has been more or less superseded by revisionist histories that instead emphasize the historical specificity of particular periods and different film practices. At the same time the failure of '**Screen theory**' to provide a totalizing theory of cinema as an **ideological apparatus** brought about a reconsideration of the historical and empirical approaches that had until then been marginalized. There are now authoritative histories of Hollywood and most (though still not all) European film industries. In particular there has been a proliferation of case studies – histories of the production and reception of specific films, analyses of previously neglected genres and cycles, critical studies of hitherto overlooked film-makers – that has done much to fill the gaps in our historical knowledge and understanding of cinema. However, as Maltby notes, the shift from grand narratives to micro-level histories – what might be termed film history from the 'bottom up' – has perhaps eclipsed some of the wider theoretical issues.

The discipline of film history is still young enough for there to be occasional 'eureka moments' that entirely reshape our thinking about the subject. The rediscovery and critical re-evaluation of early cinema in the 1970s marked perhaps the most seismic shift in the subject: the formative years of film-making were seen in an entirely new light by the simple dint of more films becoming available. Other challenges to the Standard Version have perhaps been less far-reaching in their implications for film history overall, but still represent significant historical reassessments. A good example (by no means the only one) is Eric Rentschler's revisionist study of the cinema of the Third Reich that considers the popular cinema of Nazi Germany. Rentschler examines melodramas such as *La Habanera* (1937) and fantasies such as *Münchhausen* (1943) as well as propaganda films like *Hitlerjunge Quex* (1933) and *Jud Süss* (1940). He concludes that film-making in the Third Reich was a vibrant popular cinema that 'reflected the workings of the classical cinema with its deference to character motivation, the codes of **realism**, the strictures of dramatic development and closure. It was a cinema dedicated to illusionism...Goebbels saw himself as a German David O. Selznick and sought to create a film world every bit as alluring as Hollywood.'[2] It is an important corrective to the orthodox view of Nazi-era cinema as being entirely propagandistic and pernicious.

Considering the broad trends in recent and current film-historical scholarship, three areas stand out. The first is that the old bias towards Hollywood and West European cinemas as the only sites in which culturally or aesthetically significant films have been made can no longer be sustained. The popular cinemas of non-Western countries – including Japan, Hong Kong, India, Mexico and Brazil – have started to find their place in the sun alongside the films of canonized *auteur* directors. No longer are the films of Akira Kurosawa or Satyajit Ray, for example, taken as representative of the film cultures of Japan or India. Hindi cinema (popularly if somewhat derisorily known as 'Bollywood') has been the chief beneficiary of this process, with important academic studies of the production ideologies of Hindi cinema, the visual style of Hindi films and the cultural meanings of genres and stars in Hindi cinema. A film such as *Mother India* (1957) is no longer seen as *kitsch* but as part of an ideological project in Hindi cinema of the 1950s to promote national unity and social cohesion through the vehicle of the 'All-India Film'.[3] All this said there remain significant gaps in our knowledge. The film industries of Africa and the Middle East are still largely uncharted territories (Iranian cinema is the one major exception here). The cinemas of 'small nations' such as the Scandinavian countries and the satellite states of the former Soviet bloc tend to be known only through a handful of *auteurs*. And our knowledge of film distribution and exhibition outside the West remains quite rudimentary: this is still a subject given to broad generalizations rather than specific examples.

Another recent development has been the emergence of work that goes beyond the narrow focus on national cinemas that characterizes most film-historical research and which considers instead the international scope of the film industry. Studies such as Andrew Higson and Richard Maltby's *'Film Europe' and 'Film America'* (1999), Sarah Street's *Transatlantic Crossings* (2001) and Mark Glancy's *Hollywood and the Americanization of Britain* (2013)[4] have all built upon the pioneering work of Kristin Thompson in this field. The old-fashioned Marxist interpretation of Hollywood as a hegemonic force that uses its economic and political power to impose its products upon the rest of the world has been nuanced by studies which instead emphasize the idea of economic and cultural exchange. The relationship between Hollywood and the rest of the world has as often been based on co-operation as on competition: ever since the 1950s so-called 'runaway' films (Hollywood films made overseas to benefit from production subsidies or tax incentives to encourage investment in local production sectors) have been an important industry trend. The trend of recent scholarship in this field has been to consider the 'fluid relationship between creative communities and the shared experiences of many national cinema audiences'.[5]

The third – and perhaps in the long term the most important – development has been a shift away from text-based histories – film history as the history of films – to broader-based contextual histories of exhibition and reception in which films themselves are no longer the sole focus of attention. It has been suggested that the (belated) recognition of the place of the audience in film history – exemplified by landmark conferences at University College, London in 1998 ('Hollywood and its Audiences') and the University of Ghent in 2007 ('The Glow in Their Eyes') – represents a paradigm-shifting moment in film history that 'might prove to have a comparable impact to the legendary rendezvous event at Brighton in 1978, which kindled a fundamental reconsideration of early cinema'.[6] Taken to its extreme the history of exhibition and reception removes the film text itself from film history. Robert C. Allen has suggested provocatively that – for early cinema at least – 'movies don't matter' and that the real story of the formative period is not the rise of the narrative film or the institutionalization of the **studio system** but rather the social activity of cinema-going: 'The films that have been preserved from the silent era of film history are souvenirs – mute tokens of one of the most important but least-documented cultural and social phenomena of the twentieth century.'[7] This may be going too far for some, not least because it downplays the importance of factors such as stars and **genres** in accounting for popular preferences. Nevertheless few would deny the need to consider the relationships between films and their audiences. This development has much wider implications than simply recognizing the importance of context in film history: it involves nothing less than a reconceptualization of film history away from the medium-specific discipline that is has been hitherto and its repositioning within the broader fields of economic, social and cultural history.

The recent historiography of British cinema provides some indicators of how this project might be taken forward. We have already seen how John Sedgwick has developed the 'POPSTAT' methodology based on techniques used in economic history to rank films through an index of popularity calculated from their exhibition records. Sedgwick acknowledges that his research is quantitative rather than qualitative: but in the absence of industry data regarding box-office takings it provides the best evidence of which films were most popular with British audiences of the 1930s.[8] This quantitative research complements other work examining questions of cultural and aesthetic taste. Also focusing on the 1930s, for example, Robert James's account of working-class leisure patterns locates film history within the wider fields of social and cultural history. James considers cinema-going alongside other leisure pursuits and pastimes, shows that it was not an isolated activity, and, contrary to the **Leavisite** view of popular culture as a soporific for the masses, marshals evidence that working-class consumers exercised considerable choice over their reading and viewing habits. James concludes that 'patterns of taste were never uniform, that acts of consumption are highly complex, that working-class consumers chose leisure activities to fulfil a range of cultural roles, and that these roles were never easy to define'.[9]

This trend towards historically specific studies of exhibition and reception has shifted attention away from textual analysis. In economic film history, especially, films are understood as commodities rather than as cultural artefacts. But where does this leave the place of the film itself in film history: does it mean that 'movies don't matter?' One answer – again drawn from the historiography of British cinema – is suggested by Justin Smith's research into cult films and film cults between the late 1960s and the 1990s. Smith argues that the cult film was a historically specific phenomenon that arose from a congruence of historical and cultural factors, including the fragmentation of both the film production sector and the cinema-going audience, the emergence of youth-oriented counter cultures, and the related development of 'niche taste' fan communities. While the rise of the cult film was rooted within a particular mode of consumption (fandom), however, Smith also shows that the pleasure of the text itself remained an essential aspect of the cult film experience: films such as *Performance* (1970), *The Wicker Man* (1973), *Tommy* (1975) and *Trainspotting* (1996) were celebrated for their qualities of social transgression and visual and narrative excess, while others such as *The Rocky Horror Picture Show* (1975) and *Withnail & I* (1986) can be read as celebrations of the cult phenomenon itself. Smith demonstrates that the film text still has a place in the study of audiences and reception: indeed his argument is posited on the suggestion that 'the relationship between the text and its reception is central'.[10]

For much of the history of film as an academic subject, the argument seems to have been about whether to privilege either text *or* context. At one extreme solely text-based film studies has the effect of detaching films entirely from the material conditions in which they are produced and consumed: some auteurist studies in particular tend to place films in a sort of cultural vacuum where the presence of the *auteur* alone accounts for the meaning of the films. At the other extreme, however, histories which focus solely on audiences and reception risk removing the film itself from film history. This seems equally unsatisfactory as it does not allow either for the culturally specific meanings of films for their audiences or for the very real aesthetic and stylistic differences between films. Therefore, it is my contention that only through a combination of both textual *and* contextual analysis – understanding films *as films* but also in relation to their institutional, economic, social and cultural contexts – can film history properly explore the 'larger picture of cinema's social agency in the twentieth century' that theoretical approaches alone have failed to provide.

Glossary

Actuality film Film that provides a record of real events or people that has not been restaged for the camera.

Anamorphic A **widescreen** process that uses a convex lens attached to the camera to 'squeeze' the image; when projected through another lens of the same magnification the result creates a wider image than standard projection. CinemaScope and Panavision are the best-known examples of anamorphic widescreen processes.

Art cinema An international movement in film, mostly associated with European *auteur* directors, which emerged after the Second World War. Art cinema is characterized by greater psychological realism and narrative ambiguity than **classical Hollywood cinema**, to which it is often contrasted. Art cinema directors included Michelangelo Antonioni, Ingmar Bergman, Luis Buñuel, Federico Fellini, Alain Resnais and Alain Robbe-Grillet.

***Auteur* theory** The view that the director of a film is the principal creative artist and that films reflect the world-view of their director. Associated particularly with the journal *Cahiers du Cinéma* (which termed it *la politique des auteurs*) and the US critic Andrew Sarris.

Authenticity Film that purports to be historically and/or socially accurate even when it has been restaged for the camera. In particular the term is used to describe historical films that reconstruct the past with authentic period detail and *mise-en-scène*.

Chiaroscuro A style of black-and-white cinematography associated with **German Expressionism** and *film noir* characterized by strong contrasts between light and shadow.

Cinema Nôvo A new wave movement in Brazil in the 1960s led by filmmakers such as Ruy Guerra, Glauber Rocha and Nelson Pereira dos Santos whose films dramatized the everyday lives of labourers and peasants, focusing on the rural rather than the urban.

'Cinema of attractions'   A term coined by film historian Tom Gunning to describe the style of early cinema based on spectacle rather than narrative.

Cinéma Vérité   A film movement developing in France in the 1960s, literally meaning 'cinema of truth', whose practitioners – including Jean Rouch, Edgar Morin and Jacques Rozier – aimed to record real events without directorial intervention.

Classical film aesthetics   A branch of film theory and criticism concerned with the nature of film as an art form.

Classical Hollywood cinema   A term used to describe the US film industry between the 1910s and 1950s. Classical Hollywood is both a mode of production (the **studio system**) and a particular style of film (the **classical narrative film**).

Classical narrative film   Describes the common type of feature film produced by Hollywood and other film industries. The classical narrative film is a story film where events proceed in chronological sequence and where there is a clear sense of resolution at the end. Also known as the **classic realist film**.

Close-up   A **shot** where the camera is placed close to the object, usually a person's face.

Continuity editing   The technique of constructing a film in such a way that the action proceeds naturally from one **shot** to the next – sometimes also known as 'invisible editing' because the camera remains unobtrusive and does not draw attention to itself.

Counter-cinema   A term coined by Peter Wollen to describe a theory and practice of film where everything is posited in dialectical opposition to **classical Hollywood cinema**. Thus counter cinema is characterized by non-narrative (in opposition to narrative), obscurity (in opposition to clarity), alienation (in opposition to identification) and 'un-pleasure'.

Cross-cutting   The practice of cutting between events occurring simultaneously in different screen spaces – also known as **parallel editing**.

Deep-focus cinematography A technique which creates an illusion of depth whereby images in both the foreground and background remain in sharp focus in the same **shot**.

Desaturated colour A visual style in which colours appear naturalistic rather than bright or garish.

Direct Cinema A North American equivalent of *Cinéma Vérité* emerging in parallel in the late 1950s and 1960s. Its practioners included Richard Leacock, Robert Drew, D. A. Pennebaker, and David and Albert Maysles.

Elliptical editing A technique whereby the transition between **shots** includes an ellipsis – a change of screen space or time that would usually be indicated by a fade or a dissolve.

Ethnographic A research methodology that investigates the behavior and attitudes of social groups (such as cinema audiences) based on empirical observation and focus groups.

Feature film A film that is the main or 'featured' attraction on a cinema programme – usually understood as a film with a running time over 60 minutes.

Film noir A term applied by French critics – literally meaning 'dark film' – to describe a trend in American cinema in the 1940s and 1950s characterized by psychological anxiety, social dislocation and an expressionist visual style. *Film noir* is particularly associated with crime and thriller subjects, though it is best understood as a style or mode that cuts across different genres than as a genre in its own right.

Formative film theory An approach to film aesthetics which maintains that the art of film resides in the formal properties specific to the medium, particularly *mise-en-scène* and **montage**. Formative theory was particularly influential in the 1920s and 1930s, when it was associated with the work of Rudolf Arnheim, Béla Belázs and Sergei Eisenstein.

Frankfurt School A group of German émigré academics, including Theodor Adorno, Max Horkheimer and Walter Benjamin, originally from the Institute of Cultural Research at the University of Frankfurt who moved to the United States in the 1930s. They were critical of what they perceived as the ideological conformity and low-brow nature of mass-produced popular culture, including films.

Genre   A French word meaning 'type' imported into film theory and criticism from English literature. Genres are groups of films which share broadly similar content, characters and narrative conventions. Examples include the Western, musical, comedy, gangster film, horror, science fiction, and thriller.

German Expressionism   A film movement in Germany in the early 1920s characterized by its extreme visual stylization involving acute camera angles, **chiaroscuro** lighting, deep shadows, distorted perspectives, and non-naturalistic acting.

Historical poetics   An approach to film history that analyses the relationship between film style and modes of production.

Iconography   The recurring visual motifs that characterize particular genres.

Ideological apparatus   A phrase used by Louis Althusser to refer to institutions that promote association with particular values, attitudes and beliefs.

Institutional Mode of Representation (IMR)   A term used by Noël Burch to describe a type of narrative film-making that employs realist devices and 'invisible' editing to create the illusion of an autonomous fictional world on screen.

Jump cut   A technique whereby the camera briefly stops filming without changing its position: consequently characters appear to 'jump' in the frame.

Kuleshov Experiment   An experiment in montage conducted by the Soviet film-maker Lev Kuleshov in the early 1920s. This involved placing shots of an actor looking at the camera in juxtaposition with other images. While the image of the actor's face remained the same in each case, the effect was to persuade audiences that the actor was responding differently in each case.

Leavisite   An approach to the study of culture informed by the work of literary critics F. R. and Q. D. Leavis, characterized by a preference for 'high' over 'popular' culture.

Mise-en-scène   A term used to describe the arrangement of the filmic image on screen: literally 'putting into the scene'. Aspects of *mise-en-scène* include cinematography, lighting, costumes, make-up, sets, locations, etc.

Mode of film practice   A set of shared norms and conventions about film-making that has been institutionalized within a film industry or industries.

Classical Hollywood cinema and **art cinema** are both examples of a mode of film practice.

Modernism A broad movement in the arts, literature and architecture during the first half of the twentieth century characterized by its complex formal and stylistic properties. In film modernism is associated with movements such as **German Expressionism**, **Soviet montage** and **art cinema** where aspects of form take prominence over narrative.

Montage A French term for editing, developed into a theory by Soviet film-makers of the 1920s such as Vsevolod Pudovkin and Sergei Eisenstein. Montage theory posits that the meaning of film arises from the organization of **shots** into a sequence rather than from the properties of the individual shot.

Neoformalism An approach to the history of film style which distinguishes between the story (or *fabula*) and the plot (or *syuzhet*). Neoformalism assumes that the story is retrospectively constructed by the spectator to make sense of the plot.

Neo-Realism A film movement that emerged in Italy at the end of the Second World War and lasted until the 1950s. Neo-Realism was committed to representing the real social experiences of Italian people, and was characterized by location shooting, non-professional actors and a grainy visual style. Practioners included Roberto Rossellini, Vittorio De Sica, Giuseppe De Santis and Cesare Zavattini.

New Hollywood A term used by film journalists and historians to describe the US film industry following the break-up of the **studio system**. Most regard New Hollywood as having emerged in the late 1960s when many of the studios were sold to other corporate interests.

Nickelodeon A familiar term for small cinemas in the United States in the early 1900s. Nickelodeons were often converted store fronts: they showed continuous programmes of films rather than interspersing films with variety acts.

Nouvelle Vague A new wave film movement in France in the late 1950s and early 1960s characterized by stylistic and formal innovation and by an insistence on the idea of the director as *auteur*. Major *Nouvelle Vague* film-makers included Claude Chabrol, Jean-Luc Godard, Jacques Rivette, Eric Rohmer and François Truffaut.

180-degree rule A principle of film story-telling that posits an imaginary line or axis through the middle of the scene which the camera does not cross:

this assists spectator comprehension by maintaining consistent spatial relations and movements between shots.

Paradigm   The entire range of formal and stylistic possibilities available within a **mode of film practice**.

Parallel editing   See **cross-cutting**.

Paramount Decree   The name given to the ruling of the US Supreme Court in 1948 (*United States v. Paramount Pictures et al.*) that required the major studios to relinquish their ownership of movie theatres.

Patriarchy   A system of social or political organization controlled by men.

Phantom rides   a genre of early cinema that created an illusion of movement by placing the camera on front of a moving vehicle such as a train, tram or bus.

Poetic Realism   A style of French cinema in the 1930s exemplified by the films of Marcel Carné, Julien Duvivier and Jean Renoir. Poetic Realism was characterized by narratives of despair and disillusion and featured fatalistic, often doomed, protagonists.

Point-of-view   A shot taken with the camera approximating the viewing position of a person in the film: hence the cinema spectator shares the person's point-of-view.

Primitive Mode of Representation (PMR)   A term coined by Noël Burch to describe the style of early cinema before the emergence of the **Institutional Mode of Representation**. The PMR is characterized by **tableau** framing, the prevalence of long shots, and non-closure of narrative.

'Queer Theory'   A body of work concerned with the representation of homosexual men and women and with the place of the homosexual spectator in film.

Realism   A formal and aesthetic practice in which films seem 'true to life' in terms of their stories, situations and characters.

Realist film theory   An approach to film aesthetics which maintains that the art of film is defined by its ability to capture external reality. This is achieved by techniques such as long takes and **deep-focus cinematography**. Realist film theory was at its most influential in the 1940s and 1950s, and is associated with the work of André Bazin and Siegfried Kracauer.

Scopophilia To gain pleasure, particularly sexual pleasure, from the act of looking. The idea is typically applied to feminist critiques of cinema which aver that cinema spectatorship is posited on visual pleasure: this typically arises from men looking at women.

'Screen theory' A body of film theory particularly associated with the British journal *Screen* in the 1970s. It focused on the nature of cinema as an **ideological apparatus** and was influenced by a range of theoretical perspectives, including Althusserian Marxism, Lacanian psychoanalysis and structural linguistics.

Semiotics An approach to linguistics pioneered by Ferdinand de Saussure and applied to cinema chiefly by Christian Metz. Semiotics differentiates between the 'sign' (e.g., a word), the 'signifier' (its sound or appearance) and the 'signified' (the concept attached to it).

Shot The basic formal component of film: an uninterrupted run of the camera that creates an uninterrupted run of film without an edit. Also known as a 'take'.

Shot/reverse shot A technique consisting of two or more alternating **shots** from opposite points of view. A typical example is a shot of an actor looking followed by a shot of what s/he is looking at. Also used during dialogue scenes involving two characters where the person speaking is seen from over the shoulder of the person listening and *vice versa*.

Soft-focus cinematography A visual style where the lighting avoids extremes of brightness and darkness.

Soviet montage A mode of film practice in the Soviet Union during the 1920s based on the principle that meaning in film arises from the juxtaposition between **shots**. Practioners included Lev Kuleshow, Vsevolod Pudovkin and Sergei Eisenstein.

Structuralism A theoretical approach deriving from the work of social anthropologist Claude Lévi-Strauss which maintains that the meaning of a film arises from the ideological and formal structures embedded in the text rather than through the agency of an *auteur*.

Studio system The mode of production that characterized the US film industry from the 1910s characterized by a hierarchical management system and a specialized division of labour. The studio system has often been compared to the motor car industry in the sense that it adopted mass-production methods leading to the standardization of form and content.

Sub-state cinemas   Minority cinemas within a nation state, for example Aboriginal cinema in Australia, Maori cinema in New Zealand, Québecois cinema in Canada, Welsh cinema in the United Kingdom, and Bengali, Malayalam, Punjabi, Tamil and Telugu cinemas in India.

Tableau   A **shot** where the image is framed from a front-on angle.

Typage   A device used by Soviet film-makers in which peformers are cast according to physical and social type.

Verisimilitude   The 'appearance of being real' in accordance with the conventions of the film: it suggests something that is plausible or appropriate rather than something that is necessarily realistic.

Vertical integration   A form of industrial and economic organization adopted by the US film industry in the 1920s whereby the major film companies (MGM, Paramount, Fox, Warner Bros., RKO) owned interests in each of the three sectors of the industry – production, distribution and exhibition. This system was ended by the **Paramount Decree** of 1948.

Widescreen   A process of cinematography and film projection that creates an image wider than the standard 'Academy ratio' of 4: 3 (width to height).

Zeitgeist   A German term that describes the general thought or feeling of a particular period or generation: the 'mood of the times'.

Notes

▶ Introduction

1 K. R. M. Short (ed.), *Feature Films as History* (London: Croom Helm, 1981), p. 11.

2 The history of the Society for Cinema Studies (since 2002 the Society for Cinema and Media Studies) is outlined on its own website: http://www. cmstudies.org (last accessed 8.3.2013). On the history of the journal *Screen*, see Melanie Bell, 'Fifty years of *Screen*, 1959–2009', *Journal of British Cinema and Television*, 7: 3 (2010), pp. 479–85.

3 The proceedings of the conference, chaired by A. J. P. Taylor, were published as *Film and the Historian* (London: British Universities Film Council, 1969).

4 Andrew Sarris, *The American Cinema: Directors and Directions, 1929–1968* (New York: Dutton, 1968), Peter Wollen. *Signs and Meaning in the Cinema* (London: Thames & Hudson, 1969).

5 Robert C. Allen and Douglas Gomery, *Film History: Theory and Practice* (New York: McGraw-Hill, 1985), p. 27.

6 Everson and Brownlow were both collectors who produced television programmes about the history of Hollywood and wrote numerous popular books on film. See, especially, Kevin Brownlow, *The Parade's Gone By ...* (London: Secker & Warburg, 1968).

7 Jeffrey Richards, *Visions of Yesterday* (London: Routledge & Kegan Paul, 1973), p. xv.

8 Robert C. Allen, 'From exhibition to reception: reflections on the audience in film history', *Screen*, 31: 4 (1990), p. 347.

9 David Bordwell, 'Textual analysis etc', *Enclitic*, 10–11 (1981–2), p. 135.

10 For example: Charles F. Altman, 'Toward a historiography of American film', *Cinema Journal*, 16: 1 (1977), pp. 1–25; Michael T. Isenberg, 'Toward an historical methodology for film scholarship', *Rocky Mountain Social Science Journal*, 12: 1 (1975), pp. 45–57; Vlada Petric, 'Approaches to the history of film', *Film Library Quarterly*, 6: 2 (1973), pp. 7–12; Gerald Mast, 'Film history and film histories', *Quarterly Review of Film Studies*, 1: 3 (1976), pp. 297–314.

11 David Robinson, *The History of World Cinema* (New York: Stein and Day, 1974), p. 1.
12 Allen and Gomery, *Film History*, pp. 37–8.
13 *Ibid.*, p. 5.
14 Ernest Lindgren, 'The importance of film archives', *Penguin Film Review*, 5 (1945), p. 47.
15 Derek Malcolm, *A Century of Films* (London: I. B. Tauris, 2000), p. 1.
16 In this book I follow the convention of referring to films by their common release titles: this means that some are referred to in the original language and others in their English translation. *La Grande Illusion* and *La Dolce Vita*, for example, have always been known as such rather than as 'The Great Illusion' or 'The Sweet Life'. *The Battleship Potemkin*, however, is widely known by its English title rather than as *Bronenosets Potemkin*.
17 David Bordwell, Janet Staiger and Kristin Thompson, *The Classical Hollywood Cinema: Film Style & Mode of Production to 1960* (London: Routledge, 1985), p. 10.
18 Richard Maltby, 'How can cinema history matter more?' (2007), *Screening the Past* http://www.latrobe.edu/au/screeningthepast/22/board-richard-maltby.html (accessed 27.7.2012)
19 The comment that 'movies don't matter' was made by Robert Allen at a symposium entitled 'Researching Cinema History: Perspectives and Practices in Film Historiography' at the Royal Geological Society, London, 6–7 July 2009.

▶ 1 A Brief History of Film History

1 Terry Ramsaye, *A Million and One Nights: A History of the Motion Picture* (New York: Simon & Schuster, 1926), p. xi.
2 Robert C. Allen and Douglas Gomery, *Film History: Theory and Practice* (New York: McGraw-Hill, 1985), p. 51.
3 Paul Rotha, *The Film Till Now: A Survey of World Cinema* (London: Jonathan Cape, 1930); Benjamin Hampton, *A History of the Movies* (New York: Covice, Friede, 1931); Lewis Jacobs, *The Rise of the American Film: A Critical History* (New York: Harcourt, Brace, 1939); Georges Sadoul, *Histoire générale du cinéma* (Paris: Denoël, 3 vols, 1946–52)
4 David Bordwell, *On the History of Film Style* (Cambridge MA: Harvard University Press, 1997), p. 9.
5 Lewis Jacobs, *The Rise of the American Film*, p. 35.
6 Jean Mitry, *Griffith* (Paris: Editions de l'Avant-scène, 1965), p. 68.

7 The reception of *The Birth of a Nation* is analysed in Janet Staiger, *Interpreting Films: Studies in the Historical Reception of American Cinema* (Princeton: Princeton University Press, 1991), pp. 139–53.

8 Paul Rotha, with Richard Griffith, *The Film Till Now: A Survey of World Cinema* (London: Spring Books, 3rd edn, 1969 [1930]), p. 15.

9 *Ibid.*, pp. 93, 126.

10 *Ibid.*, pp. 110, 112.

11 Jacobs, *The Rise of the American Film*, p. 302.

12 *Ibid.*, p. 433.

13 Larry Swindell, '1939: A very good year', *American Film*, 1: 3 (1975), p. 28.

14 Jacobs, *The Rise of the American Film*, p. 539.

15 Roger Manvell, *The Film and the Public* (Harmondsworth: Penguin, 1955), pp. 13–14.

16 Rotha, *The Film Till Now*, p. 41.

17 Gerald Mast, *A Short History of the Movies* (Indianapolis: Bobbs-Merrill, 1971); David Robinson, *The History of World Cinema* (New York: Stein and Day, 1973); Basil Wright, *The Long View: A Personal Perspective on World Cinema* (London: Secker & Warburg, 1974); Eric Rhode, *A History of the Cinema from its Origins to 1970* (London: Allen Lane, 1976).

18 Basil Wright, *The Long View*, p. 694.

19 Thorold Dickinson, *A Discovery of Cinema* (London: Oxford University Press, 1971), pp. 13–105.

20 Geoffrey Nowell-Smith (ed.), *The Oxford History of World Cinema* (Oxford: Oxford University Press, 1995), p. xx.

21 See Jon Gartenberg, 'The Brighton Project: Archives and historians', *Iris*, 2: 1 (1984), pp. 5–16. A selection of the most important work can be found in Thomas Elsaesser (ed.), *Early Cinema: Space, Frame, Narrative* (London: British Film Institute, 1990). Another volume, complementing rather than duplicating the Elsaesser collection, is Lee Grieveson and Peter Krämer (eds), *The Silent Cinema Reader* (London: Routledge, 2004).

22 Rotha, *The Film Till Now*, p. 67.

23 Charles Barr, 'Before *Blackmail*: Silent British Cinema', in Robert Murphy (ed.), *The British Cinema Book* (London: British Film Institute, 1997), pp. 7–8.

24 Charles Musser, *Before the Nickelodeon: Edwin S. Porter and the Edison Manufacturing Company* (Berkeley: University of California Press, 1991), p. 405.

25 André Gaudreault, 'Temporality and Narrative in Early Cinema, 1895–1908', in John Fell (ed.), *Film Before Griffith* (Berkeley: University of California Press, 1984), p. 322.

26 Noël Burch, *Life to Those Shadows*, trans. Ben Brewster (London: British Film Institute, 1990), p. 186.

27 Noël Burch, 'Porter, or ambivalence', trans. Tom Milne, *Screen*, 19: 4 (1978/79), p. 91.

28 Tom Gunning, 'The cinema of attractions: early cinema, its spectator and the avant-garde', *Wide Angle*, 8: 3–4 (1986), pp. 63–70.

29 *Ibid.*

30 Margaret Thorp, *America at the Movies* (London: Faber & Faber, 1946); Hortense Powdermaker, *Hollywood the Dream Factory* (New York: Grosset & Dunlap, 1950); Siegfried Kracauer, *From Caligari to Hitler: A Psychological History of the German Film* (Princeton: Princeton University Press, 1947)

31 Kracauer, *From Caligari to Hitler*, p. 6.

32 *Ibid.*, p. 65.

33 *Ibid.*, p. 272.

34 Allen and Gomery, *Film History*, p. 159.

35 Paul Monaco, *Cinema and Society: France and Germany During the Twenties* (New York: Elsevier, 1976), p. 160.

36 Arthur Marwick, *Class: Image and Reality in Britain, France and the USA Since 1930* (New York: Oxford University Press, 1980), p. 22.

37 Kristin Thompson, *Exporting Entertainment: America in the World Film Market 1907–1934* (London: British Film Institute, 1985), p. 168.

38 Thomas Elsaesser, *Weimar Cinema and After: Germany's Historical Imaginary* (London: Routledge, 2000), pp. 106–42.

39 This work includes (but is not limited to): Tino Balio, *United Artists: The Company Built by the Stars* (Madison: University of Wisconsin Press, 1976); Rudy Behlmer (ed.), *Inside Warner Bros. 1935–1951* (New York: Simon & Schuster, 1985); Douglas Gomery, *The Hollywood Studio System* (London: Macmillan, 1986); and Thomas Schatz, *The Genius of the System: Hollywood Filmmaking in the Studio Era* (New York: Pantheon, 1988). Balio was also general editor of the Wisconsin/Warner Bros. Screenplay series published by the University of Wisconsin Press in the 1970s and 1980s.

40 The Margaret Herrick Library is part of the Douglas Fairbanks Centre for the Perfoming Arts, the reference and research arm of the Academy of Motion Picture Arts and Sciences in Beverly Hills, Los Angeles. Other archives holding significant collections of studio and personal papers in the United States include the Cinematic Arts Library, University of Southern California; the Performing Arts Special Collection, University of California Los Angeles; the Wisconsin Center for Film and Theater Research, University of Wisconsin, Madison; and the Humanities Research Center, University of Texas, Austin.

The largest collection of archive materials in Britain is at the British Film Institute Library, London.

41 Ernest Borneman, 'United States versus Hollywood: The case study of an antitrust suit', in Tino Balio (ed.), *The American Film Industry* (Madison: University of Wisconsin Press, 1976), pp. 332–45.

42 See Klaus Kreimeier, *The UFA Story: A History of Germany's Greatest Film Company, 1918–1945*, trans. Robert and Rita Kimber (Berkeley: University of California Press, 1999 [1992]); Colin Crisp, *The Classic French Cinema, 1930–1960* (London: I. B. Tauris, 1993); and Rachael Low, *The History of the British Film 1929–1939: Film Making in 1930s Britain* (London: George Allen & Unwin, 1985). There is currently no equivalent institutional and economic history of the Japanese film industry.

43 Thomas Guback, 'Hollywood's international market', in Balio (ed.), *The American Film Industry*, p. 387.

44 Kerry Segrave, *American Films Abroad: Hollywood's Domination of the World's Movie Screens* (Jefferson: McFarland, 1997), p. 282.

45 Nick Roddick, *A New Deal in Entertainment: Warner Brothers in the 1930s* (London: British Film Institute, 1983), p. 14.

46 Thompson, *Exporting Entertainment*, p. 100.

47 Raymond Fielding, 'The technological antecedents of the coming of sound: An introduction', in Evan W. Cameron (ed.), *Sound and the Cinema* (Pleasantville: Redgrave, 1982), p. 2.

48 The history of widescreen technology is expertly explained in John Belton, *Widescreen Cinema* (Cambridge MA: Harvard University Press, 1992).

49 Jacobs, *The Rise of the American Film*, p. 299.

50 J. Douglas Gomery, 'Writing the history of the American film industry: Warner Bros. and sound', *Screen*, 17: 1 (1976), pp. 40–53 (52). See also Gomery, 'The coming of the talkies: Invention, innovation and diffusion', in Balio (ed), *The American Film Industry*, pp. 193–211.

51 Robert C. Allen, 'William Fox presents *Sunrise*', *Quarterly Review of Film Studies*, 2: 3 (1977), pp. 327–38.

52 Donald Crafton, *History of the American Cinema Volume 4. The Talkies: American Cinema's Transition to Sound 1926–1931* (Berkeley: University of California Press, 1997), p. 4.

53 Gomery, 'Writing the history of the American film industry', p. 53.

54 The best summary of 'Screen theory' (although it does not actually use the term) is Sheila Johnston, 'Film narrative and the structuralist controversy', in the first edition of Pam Cook (ed.), *The Cinema Book* (London: British Film Institute, 1985), pp. 222–50. Note that this material has been substantially abridged in later editions of *The Cinema Book*. See also Mark Jancovich, 'Screen theory', in Joanne Hollows and Mark Jancovich (eds),

Approaches to Popular Film (Manchester: Manchester University Press, 1995), pp. 124–50, and Annette Kuhn, '*Screen* and screen theorizing today', *Screen*, 50: 1 (2009), pp. 1–12.

55 In 1976, for instance, Edward Buscombe, Christine Gledhill, Alan Lovell and Christopher Williams issued a statement 'Why we have resigned from the Board of *Screen*', *Screen*, 17: 2 (1976), pp. 106–9. They complained that the journal 'is unnecessarily obscure and inaccessible', that the 'politico-cultural analysis that has increasingly come to underpin *Screen*'s whole theoretical effort is intellectually unsound and unproductive', and that '*Screen* has no serious interest in educational matters'. A 'Reply' by other members of the editorial board (Ben Brewster, Elizabeth Cowie, Jon Halliday, Kari Hanet, Stephen Heath, Colin MacCabe, Paul Willemen, Peter Wollen) defended the charge of obscurity on the grounds that 'Understanding ... has itself to be constructed or produced, it is not simple, and we ourselves continue to be unable to espouse a condescending stance to our readers as passive targets'. *Screen*, 17: 2 (1976), pp. 110–16.

56 For a critique of the language of high theory, see Michael Pursell, 'The tyranny of screenspeak', *Literature/Film Quarterly*, 14: 1 (1986), pp. 10–16, and, more polemically, Kevin Brownlow, 'Cinematic theology', *Cineaste*, 10: 4 (1980), pp. 20–1.

57 Laura Mulvey, 'Visual pleasure and narrative cinema', *Screen*, 16: 3 (1975), pp. 6–18.

58 James Curran and Vincent Porter (eds), *British Cinema History* (London: Weidenfeld and Nicolson, 1983).

59 Andrew Higson, 'Critical theory and "British cinema"', *Screen*, 24: 4–5 (1983), pp. 80– 95.

60 'Letters', *Screen*, 25: 1 (1984), pp. 86–8.

61 *Ibid.*, p. 86.

62 *Ibid.*

63 Contrast, for example, Steve Neale's book *Genre* (London: British Film Institute, 1980), a highly theorized discussion of genre with relatively few references to actual films, to his later *Genre and Hollywood* (London: Routledge, 2000), where he draws extensively upon the trade press to analyse how genre terminology developed in the industry itself.

64 Charles Barr, '*Straw Dogs*, *A Clockwork Orange* and the critics', *Screen*, 13: 2 (1972), pp. 17–31; Edward Buscombe, 'Notes on Columbia Pictures Corporation, 1926–41', *Screen*, 16: 3 (1975), pp. 65–82; Patrick Ogle, 'Technological and aesthetic influences upon the development of deep focus cinematography in the United States', *Screen*, 13: 1 (1972), pp. 45–74; John Ellis, 'Art, culture, quality: Terms for a cinema in the Forties and Seventies', *Screen*, 19: 3 (1978), pp. 9–49.

65 Thomas Elsaesser, 'The new film history', *Sight & Sound*, 55: 4 (1985), p. 246.

66 *Ibid.*, p. 251.

67 Jeffrey Richards, 'Rethinking British Cinema', in Justine Ashby and Andrew Higson (eds), *British Cinema, Past and Present* (London: Routledge, 2000), p. 21. The fact that Richards was contributing to a volume co-edited by Andrew Higson is itself evidence of the *rapprochement* between film history and film theory. Richards had been one of the contributors to the *British Cinema History* volume, while his own book *The Age of the Dream Palace: Cinema and Society in Britain, 1930–1939* (London: Routledge & Kegan Paul, 1984) had also been criticized for its 'familiar and naive idea of cinema "reflecting" society'. Andrew Higson and Steve Neale, 'Introduction: Components of the national film culture', *Screen*, 26: 1 (1985), p. 6.

68 David Bordwell, Janet Staiger and Kristin Thompson, *The Classical Hollywood Cinema: Film Style & Mode of Production to 1960* (London: Routledge, 1985), p. xiv.

69 *Ibid.*, p. 9.

70 *Ibid.*, p. 306.

71 *Ibid.*, p. 10.

72 *Ibid*, p. 388.

73 See Kristine Brunslova Karnack and Henry Jenkins (eds), *Classical Hollywood Comedy* (New York: Routledge, 1994), especially the chapters by Peter Krämer and Frank Krutnik; Rick Altman, *The American Film Musical* (Bloomington: University of Indiana Press, 1987); and Jane Feuer, *The Hollywood Musical* (London: Macmillan, 1982).

74 See James Naremore, *More Than Night: Film Noir in its Contexts* (Berkeley: University of California Press, 1998); Neale, *Genre and Hollywood*, pp. 151–77; and R. Barton Palmer, *Hollywood's Dark Cinema: The American Film Noir* (New York: Twayne, 1994).

75 Bordwell, Staiger and Thompson, *The Classical Hollywood Cinema*, p. 367.

76 Thomas Elsaesser, *New German Cinema: A History* (New Brunswick: Rutgers University Press, 1989); Crisp, *The Classic French Cinema*; David Bordwell, *Planet Hong Kong: Popular Cinema and the Art of Entertainment* (Cambridge MA: Harvard University Press, 2000).

77 Sue Harper, *Picturing the Past: The Rise and Fall of the British Costume Film* (London: British Film Institute, 1994), p. 1.

78 See the 'Introduction' to James Chapman, Mark Glancy and Sue Harper (eds), *The New Film History: Sources, Methods, Approaches* (Basingstoke: Palgrave Macmillan, 2007), pp. 1–10.

79 Melanie Bell, *Femininity in the Frame: Women and 1950s British Popular Cinema* (London: I. B. Tauris, 2010); Laurie N. Ede, *British Film Design: A*

History (London: I. B. Tauris, 2010); Mark Glancy, *Temporary American Citizens? Hollywood and the Americanization of Britain* (London: I. B. Tauris, 2013); Lawrence Napper, *British Cinema and Middlebrow Culture in the Interwar Years* (Exeter: University of Exeter Press, 2009); Justin Smith, *Withnail and Us: Cult Films and Film Cults in British Cinema* (London: I. B. Tauris, 2010); Andrew Spicer, *Typical Men: The Representation of Masculinity in Popular British Cinema* (London: I. B. Tauris, 2006).

▶ 2 Film as an Art Form

1 Gerald Mast, *A Short History of the Movies* (Indianapolis: Bobbs-Merrill, 1971), p. 10.

2 Terry Ramsaye, *A Million and One Nights: A History of the Motion Picture* (New York: Simon & Schuster, 1926), p. v.

3 Mark Cousins, *The Story of Film* (London: Pavilion, 2004), p. 7.

4 Theodor Adorno and Max Horkheimer, *Dialectic of Enlightenment*, trans. John Cumming (London: Allen Lane, 1973 [1944]), p. 121.

5 J. Dudley Andrew, *The Major Film Theories: An Introduction* (Oxford: Oxford University Press, 1976), pp. 11–13.

6 David Bordwell, '*Citizen Kane*', *Film Comment*, 7: 2 (1971), p. 39.

7 Béla Belázs, *Theory of the Film: Character and Growth of a New Art*, trans. Edith Bone (London: Dobson, 1952), p. 161.

8 Lev Kuleshov, 'Montage as the Foundation of Film-Making', in *Lev Kuleshov: Fifty Years in Films: Selected Works*, trans. Dmitri Agrachev and Nina Belenkaya (Moscow: Raduga, 1986), pp. 134–5.

9 Rudolf Arnheim, *Film as Art*, trans. L. M. Sieveking and Ian F. D. Morrow (London: Faber and Faber, 1958 [1932]), p. 55.

10 See Lotte H. Eisner, *The Haunted Screen: Expressionism in the German Cinema and the Influence of Max Reinhardt*, trans. Roger Greaves (Berkeley: University of California Press, 1969 [1952]); Thomas Elsaesser, *Weimar Cinema and After: Germany's Historical Imaginary* (London: Routledge, 2000); David Robinson, *Das Cabinet des Dr Caligari* (London: British Film Institute, 1997).

11 See Jay Leda, *Kino: A History of the Russian and Soviet Film* (Princeton: Princeton University Press, 3rd edn, 1983); Richard Taylor, *The Politics of Soviet Cinema* (Cambridge: Cambridge University Press, 1979); Denise J. Youngblood, *Soviet Cinema in the Silent Era, 1918–1935* (Ann Abor: UMI Research Press, 1985).

12 Kuleshov, 'Report for the First Half of 1923 and catalogue of the Work and Human Material of the Kuleshov Film Workshop', *Fifty Years in Films*, p. 105.

13 *Ibid.*, pp. 101–13.

14 Kristin Thompson and David Bordwell, *Film History: An Introduction* (New York: McGraw-Hill, 1994), p. 142.

15 Vsevolod Pudovkin, *Film Technique and Film Acting*, trans. Ivor Montagu (London: Vision Press, 1954 [1929]), p. 121.

16 Sergei M. Eisenstein, *The Film Sense*, trans. Jay Leda (London: Faber and Faber, 1943), p. 140.

17 D. Mayer, *Sergei M. Eisenstein's Potemkin: A Shot-by-Shot Presentation* (New York: Da Capo Press, 1990 [1988]); D. L. Selden, 'Vision and violence: The rhetoric of *Potemkin*', *Quarterly Review of Film Studies*, 7: 4 (1982), pp. 309–25; Richard Taylor, *The Battleship Potemkin: The Film Companion* (London: I. B. Tauris, 2000), pp. 35–54.

18 Sergei Eisenstein, 'The dialectical approach to film form', *Sergei Eisenstein: Selected Works Volume 1: Writings 1922–34*, trans. Richard Taylor (Bloomington: University of Indiana Press, 1988), p. 172.

19 Eisenstein, *The Film Sense*, pp. 15–57.

20 *Ibid.*, pp. 114–55.

21 *Ibid.*, pp. 58–9.

22 François Truffaut, with Helen G. Scott, *Hitchcock* (London: Paladin, 1986 [1968]), p. 321.

23 Siegfried Kracauer, *Theory of Film: The Redemption of Physical Reality* (New York: Oxford University Press, 1960), p. 53.

24 André Bazin, 'The myth of total cinema', *What is Cinema? Volume 1*, trans. Hugh Gray (Berkeley: University of California Press, 1967), p. 21.

25 André Bazin, 'The ontology of the photographic image', *What Is Cinema? Vol 1*, p. 13.

26 André Bazin, 'The evolution of the language of cinema', *What Is Cinema? Vol 1*, p. 26.

27 *Ibid.*, p. 37.

28 *Ibid.*, p. 23.

29 *Ibid.*, p. 30.

30 *Ibid.*, p. 28.

31 *Ibid.*, p. 35.

32 *Ibid.*, p. 34.

33 André Bazin, 'William Wyler, or the Jansenist of *mise en* scene', in Christopher Williams (ed.), *Realism and the Cinema: A Reader* (London: Routledge & Kegan Paul, 1980), pp. 48–50.

34 André Bazin, 'An aesthetic of reality: Neo-realism', *What Is Cinema? Volume II*, trans. Hugh Gray (Berkeley: University of California Press, 1971), pp. 20–1.

35 André Bazin, '*Bicycle Thief*', *What Is Cinema? Vol II*, p. 60.

36 André Bazin, '*Umberto D*: A great work', *What Is Cinema? Vol II*, p. 81.

37 *Ibid.*, p. 82.

38 Christopher Williams, 'Bazin on neo-realism', *Screen*, 14: 4 (1973), pp. 61–8.

39 Mast, *A Short History of the Movies*, p. 3.

40 C. A. Lejeune, *Chestnuts in Her Lap: 1936–1946* (London: Pheonix House, 1947), p. 169.

41 Strictly '*la politique des auteurs*' is a term associated with *Cahiers du Cinéma*, while '*auteur* theory' was a term coined by Andrew Sarris. While there are different emphases between the bodies of critical writing, the underlying ideas are similar.

42 Eric Rohmer, 'Rediscovering America', in Jim Hillier (ed.), *Cahiers du Cinéma. The 1950s: Neo-Realism, Hollywood, New Wave* (Cambridge MA: Harvard University Press, 1985), p. 89.

43 André Bazin, 'On the politique des auteurs', in Hillier (ed.), *Cahiers du Cinéma. The 1950s*, pp. 248–58.

44 John Grierson, 'Hitchcock, Asquith and the English cinema', in Forsyth Hardy (ed.), *Grierson on the Movies* (London: Faber and Faber, 1981), p. 108.

45 Robin Wood, *Hitchcock's Films* (London: Zwemmer, 1965), p. 19.

46 Andrew Sarris, 'Notes on the *auteur* theory in 1962', *Film Culture*, 27 (1962), pp. 5–6.

47 Andrew Sarris, *The American Cinema: Directors and Directions 1929–1968* (New York: De Capo Press, 1996 [1968]), p. 30.

48 *Ibid.*, pp. 39, 83.

49 *Ibid.*, p. 155.

50 *Ibid.*, p. 30.

51 David Bordwell, *Poetics of Cinema* (New York: Routledge, 2008), p. 254.

52 Jim Kitses, *Horizons West: Studies of Authorship within the Western* (London: Thames and Hudson, 1969); Colin McArthur, *Underworld USA* (London: Secker & Warburg, 1972); Will Wright, *Sixguns and Society: A Structural Study of the Western* (Berkeley: University of California Press, 1975).

53 Roland Barthes, 'The death of the author', in *Image/Music/Text*, trans. Stephen Heath (London: Collins, 1977), pp. 142–8.

54 Peter Krämer, 'When "Hanoi Jane" conquered Hollywood: Jane Fonda's films and activism, 1977–81', in James Chapman, Mark Glancy and Sue Harper (eds), *The New Film History: Sources, Methods, Approaches* (Basingstoke: Palgrave Macmillan, 2007), pp. 104–16.

55 Gilles Deleuze, *Cinema 1: The Movement-Image*, trans. Hugh Tomlinson and Barbara Habbermas (London: Continuum, 1988 [1983]), p. xiv.

56 *Ibid.*, pp. 67–89.

57 Gilles Deleuze, *Cinema 2: The Time-Image*, trans. Hugh Tomlinson and Robert Galeta (London: Continuum, 1989 [1985]), p. 7.

58 *Ibid.*, pp. 268–9.

59 Series editors' foreword to, for example, Andrew Spicer, *Sydney Box* (Manchester: Manchester University Press, 2006), p. x.

60 David Bordwell, *Narration in the Fiction Film* (London: Methuen, 1985); David Bordwell, *Making Meaning: Inference and Rhetoric in the Interpretation of Cinema* (Cambridge MA: Harvard University Press, 1989); David Bordwell, *On the History of Film Style* (Cambridge MA: Harvard University Press, 1997); David Bordwell *The Way Hollywood Tells It: Story and Style in Modern Movies* (Berkeley: University of California Press, 2006).

61 Bordwell, *Narration in the Fiction Film*, p. ix.

62 David Bordwell, 'Historical poetics of cinema', in R. Barton Palmer (ed.), *The Cinematic Text: Methods and Approaches* (New York: AMS Press, 1989), p. 385.

63 Bordwell, *Narration in the Fiction Film*, pp. 49–53.

64 Bordwell, 'Historical poetics of cinema', p. 371.

65 Bordwell, *Poetics of Cinema*, pp. 337–93. See also Kristin Thompson and David Bordwell, 'Space and narrative in the films of Ozu', *Screen*, 17: 3 (1976), pp. 41–73.

66 David Bordwell, 'Art cinema as a mode of film practice', *Film Criticism*, 4: 1 (1979), p. 56.

67 Bordwell, 'Historical poetics of cinema', p. 382.

68 David Bordwell, Janet Staiger and Kristin Thompson, *The Classical Hollywood Cinema: Film Style & Mode of Production to 1960* (London: Routledge, 1985), p. 78.

69 Bordwell, *Poetics of Cinema*, p. 30.

70 Sarris, *The American Cinema*, p. 78.

71 Quoted in Robert L. Carringer, *The Making of 'Citizen Kane'* (Berkeley: University of California Press, rev. edn, 1996), p. 117.

72 Bazin, 'The evolution of the language of cinema', p. 37.

73 André Bazin, *Orson Welles: A Critical View* (Los Angeles: Acrobat, 1991 [1972]), p. 81.

74 Bazin, 'The evolution of the language of cinema', p. 36.

75 Bordwell, *'Citizen Kane'*, p. 40.

76 Deleuze, *Cinema 2*, p. 102.

77 *Ibid.*, pp. 107–8.

78 Sarris, *The American Cinema*, p. 78.

▶ **3   Film and Ideology**

1 Jean-Luc Comolli and Jean Narboni, 'Cinema/ideology/criticism', *Screen*, 12: 1 (1971), p. 30.

2 *Ibid.*, p. 28.

3 The Langlois affair and its consequences are discussed in Sylvia Harvey, *May '68 and Film Culture* (London: British Film Institute, 1978). See also Sam Rohdie, 'The Estates General of the French cinema, May 1968', *Screen*, 13: 4 (1972/73), pp. 79–85.

4 'Editorial', *Screen*, 12: 1 (1971), p. 5.

5 Geoffrey Nowell-Smith, 'On the writing of the history of the cinema: Some problems', in *Edinburgh '77 Magazine: History/Production/Memory* (Edinburgh: Edinburgh Film Festival, 1977), p. 10.

6 Dwight Macdonald, 'A theory of mass culture' in Bernard Rosenberg and David Manning White (eds), *Mass Culture: The Popular Arts in America* (New York: Macmillan, 1957), p. 60.

7 Louis Althusser, *Lenin and Philosophy and Other Essays* (London: NLB, 1971), p. 159.

8 Comolli and Narboni, 'Cinema/ideology/criticism', p. 30.

9 *Ibid.*, pp. 31–4.

10 *Ibid.*, p. 33.

11 See, for example: Barbara Klinger, *Melodrama and Meaning: History, Culture and the Films of Douglas Sirk* (Bloomington: University of Indiana Press, 1994); Laura Mulvey and John Halliday (eds), *Douglas Sirk* (Edinburgh: Edinburgh Film Festival, 1972).

12 'John Ford's *Young Mr Lincoln*: A collective text by the Editors of *Cahiers du Cinéma*', trans. Helen Lackner and Diana Matias, *Screen*, 13: 3 (1972), p. 6.

13 *Ibid.*, p. 44.

14 Ben Brewster, 'Notes on the text "John Ford's *Young Mr Lincoln*" by the Editors of *Cahiers du Cinéma*', *Screen*, 14: 3 (1973), p. 41.

15 Stephen Heath, 'Film and system: Terms of analysis', *Screen*, 16: 1 (1975), pp. 7–77.

16 Edward Buscombe, 'Notes on Columbia Pictures Corporation 1926–41', *Screen*, 16: 3 (1975), p. 67.

17 Robin Wood, 'Ideology, genre, auteur', *Film Comment*, 12: 6 (1976), p. 671.

18 For a concise introduction to 'Neo-Gramscian cultural studies' see John Storey, *An Introduction to Cultural Theory and Popular Culture* (Hemel Hempstead: Prentice Hall/Harvester Wheatsheaf, 2nd edn, 1997), pp. 123–30.

19 Tony Bennett and Janet Woollacott, *Bond and Beyond: The Political Career of a Popular Hero* (London: Macmillan, 1987), p. 4.

20 *Ibid.*, p. 29.

21 Marcia Landy, *British Genres: Cinema and Society, 1930–1960* (Princeton: Princeton University Press, 1991), p. 21.

22 Marcia Landy, *Cinematic Uses of the Past* (Minneapolis: University of Minnesota Press, 1996), p. 3.

23 Arthur Marwick, *The Nature of History* (London: Macmillan, 3rd edn, 1989), p. 308.

24 Peter Wollen, *Signs and Meaning in the Cinema* (London: Secker & Warburg, 2nd edn, 1972 [1969]), p. 104.

25 *Ibid.*, p. 102.

26 *Ibid.*, p. 168.

27 Will Wright, *Sixguns and Society: A Structural Study of the Western* (Berkeley: University of California Press, 1975), p. 2.

28 *Ibid.*, pp. 41–8.

29 *Ibid.*, p. 49.

30 *Ibid.*, p. 12.

31 Michael Coyne, *The Crowded Prairie: American National Identity in the Hollywood Western* (London: I. B. Tauris, 1997), p. 11. For a critique of Wright's methodology, see also Christopher Frayling, 'The American western and American society', in Philip Davies and Brian Neve (eds), *Cinema, Politics and Society in America* (Manchester: Manchester University Press, 1981), pp. 136–62.

32 The films are *Rio Bravo* (a parenthetical reference), *2001: A Space Odyssey* and *North by Northwest* (both mentioned in the context of other critics' analysis of the films).

33 Christian Metz, 'The imaginary signifier', trans. Ben Brewster, *Screen*, 16: 2 (1975), pp. 18–19.

34 Wollen, *Signs and Meaning in the Cinema*, p. 159.

35 Molly Haskell, *From Reverence to Rape: The Treatment of Women in the Movies* (New York: Holt, Rinehard and Winston, 1973); Marjorie Rosen, *Popcorn Venus; Women, Movies and the American Dream* (New York: Coward, McCann & Geoghegan, 1973).

36 Molly Haskell, *From Reverence to Rape* (Chicago: University of Chicago Press, 2nd edn, 1987), p. 4.

37 'Camera obscura collective', *Camera Obscura* 1 (1976), p. 3.

38 Pam Cook, 'Melodrama and the women's picture', in Marcia Landy (ed.), *Imitations of Life: A Reader in Film and Television Melodrama* (Detroit: Wayne State University Press 1991), p. 251.

39 Laura Mulvey, 'Visual pleasure and narrative cinema', *Screen*, 16: 3 (1975), p. 6.

40 *Ibid.*, p. 11.

41 *Ibid.*, p. 13.

42 Laura Mulvey, 'Afterthoughts on "Visual pleasure and narrative cinema": Inspired by *Duel in the Sun*', *Framework*, 15/16/17 (1981), pp. 12–15.

43 Tania Modleski, *The Women Who Knew Too Much: Hitchcock and Feminist Theory* (New York: Methuen, 1988), p. 85.

44 *Ibid.*, p. 120.

45 Haskell, *From Reverence to Rape*, p. 146.

46 Claire Johnston, 'Dorothy Arzner: Critical strategies', in Claire Johnston (ed.), *Dorothy Arzner: Towards a Feminist Cinema* (London: British Film Institute, 1975), p. 4.

47 Peter Wollen, *Readings and Writings: Semiotic Counter-Strategies* (London: Verso, 1982), p. 132.

48 Laura Mulvey, *Visual and Other Pleasures* (London: Macmillan, 1989), p. 26.

49 Mulvey, 'Visual pleasure and narrative cinema', p. 7.

50 See Kenneth M. Cameron, *Africa on Film: Beyond Black and White* (New York: Continuum, 1994), pp. 33–44.

51 Edward Said, *Orientalism* (Harmondsworth: Penguin, 1985 [1978]), p. 3.

52 Stephen Crofts, 'Reconceptualising national cinema/s', *Quarterly Review of Film and Video*, 14: 3 (1993), p. 50.

53 Fredric Jameson, 'Third World literature in the era of multinational capitalism', *Social Text*, 15 (1986), p. 69.

54 Mike Wayne, *Political Film: The Dialectics of Third Cinema* (London: Pluto Press, 2001), p. 9.

55 Teshome Gabriel, 'Towards a critical theory of Third World films', in Jim Pines and Paul Willemen (eds), *Questions of Third Cinema* (London: British Film Institute, 1989), p. 31.

56 *Ibid.*, p. 37.

57 *Ibid.*, p. 34.

58 Fernando Solanas and Octavio Getino, 'Towards a third cinema' [1969], in Bill Nichols (ed.), *Movies and Methods Volume 1* (Berkeley: University of California Press, 1976), p. 52.

59 *Ibid.*, p. 47.

60 Glauber Rocha, 'Aesthetics of Hunger', http://www.tempoglauber.com.br/ english/t_estetica.html (accessed 21.5.2013); Julio Garcia Espinoza, 'For an imperfect cinema', *Jump Cut: A Review of Contemporary Media*, 20 (1979), pp. 24–6.

61 'Third World on screen', in Ann Lloyd (ed.), *The History of the Movies* (London: Macdonald Orbis, 1988), p. 351.

62 Solanas and Getino, 'Towards a third cinema', p. 61.

63 *Ibid.*, p. 47.

64 Jonathan Buchsbaum, 'A closer look at third cinema', *Historical Journal of Film, Radio and Television*, 21: 2 (2001), p. 161.

▶ **4 Film as a Historical Source**

1 Quoted in Anthony Aldgate, *Cinema and History: British Newsreels and the Spanish Civil War* (London: Scolar Press, 1979), p. 1.

2 Boleslas Matuszewski, 'A new source of history' [25 March 1898], trans. Laura U. Marks and Diane Koszarski, *Film History*, 7: 3 (1995), p. 322.

3 *Ibid.*, p. 323.

4 Erik Barnouw, *Documentary: A History of the Non-Fiction Film* (New York: Oxford University Press, rev. edn 1993), pp. 24–5.

5 Matuszewski, 'A new source of history', p. 322.

6 Quoted in Aldgate, *Cinema and History*, pp. 5–6.

7 Quoted in Sue Harper, *Picturing the Past: The Rise and Fall of the British Costume Film* (London: British Film Institute, 1994), p. 66

8 Charles R. Beard, 'Why get it wrong?', *Sight & Sound*, 2: 8 (1934), p. 124.

9 Arthur Elton, 'The film as source material for history', *Aslib Proceedings*, 7: 4 (1955), pp. 207–16.

10 The first issue of *University Vision* in 1968 included short pieces by C. H. Roads and David Adams supporting the use of film in university teaching. *Annales* 23 (1968) and 28 (1973) included articles by Marc Ferro. See also Christopher H. Roads, 'Film as historical evidence', *Journal of the Society of Archivists*, 3: 4 (1966).

11 *Film and the Historian* (London: British Universities' Film Council, 1968), p. 1.

12 See Arthur Marwick, 'History at the Open University', *Oxford Review of Education*, 2: 2 (1976), pp. 129–37, and Anthony Aldgate, 'Teaching film history in the history curriculum', in John E. O'Connor (ed.), *Image As Artifact: The Historical Analysis of Film and Television* (Malabar: Robert E. Krieger, 1990), pp. 276–83.

13 Quoted on the page for *Film and History* on the American Historical Association website: http://www.historians.org/affiliates/hisn_film_comt.htm (accessed 4.7.2012).

14 James Chapman, 'Television and history: *The World at War*', *Historical Journal of Film, Radio and Television*, 31: 2 (2011), pp. 247–75.

15 J. A. S. Grenville, *Film as History* (Birmingham: University of Birmingham, 1971), p. 9.

16 William Hughes, 'The evaluation of film as evidence', in Paul Smith (ed.), *The Historian and Film* (Cambridge: Cambridge University Press, 1976), p. 51.

17 Nicholas Pronay, 'The newsreels: The illusion of actuality', in Smith (ed.), *The Historian and Film*, p. 96.

18 Arthur Marwick, *The Nature of History* (London: Macmillan, 3rd edn, 1989), p. 216.

19 Karsten Fledelius, 'Film and History: An Introduction to the Theme', in Fledelius *et al.* (eds), *History and the Audio-Visual Media* (Copenhagen: University of Copenhagen, 1979), p. 9.

20 K. R. M. Short, 'The *Historical Journal of Film, Radio and Television*: A personal recollection of the early years', *Historical Journal of Film, Radio and Television*, 20: 1 (2000), pp. 89–99.

21 See Christopher Williams (ed.), *Realism and the Cinema: A Reader* (London: Routledge & Kegan Paul, 1980).

22 The making of the film is documented in S. D. Badsey, '*The Battle of the Somme*: British war-propaganda', *Historical Journal of Film, Radio and Television*, 3: 2 (1983), pp. 99–115. On its reception, see Nicholas Reeves, 'Cinema, spectatorship and propaganda: *Battle of the Somme* (1916) and its contemporary audience', *Historical Journal of Film, Radio and Television*, 17: 1 (1997), pp. 5–28.

23 D. S. Higgins (ed.), *The Private Diaries of Sir H. Rider Haggard, 1914–1925* (London: Cassell, 1980), p. 84.

24 Roger Smither, '"A wonderful idea of the fighting": The question of fakes in *The Battle of the Somme*', *Historical Journal of Film, Radio and Television*, 13: 2 (1993), pp. 149–68.

25 Phil Landon, 'Realism, genre and *Saving Private Ryan*', *Film and History*, 28: 3–4 (1998), p. 58.

26 Ambrose's endorsement is quoted in the press book for the film by the UK distributor UIP: *Saving Private Ryan* (London: UIP, 1998), p. 15.

27 Toby Haggith, 'D-Day filming – for real: A comparison of "truth" and "reality" in *Saving Private Ryan* and combat film by the British Army's Film and Photographic Unit', *Film History*, 14: 3–4 (2002), pp. 332–53.

28 The Zapruder footage is one of the few examples (others relate to twentieth-century genocide) where the minute examination of a piece of film is of interest beyond the narrow halls of film scholarship. There is extensive commentary: see the review essay 'Zaprudered: The Kennedy Assassination Film in Visual Culture', *Film and History*, 42: 2 (2012), pp. 72–3.

29 See Vanessa Toulmin, Simon Popple and Patrick Russell (eds), *The Lost World of Mitchell and Kenyon: Edwardian Britain on Film* (London: British Film Institute, 2005).

30 Hughes, 'The evaluation of film as evidence', p. 59.

31 Nicholas Pronay, 'British newsreels in the 1930s: 1. Audiences and producers', *History*, 56 (1971), pp. 411–18; 'British newsreels in the 1930s: 2. Their policies and impact', *History*, 57 (1972), pp. 63–72.

32 Aldgate, *Cinema and History*, p. 193.

33 John Grierson, 'The course of realism', in Forsyth Hardy (ed.), *Grierson on Documentary* (London: Faber and Faber, 1966), p. 72.

34 On *Cinéma Vérité*, see Kristin Thompson and David Bordwell, *Film History: An Introduction* (New York: McGraw-Hill, 1994), pp. 570–3.

35 Richard Taylor, *Film Propaganda: Soviet Russia and Nazi Germany* (London: Croom Helm, 1979), p. 177.

36 Hughes, 'The evaluation of film as evidence', p. 65.

37 *Ibid.*, p. 67.

38 Marc Ferro, *Cinema and History*, trans. Naomi Greene (Detroit: Wayne State University Press, 1988 [1977]), p. 161.

39 Pierre Sorlin, *The Film in History: Restaging the Past* (Oxford: Basil Blackwell, 1980), p. 27.

40 *Ibid.*, p. 209.

41 Quoted in Andrew Kelly, *Cinema and the Great War* (London: Routledge, 1997), p. 125.

42 Robert A. Rosenstone, *History on Film/Film on History* (Harlow: Pearson Education, 2006), p. 3.

43 Robert A. Rosenstone, 'Introduction', in Robert A. Rosenstone (ed.), *Revisioning History: Film and the Construction of a New Past* (Princeton: Princeton University Press, 1995), p. 8.

44 Rosenstone, *History on Film/Film on History*, p. 8.

45 'Author's response' to review of *History on Film/Film on History* by James Chapman, *Reviews in History*, www.history.ac.uk/reviews/review/629 (last accessed 6.9.2012).

46 For a close reading of the film and its representation of historical events that also takes into account the political and ideological contexts of its production, see Richard Taylor, *October* (London: British Film Institute, 2002).

47 On the making of the film, see Kevin Brownlow, 'Before the deluge', *Sight and Sound*, 41: 4 (1972), pp. 186–7. For contextualization, see James Chapman, 'The world turned upside down: *Cromwell* (1970), *Winstanley* (1975), *To Kill A King* (2003) and the British historical film', in Leen Engelen and Roel Vande Winkel (eds), *Perspectives on European Film and History* (Ghent: Academia Press, 2007), pp. 111–31.

48 'Notes and comments', *Past and Present*, 69 (1975), p. 132.

49 John C. Tibbetts, 'Kevin Brownlow's historical films: *It Happened Here* (1965) and *Winstanley* (1975)', *Historical Journal of Film, Radio and Television*, 20: 2 (2000), p. 244.

50 L. Rubenstein, '*Winstanley* and the historical film: An interview with Kevin Brownlow', *Cineaste*, 10: 4 (1980), p. 25.

▶ 5 Film as a Social Practice

1 Marc Ferro, 'Film as an agent, product and source of history', trans. Anthony Wells, *Journal of Contemporary History*, 18: 3 (1983), p. 358.

2 Robert C. Allen and Douglas Gomery, *Film History: Theory and Practice* (New York: McGraw-Hill, 1985), p. 158.

3 Jeffrey Richards, *Visions of Yesterday* (London: Routledge & Kegan Paul, 1973), p. xv.

4 Lewis Jacobs, *The Rise of the American Film: A Critical History* (New York: Harcourt, Brace, 1939), p. ??.

5 Raymond Durgnat, *A Mirror for England: British Movies from Austerity to Affluence* (London: Faber and Faber, 1970), p. 10.

6 Richards, *Visions of Yesterday*, p. xv.

7 Robert Sklar, *Movie-Made America: A Cultural History of American Movies* (New York: Random House, 1975), p. 316.

8 Arthur Marwick, *Class: Image and Reality in Britain, France and the USA Since 1930* (New York: Oxford University Press, 1980), p. 22.

9 *Ibid.*, pp. 293–4.

10 Justine Ashby and Andrew Higson, 'Introduction', to Justine Ashby and Andrew Higson (eds), *British Cinema, Past and Present* (London: Routledge, 2000), p. 15

11 Graeme Turner, *Film As Social Practice* (London: Routledge, 1988), p. 129.

12 John Hill, *Sex, Class and Realism: British Cinema 1956–1963* (London: British Film Institute, 1986), p. 2.

13 Segond's remarks are from his review of Richards's *Visions of Yesterday* in *Monogram*, 6 (1975), pp. 43–4.

14 Andy Medhurst, '*Victim*: Text as context', *Screen*, 25: 4–5 (1984), p. 23.

15 Elizabeth Grottle Strebel, 'Jean Renoir and the Popular Front', in K. R. M. Short (ed.), *Feature Films as History* (London: Croom Helm, 1981), p. 92.

16 Arthur Marwick, *The Nature of History* (London: Macmillan, 3rd edn, 1989), p. 305.

17 John Belton, *American Cinema/American Culture* (New York: McGraw-Hill, 1994), p. xxi.

18 *Ibid.*

19 Hill, *Sex, Class and Realism*, p. 2.

20 Prem Chowdhry, *Colonial India and the Making of Empire Cinema: Image, Ideology and Identity* (Manchester: Manchester University Press, 2000), p. 3.

21 John E. O'Connor and Martin A. Jackson (eds), *American History/American Film* (New York: Ungar, 1979); K. R. M. Short (ed.), *Feature Films as History*; Peter C. Rollins (ed.), *Hollywood As Historian: American Film in a Cultural Context* (Lexington: University Press of Kentucky, 1983); Jeffrey Richards and Anthony Aldgate, *Best of British: Cinema and Society 1930–1960* (Oxford: Basil Blackwell, 1983); and Anthony Aldgate and Jeffrey Richards, *Britain Can Take It: British Cinema in the Second World War* (Oxford: Basil Blackwell, 1986).

22 For example K. R. M. Short, *'The White Cliffs of Dover*: promoting the Anglo-American alliance in World War II', *Historical Journal of Film, Radio and Television*, 2: 1 (1982), pp. 4–25; Jeffrey Richards, 'Wartime British cinema audiences and the class system: The case of *Ships With Wings* (1941), *Historical Journal of Film, Radio and Television*, 7: 2 (1987), pp. 129–41; Andrew Kelly, '*All Quiet on the Western Front*: "brutal cutting, stupid censors and bigoted politicos"', *Historical Journal of Film, Radio and Television*, 9: 2 (1989); pp. 135–50; K. R. M. Short, '*That Hamilton Woman* (1941): propaganda, feminism and the Production Code', *Historical Journal of Film, Radio and Television*, 11: 1 (1991), pp. 3–19.

23 Richards and Aldgate, *Best of British*, p. 8.

24 Richard Taylor, *Film Propaganda: Soviet Russia and Nazi Germany* (London: Croom Helm, 1979), p. 15.

25 *Ibid.*, p. 17.

26 David Welch, *Propaganda and the German Cinema 1933–1945* (Oxford: Clarendon Press 1983), pp. 47–93.

27 *Ibid.*, pp. 280–304.

28 Steve Neale, 'Propaganda', *Screen*, 18: 3 (1977), pp. 9–40.

29 On Grierson's aesthetic and ideological influences, see Ian Aitken, *Film and Reform: John Grierson and the Documentary Film Movement* (London: Routledge, 1990). For a political and institutional history, see Paul Swann, *The British Documentary Film Movement, 1926–1946* (Cambridge: Cambridge University Press, 1989).

30 See Jeffrey Richards, 'The British Board of Film Censors and content control in the 1930s: Images of Britain', *Historical Journal of Film, Radio and Television*, 1: 2 (1981), pp. 95–116, and 'The British Board of Film Censors and content control in the 1930s: Foreign affairs', *Historical Journal of Film, Radio and Television*, 2: 1 (1982), pp. 29–48. The case of *Love on the Dole* – which the BBFC would allow only after the outbreak of the Second World War when it became a backward-looking rather than present-day story – is discussed in Sarah Street, *British Cinema in Documents* (London: Routledge, 2000), pp. 23–38.

31 Tony Aldgate, 'Ideological consensus in British feature films, 1935–1947', in Short (ed.), *Feature Films as History*, p. 111.

32 Richard Maltby, *Harmless Entertainment: Hollywood and the Ideology of Consensus* (Metuchen: Scarecrow Press, 1983), p. 13.

33 Edward Buscombe, 'Walsh and Warner Bros.', in Phil Hardy (ed.), *Raoul Walsh* (Edinburgh: Edinburgh Film Festival, 1974), p. 54.

34 Ruth Vasey, 'Beyond sex and violence: "Industry policy" and the regulation of Hollywood movies, 1922–1939', *Quarterly Review of Film and Video*, 15: 4 (1995), pp. 65–85.

35 Gregory D. Black, *Hollywood Censored: Morality Codes, Catholics, and the Movies* (Cambridge: Cambridge University Press, 1994), pp. 299–300.

36 Arthur Marwick, '*Room at the Top, Saturday Night and Sunday Morning*, and the "Cultural Revolution" in Britain', *Journal of Contemporary History*, 19: 1 (1984), p. 49.

37 Anthony Aldgate, *Censorship and the Permissive Society: British Cinema and Theatre 1955–1965* (Oxford: Clarendon Press, 1995), *passim*. See also Anthony Aldgate, 'Defining the parameters of "quality" cinema for "the permissive society": The British Board of Film Censors and *This Sporting Life*', in Anthony Aldgate, James Chapman and Arthur Marwick (eds), *Windows on the Sixties: Exploring Key Texts of Media and Culture* (London: I. B. Tauris, 2000), pp. 19–36.

38 Barry Keith Grant, 'Introduction', *Film Genre Reader II* (Austin: University of Texas Press, 1995), p. xv.

39 Robert Warshaw, *The Immediate Experience* (New York: Atheneum, 1970), p. 129.

40 Jim Kitses, *Horizons West: Studies of Authorship within the Western* (London: Thames and Hudson, 1969); Colin McArthur, *Underworld USA* (London: Secker & Warburg, 1972); Will Wright, *Sixguns and Society: A Structural Study of the Western* (Berkeley: University of California Press, 1975).

41 Peter Wollen, *Signs and Meaning in the Cinema* (London: Secker & Warburg, 2nd edn 1972), p. 94.

42 Kitses, *Horizons West*, p. 19.

43 McArthur, *Underworld USA*, p. 18.

44 Thomas Schatz, *Hollywood Genres: Formulas, Filmmaking and the Studio System* (New York: Random House, 1981), p. 261.

45 Belton, *American Cinema/American Culture*, p. 116.

46 André Bazin, 'The Western; or the American film *par excellence*', *What is Cinema? Volume II*, trans. Hugh Gray (Berkeley: University of California Press, 1971), pp. 140–8.

47 Michael Coyne, *The Crowded Prairie: American National Identity in the Hollywood Western* (London: I. B. Tauris, 1997), p. 184.

48 Jane Feuer, *The Hollywood Musical* (London: Macmillan, 1982), p. vii.

49 Wright, *Sixguns and Society*, p. 32.

50 Andrew Tudor, *Theories of Film* (London: Secker & Warburg, 1974), p. 135.

51 Tino Balio, *History of the American Cinema Volume 5. Grand Design: Hollywood as a Modern Business Enterprise 1930–1939* (Berkeley: University of California Press, 1993), p. 179.

52 Richard Maltby, *Hollywood Cinema: An Introduction* (Oxford: Blackwell, 1995), p. 111.

53 Jeanine Basinger, *The World War II Combat Film: Anatomy of a Genre* (Middletown: Wesleyan University Press, rev. edn 2003), pp. 14–75.

54 Richard Dyer and Ginette Vincendeau, 'Introduction', to Richard Dyer and Ginette Vincendeau (eds), *Popular European Cinema* (London: Routledge, 1992), p. 1.
55 André Bazin, Jacques Doniol-Valcroze, Pierre Kast, Roger Leenhardt, Jacques Rivette and Eric Rohmer, 'Six characters in search of *auteurs*: a discussion about the French cinema', in Jim Hillier (ed.), *Cahiers du Cinéma Volume 1. The 1950s: Neo-Realism, Hollywood, New Wave* (Cambridge MA: Harvard University Press, 1985), p. 32.
56 Julian Petley and Alan Burton, 'Introduction', *Journal of Popular British Cinema*, 1 (1998), p. 4.
57 Sue Harper, *Picturing the Past: The Rise and Fall of the British Costume Film* (London: British Film Institute, 1994), pp. 119–35; Pam Cook, *Fashioning the Nation: Costume and Identity in British Cinema* (London: British Film Institute, 1996), pp. 80–115; Peter Hutchings, *Hammer and Beyond: The British Horror Film* (Manchester: Manchester University Press, 1993).
58 David Pirie, *A Heritage of Horror: The English Gothic Cinema 1946–1972* (London: Gordon & Fraser, 1973), p. 9.
59 Raymond Borde and Etienne Chaumeton, *Panorama du Film Noir Américain* (Paris: Editions de Minuit, 1955), pp. 205–9.
60 Alain Silver and Elizabeth Ward (eds), *Film Noir: An Encyclopedic Reference Guide to the American Style* (London: Secker & Warburg, 3rd edn 1992), pp. 393–7.
61 John Houseman, 'Today's Hero: A review', *Hollywood Quarterly*, 2: 2 (1947), p. 161.
62 Richard Winnington, *Drawn and Quartered: A Selection of Weekly Film Reviews and Drawings* (London: Saturn Press, 1949), p. 93.
63 Schatz, *Hollywood Genres*, p. 113.
64 David A. Cook, *A History of Narrative Film* (London: W. W. Norton, 2nd edn 1990), p. 471.
65 Lester Asheim, 'Film and the zeitgeist', *Hollywood Quarterly*, 2: 4 (1947), p. 415.
66 Steve Neale, *Genre and Hollywood* (London: Routledge, 2000), p. 158.
67 Robert B. Ray, *A Certain Tendency of the Hollywood Cinema, 1930–1980* (Princeton: Princeton University Press, 1985), p. 141.
68 J. A. Place and L. S. Pearson, 'Some visual motifs of *film noir*', *Film Comment*, 10: 1 (1974), p. 31.
69 Paul Schrader, 'Notes on *film noir*', *Film Comment*, 8: 1 (1972), p. 13.
70 Ray, *A Certain Tendency of the Hollywood Cinema*, p. 160.
71 Paul Kerr, 'Out of what past? Notes on the B *film noir*', *Screen Education*, 32–33 (1979–80), p. 65.

► **6 A Historical Sociology of Film**

1 Hortense Powdermaker, *Hollywood the Dream Factory: An Anthropologist Looks at the Movie-Makers* (London: Secker & Warburg, 1951), p. 15.

2 *Ibid.*, p. 3.

3 *Ibid.*, pp. 330–1.

4 Ian Jarvie, *Movies and Society* (New York: Basic Books, 1970), p. 14.

5 Robert C. Allen and Douglas Gomery, *Film History: Theory and Practice* (New York: McGraw-Hill, 1985), p. 154.

6 *Ibid.*, p. 186.

7 Neal Gabler, *An Empire of Their Own: How the Jews Invented Hollywood* (New York: Crown, 1988), p. 5.

8 Richard Maltby, 'The political economy of Hollywood: The studio system', in Philip Davies and Brian Neve (eds), *Cinema, Politics and Society in America* (Manchester: Manchester University Press, 1981), p. 54.

9 Thomas Schatz, *The Genius of the System: Hollywood Filmmaking in the Studio Era* (New York: Pantheon, 1988), pp. 452–8.

10 Aljean Harmeatz, *The Making of The Wizard of Oz* (London: Pavilion, 1989), and *Round Up the Usual Suspects: The Making of Casablanca – Bogart, Bergman and World War II* (London: Weidenfeld & Nicolson, 1993).

11 Rudy Behlmer, 'Introduction: The heroic virtues', *The Sea Hawk* (Madison: University of Wisconsin Press, 1980), pp. 11–43.

12 Tino Balio, 'Foreword', *The Sea Hawk*, p. 7.

13 David Bordwell and Kristin Thompson, *Film Art: An Introduction* (New York: Alfred A. Knopf, 2nd edn, 1979), p. 22.

14 Pauline Kael, 'Raising *Kane*', in *The Citizen Kane Book* (London: Secker & Warburg, 1971), p. 8.

15 *Ibid.*, p. 39.

16 Richard B. Jewell, 'A History of RKO Radio Pictures, Incorporated, 1928–1942', PhD thesis, University of Southern California, 1978.

17 Robert L. Carringer, *The Making of Citizen Kane* (Berkeley: University of California Press, rev. edn 1996 [1984]), p. 117.

18 *Ibid.*, p. 29.

19 *Ibid.*, p. 35.

20 Janet Staiger, *Interpreting Films: Studies in the Historical Reception of American Cinema* (Princeton: Princeton University Press, 1992); Miriam Hansen, *Babel and Babylon: Spectatorship in American Silent Film* (Cambridge MA: Harvard University Press, 1991); Barbara Klinger, *Melodrama and Meaning: History, Culture and the Films of Douglas Sirk* (Bloomington: Indiana University Press, 1994); Jackie Stacey, *Star Gazing: Hollywood Cinema and Female Spectatorship* (London: Routledge, 1994).

21 Staiger, *Interpreting Films*, p. 80.
22 *Ibid.*, p. 152.
23 Klinger, *Melodrama and Meaning*, pp. 36–68.
24 Staiger, *Interpreting Films*, p. 212.
25 Hansen, *Babel and Babylon*, p. 130.
26 *Ibid.*, p. 241.
27 Stacey, *Star Gazing*, p. 80.
28 Helen Taylor, *Scarlet's Women: 'Gone With the Wind' and its Female Fans* (London: Virago, 1989), p. 232.
29 Robert E. Kapsis, *Hitchcock: The Making of a Reputation* (Chicago: University of Chicago Press, 1992), p. 27.
30 Robin Wood, *Hitchcock's Films* (London: Zwemmer, 1965), p. 62.
31 Eric Rohmer and Claude Chabrol, *Hitchcock: The First Forty-Four Films*, trans. Stanley Hochman (New York: Ungar, 1988 [1957]), pp. 122–8.
32 François Truffaut, *The Films in My Life*, trans. Leonard Mayhew (New York: Simon & Schuster, 1978), p. 82.
33 Robert Stam and Roberta Pearson, 'Hitchcock's *Rear Window*: Reflexivity and the critique of voyeurism', *Enclitic*, 7: 1 (1983), p. 136.
34 Justin Smith, '*The Wicker Man* (1973) Email digest: A case study in web ethnography', in James Chapman, Mark Glancy and Sue Harper (eds), *The New Film History: Sources, Methods, Approaches* (Basingstoke: Palgrave Macmillan, 2007), p. 243.
35 Robert C. Allen, 'From exhibition to reception: Reflections on the audience in film history', *Screen*, 31: 4 (1990), p. 348.
36 Margaret Thorp, *America at the Movies* (London: Faber & Faber, 1946); J. P. Mayer, *British Cinemas and their Audiences: Sociological Studies* (London: Dobson, 1948).
37 Jeffrey Richards and Dorothy Sheridan (eds), *Mass-Observation at the Movies* (London: Routledge & Kegan Paul, 1987).
38 Eileen Bowser, *History of the American Cinema Volume 2: The Transformation of Cinema 1907–1915* (Berkeley: University of California Press, 1990), p. 6.
39 Local studies include Robert C. Allen, 'Motion picture exhibition in Manhattan: Beyond the nickelodeon', *Cinema Journal*, 18: 2 (1979), pp. 2–15; Douglas Gomery, 'The growth of movie monopolies: The case of Balaban & Katz', *Wide Angle*, 3: 1 (1979), pp. 54–63; Burnes St Patrick Hollyman, 'The first picture shows: Austin, Texas, 1894–1913', *Journal of the University Film Association*, 19: 3 (1977), pp. 3–8; Ben Singer, 'Manhattan nickelodeons: New data on audiences and exhibitors', *Cinema Journal*, 34: 3 (1995), pp. 5–35.
40 Kathy Peiss, *Cheap Amusements: Working Women and Leisure in Turn-of-the Century New York* (Philadelphia: 1986), *passim*.

41 Kristin Thompson and David Bordwell, *Film History: An Introduction* (New York: McGraw-Hill, 1994), p. 33.
42 *Going to the Show: Mapping Moviegoing in North Carolina*, http://docsouth. unc.edu/gtts/ (accessed 21.5.2013).
43 *Ibid.*
44 Jeffrey Richards, *The Age of the Dream Palace: Cinema and Society in Britain, 1930– 1939* (London: Routledge & Kegan Paul, 1984), p. 15.
45 *Ibid.*, p. 7.
46 *Ibid.*, p. 323.
47 *Ibid.*, pp. 160–1.
48 *Ibid.*, p. 324.
49 John Sedgwick, *Popular Filmgoing in 1930s Britain: A Choice of Pleasures* (Exeter: Universiy of Exeter Press, 2000), pp. 266–76.
50 *Ibid.*, pp. 192–3.
51 Annette Kuhn, *An Everyday Magic: Cinema and Cultural Memory* (London: I. B. Tauris, 2002), p. 118.
52 Simon Rowson, 'A statistical survey of the cinema industry in Great Britain in 1934', *Journal of the Royal Statistical Society*, 99 (1936), pp. 67–129.
53 Sue Harper, 'A lower middle-class taste community in the 1930s: Admissions figures at the Regent Cinema, Portsmouth, UK', *Historical Journal of Film, Radio and Television*, 24: 4 (2004), pp. 565–87.
54 Sue Harper, 'Fragmentation and crisis: 1940s admissions figures at the Regent Cinema, Portsmouth, UK', *Historical Journal of Film, Radio and Television*, 26: 3 (2006), pp. 361–94.
55 Mark Glancy, '*Picturegoer*: The fan magazine and popular film culture in Britain during the Second World War', *Historical Journal of Film, Radio and Television*, 31: 4 (2011), p. 474.
56 *Ibid.*

▶ Conclusion

1 Richard Maltby, 'How can cinema history matter more?' (2007), *Screening the Past*, http://tlweb.latrobe.edu.au/humanities/screeningthepast/22/ board-richard-maltby.html (accessed 21.5.2013).
2 Eric Rentschler, *The Ministry of Illusion: Nazi Cinema and its Afterlife* (Cambridge MA: Harvard University Press, 1996), p. 217.
3 Ashish Rajadhyaksha, 'Indian cinema', in John Hill and Pamela Church Gibson (eds), *World Cinemas: Critical Approaches* (Oxford: Oxford University Press, 2000), p. 153.
4 Andrew Higson and Richard Maltby, *'Film Europe' and 'Film America': Cinema, Commerce and Cultural Exchange, 1920–1939* (Exeter: University of

Exeter Press, 1999); Sarah Street, *Transatlantic Crossings: British Feature Films in the USA* (London: Continuum, 2001); Mark Glancy, *Hollywood and the Americanization of Britain: From the 1920s to the Present* (London: I. B. Tauris, 2013).

5 Geoffrey Nowell-Smith and Steven Ricci (eds), *Hollywood and Europe: Economics, Culture, National Identity 1945–95* (London: British Film Institute, 1998), p. ix.

6 This comment is made by Maria A. Vélez-Serna in a review of Richard Maltby, Daniel Biltereyst and Philippe Meers (eds), *Explorations in New Cinema History: Approaches and Case Studies* (Oxford: Wiley-Blackwell, 2011), in the *Historical Journal of Film, Radio and Television*, 32: 3 (2012), p. 489.

7 *Going to the Show: Mapping Moviegoing in North Carolina*, http://docsouth. unc.edu/gtts (accessed 20.5.2013). Allen's remark that 'movies don't matter' was made at a symposium entitled 'Researching Cinema History: Perspectives and Practices in Film Historiography' at the Royal Geological Society, London, 6–7 July 2009.

8 John Sedgwick, *Popular Film-going in 1930s Britain: A Choice of Pleasures* (Exeter: University of Exeter Press, 2000). Sedgwick has recently extended this method to consider exhibition patterns in 1930s Sydney: see his 'Patterns in first-run and suburban filmgoing in Sydney in the mid-1930s', in Maltby, Biltereyst and Meers (eds), *Explorations in New Cinema History*, pp. 140–58.

9 Robert James, *Popular Culture and Working-Class Taste in Britain, 1930–39: A Round of Cheap Diversions?* (Manchester: Manchester University Press, 2010), p. 207.

10 Justin Smith, *Withnail and Us: Cult Films and Film Cults in British Cinema* (London: I.B. Tauris, 2010), p. 3.

Further Reading

▶ **Introduction**

To date the only methodological study of the discipline of film history is Robert C. Allen and Douglas Gomery, *Film History: Theory and Practice* (New York: McGraw-Hill, 1985), a highly didactic work whose case studies reflect the authors' expertise in American cinema, particularly early cinema history. An alternative overview of the field, including a critique of Allen and Gomery, can be found in Robert Sklar, '*Oh! Althusser!*: Historiography and the Rise of Cinema Studies', in Robert Sklar and Charles Musser (eds), *Resisting Images: Essays on Cinema and History* (Philadelphia: Temple University Press, 1990), pp. 12–35. This book is one of several anthologies that include essays on particular aspects of film history within a methodological framework: others include Annette Kuhn and Jackie Stacey (eds), *Screen Histories: A Reader* (Oxford: Clarendon Press, 1998) – an anthology of articles originally published in the journal *Screen* here grouped thematically into sections on 'Reception Histories', 'Social Histories', 'Institutional Histories' and 'Textual Histories' – and James Chapman, Mark Glancy and Sue Harper (eds), *The New Film History: Sources, Methods, Approaches* (Basingstoke: Palgrave Macmillan, 2007), which comprises newly commissioned essays grouped thematically into 'History', 'Genre', 'Authorship' and 'Reception'. Paul Grainge, Mark Jancovich and Sharon Monteith (eds), *Film Histories: An Introduction and Reader* (Edinburgh: Edinburgh University Press, 2007) is a somewhat eclectic collection of extracts from film-history texts. A more theoretical take on the relationship between cinema and history, focusing on issues of reality and subjectivity, is Geoffrey Nowell-Smith, 'On history and the cinema', *Screen*, 31: 2 (1990), pp. 160–71. See also the 'In Focus' (debates) section of *Cinema Journal*, 44: 1 (2004), entitled 'Film History, or a Baedeker Guide to the Historical Turn', which includes a series of short essays by both established scholars (Richard Abel, Charles Musser, Robert Sklar, Janet Staiger) and newcomers (Jane M. Gaines, Lee Grieveson, Sumiko Higashi) that map the field of current film historiography, again with particular reference to early American cinema. A critique of this work is offered by David Bordwell, 'Film and the Historical Return' (http://www.davidbordwell.net/essays/return.php)

on Bordwell's useful cinema website (last accessed 8.3.2013). The British context is outlined by Justin Smith, 'Film History', for the *Making History* website
(http://www.history.ac.uk/makinghistory/resources/articles/film_history.html)
hosted by the Institute of Historical Research (last accessed 30.8.2012).

▶ **Chapter 1**

The best way of understanding the growth of film history as a discipline is of
course to read a wide range of film histories. The foundational texts of film
history include Terry Ramsaye, *A Million and One Nights: A History of the Motion
Picture* (New York: Simon and Schuster, 1926), Paul Rotha, *The Film Till Now: A
Survey of World Cinema* (London: Jonathan Cape, 1930), Benjamin Hampton,
A History of the Movies (New York: Covice, Friede, 1931) – republished as *The
History of the American Film Industry from its Beginnings to 1931* (New York:
Dover, 1970) – and Lewis Jacobs, *The Rise of the American Film: A Critical History*
(New York: Harcourt, Brace, 1939). These books are now best read for what
they reveal about critical assumptions and aesthetic tastes, rather than as reliable repositories of fact. There is currently no English translation of Georges
Sadoul's *Histoire générale du cinéma* (Paris: Denoël, 3 vols, 1946–52). The pick of
the second wave of synoptic histories from the 1970s is Eric Rhode, *A History of
the Cinema from its Origins to 1970* (London: Allen Lane, 1976), which is valuable as it considers film from a social-historical as well as an aesthetic angle. See
also David Robinson, *The History of World Cinema* (New York: Stein and Day,
1973), and Basil Wright, *The Long View: A Personal Perspective on World Cinema*
(London: Secker & Warburg, 1974), perhaps the most idiosyncratic of the many
single-author histories but also one which includes more coverage of non-
Western cinemas. There are two excellent (and more recent) synoptic scholarly histories in David A. Cook, *A History of Narrative Film* (New York: W. W.
Norton, 1981 and later editions), and Kristin Thompson and David Bordwell,
Film History: An Introduction (New York: McGraw-Hill, 1994 and later editions),
which focus on the international history of film form and style: both include
comprehensive bibliographies. Finally, Geoffrey Nowell-Smith (ed.), *The Oxford
History of World Cinema* (Oxford: Oxford University Press, 1995) is particularly
strong on the institutional and cultural contexts of national cinemas though
with fewer close readings of films.

Once the general histories are exhausted, there is an abundance of historical
material on particular periods and different national cinemas. A good selection
of the revisionist work on early cinema following the landmark FIAF conference
of 1978 is anthologized in Thomas Elsaesser (ed.), *Early Cinema: Space, Frame,
Narrative* (London: British Film Institute, 1990). For an archival perspective

on early film, see Paulo Cherchi Usai, *Burning Passions: An Introduction to the Study of Silent Cinema*, trans. Elizabeth Sansone (London: British Film Institute, 1994). The foundational text of sociological film history is Siegfried Kracauer, *From Caligari to Hitler: A Psychological History of the German Film* (Princeton: Princeton University Press, 1947), which, for all its methodological flaws, remains essential reading. Other social histories, largely shorn of the psychoanalytical baggage of Kracauer, include: Paul Monaco, *Cinema and Society: France and Germany During the Twenties* (New York: Elsevier, 1976): Keith Reader, *Cultures on Celluloid* (London: Quartet, 1981), which is valuable as a rare example of comparative film history, covering America, Britain, France and Japan; Robert Sklar, *Movie-Made America: A Cultural History of American Movies* (New York: Random House, 1975); and another comparative history, Pierre Sorlin, *European Cinemas, European Societies 1939–1990* (London: Routledge, 1991). There is a series of useful introductions to national cinemas, including critical debates as well as film-making, in Robert Murphy (ed.), *The British Cinema Book* (London: British Film Institute, 1997), Tim Bergfelder, Erica Carter and Deniz Göktürk (eds), *The German Cinema Book* (London: British Film Institute, 2002), and Michael Temple and Michael Witt (eds), *The French Cinema Book* (London: British Film Institute, 2004). Routledge's 'National Cinemas' series (general editor: Susan Hayward) tends on the whole towards more theoretical approaches, though Sarah Street, *British National Cinema* (London: Routledge, 1997), and Sabine Hake, *German National Cinema* (London: Routledge, 2002), are more historically based.

Most institutional and economic histories have focused on the US film industry. The 'History of the American Cinema' project, sponsored by the American Film Institute, has produced a series of highly authoritative studies by period, beginning with Charles Musser, *History of the American Cinema Volume 1. The Emergence of Cinema: The American Screen to 1907* (Berkeley: University of California Press, 1994). David Bordwell, Janet Staiger and Kristin Thompson, *The Classical Hollywood Cinema: Film Style & Mode of Production to 1960* (London: Routledge, 1985) is essential reading not only for Hollywood but also from a methodological perspective as a historical analysis of film-making in both its formal and industrial contexts. For this approach applied to other national cinemas, see (again) David Bordwell, *Planet Hong Kong: Popular Cinema and the Art of Entertainment* (Cambridge MA: Harvard University Press, 2000), Colin Crisp, *The Classic French Cinema, 1930–1960* (Bloomington: Indiana University Press, 1993), and Thomas Elsaesser, *New German Cinema: A History* (New Brunswick: Rutgers University Press, 1989). The standard history of the foreign policy of the US film industry is Thomas H. Guback, *The International Film Industry: Western Europe and America Since 1945* (Bloomington: Indiana University Press, 1969). For an alternative to Guback's Marxist approach, see Kristin

Thompson, *Exporting Entertainment: America in the World Film Market 1907–1934* (London: British Film Institute, 1985), and Ian Jarvie, *Hollywood's Overseas Campaign: The North Atlantic Movie Trade, 1920–1950* (Cambridge: Cambridge University Press, 1992). The economic and cultural relations between the United States and other film industries are analysed in Andrew Higson and Richard Maltby (eds), *'Film Europe' and 'Film America': Cinema, Commerce and Cultural Exchange 1920–1939* (Exeter: University of Exeter Press, 1999), an excellent study of the various attempts to create a pan-European film industry as an alternative to the economic and cultural hegemony of Hollywood, and for the post-war period in Geoffrey Nowell-Smith and Steven Ricci (eds), *Hollywood and Europe: Economics, Culture, National Identity 1945–95* (London: British Film Institute, 1998).

► Chapter 2

There is an abundant critical literature on film as an art form. The best starting point is David Bordwell and Kristin Thompson, *Film Art: An Introduction* (New York: Alfred A. Knopf, 1979 and subsequent editions), which covers aspects of form and style, features plentiful case studies, and includes a useful short history of the major movements. V. F. Perkins, *Film as Film: Understanding and Judging Movies* (Harmondsworth: Penguin, 1972) remains perhaps the best introduction to formal/textual analysis. A compact, still useful, introduction to the formative and realist schools of classical film aesthetics is provided by J. Dudley Andrew, *The Major Film Theories: An Introduction* (Oxford: Oxford University Press, 1976). Otherwise the best sources are the original texts themselves – most of which are available in English translations. The key texts can be traced through the endnotes to chapter 2, but particularly important are: Sergei Eisenstein, *The Film Sense*, trans. Jay Leda (London: Faber and Faber, 1943) and *Film Form: Essays in Film Theory*, trans. Jay Leda (London: Faber and Faber, 1949); Siegfried Kracauer, *Theory of Film: The Redemption of Physical Reality* (New York: Oxford University Press, 1960); and André Bazin, *What is Cinema?*, trans. Hugh Gray (Berkeley: University of California Press, 2 vols, 1967 & 1971). Extracts from these theorists are widely anthologized, for example in Gerald Mast, Marshall Cohen and Leo Braudy (eds), *Film Theory and Criticism: Introductory Readings* (New York: Oxford University Press, 4th edn, 1992), and Bill Nichols (ed.), *Movies and Methods* (Berkeley: University of California Press, 2 vols, 1976 & 1985). Christopher Williams (ed.) *Realism and the Cinema: A Reader* (London: Routledge & Kegan Paul, 1980) is the standard introduction to realist film theories. An alternative taxonomy of film aesthetics is offered by Gilles Deleuze: *Cinema 1: The Movement Image*, trans. Hugh Tomlinson and

Barbara Habbermas (London: Athlone Press, 1986 [1983]), and *Cinema 2: The Time-Image*, trans. Hugh Tomlinson and Robert Galeta (London: Athlone Press, 1989 [1985]). The large critical literature on rather than by Deleuze is of little interest in its own right other than for extending his taxonomy to other films: this work rarely if ever seems to engage in dialogue with any theory other than itself.

There are two useful collections of *auteur* criticism: John Caughie (ed.), *Theories of Authorship: A Reader* (London: Routledge & Kegan Paul, 1981), and Virginia Wright Wexman (ed.), *Film and Authorship* (New Brunswick: Rutgers University Press, 2003). Andrew Sarris, *The American Cinema: Directors and Directions 1929–1968* (New York: Dutton, 1968) includes the infamous 'Pantheon': see also his article 'Notes on the *auteur* theory in 1962', *Film Culture*, 27 (1962), pp. 1–8. Other foundational texts of *auteur* criticism include Eric Rohmer and Claude Chabrol, *Hitchcock: The First Forty-Four Films*, trans. Stanley Hochman (New York: Continuum, 1988 [1957]), Robin Wood, *Hitchcock's Films* (London: Zwemmer, 1965) – see also Wood's *Hitchcock's Films Revisited* (London: Faber and Faber, 1991) – and Robin Wood, *Howard Hawks* (London: Secker & Warburg, 1968). There is a vast (and ever expanding) critical literature on Alfred Hitchcock: see the 'annotated bibliography' in Jane E. Sloan, *Alfred Hitchcock: A Filmography and Bibliography* (Berkeley: University of California Press, 1993). Robert E. Kapsis, *Hitchcock: The Making of a Reputation* (Chicago: University of Chicago Press, 1992) charts the director's changing critical fortunes as he progressed from being regarded as a mere technician to the *auteur par excellence*. The work of David Bordwell on historical poetics can be traced through the endnotes: see in particular *Narration in the Fiction Film* (London: Methuen, 1985), *Making Meaning: Inference and Rhetoric in the Interpretation of Cinema* (Cambridge MA: Harvard University Press, 1989), and *Poetics of Cinema* (New York: Routledge, 2008).

There is, not surprisingly, an extensive critical literature on *Citizen Kane*: perhaps the best starting point is the short essay by (again) David Bordwell, '*Citizen Kane*', *Film Comment* 7: 2 (1971), pp. 39–46. See also Peter Wollen, 'Introduction to *Citizen Kane*', *Readings and Writings: Semiotic Counter-Strategies* (London: Verso, 1982), pp. 46–61, and Laura Mulvey, *Citizen Kane* (London: British Film Institute, 1992). Pauline Kael, *The Citizen Kane Book* (London: Secker & Warburg, 1971), includes the screenplay and Kael's famous essay 'Raising *Kane*' in which she argues that the screenplay was the work of Herman J. Mankiewicz rather than Welles: the essay is as much a polemic against the *auteur* theory as it is an attack on Welles personally. A range of critical essays can be found in both Ronald Gottesman (ed.), *Focus on Citizen Kane* (Englewood Cliffs: Prentice-Hall, 1976) and James Naremore (ed.), *Orson Welles's Citizen Kane: A Casebook* (Oxford: Oxford University Press, 2004).

► Chapter 3

Pam Cook (ed.), *The Cinema Book* (London: British Film Institute, 1985; 1999; 2007) is a good introduction to the major theoretical issues in film studies, particularly the first edition which includes a section on 'Film Narrative and the Structuralist Controversy' that has been somewhat abridged in later editions. Michael Lapsley and Robert Westlake, *Film Theory: An Introduction* (Manchester: Manchester University Press, 1988), provides a good overview of politics, semiotics and psychoanalysis, though it is best read as a follow-up to a more basic introductory text such as Joanne Hollows and Mark Jancovich (eds), *Approaches to Popular Film* (Manchester: Manchester University Press, 1995). The radicalization of intellectual film culture in France is discussed in Sylvia Harvey, *May '68 and Film Culture* (London: British Film Institute, 2nd edn 1980). Peter Wollen, *Signs and Meaning in the Cinema* (London: Secker & Warburg, 1969) remains essential reading as the text that introduced structuralism and semiotics into English-language film theory. References from *Screen* and other journals can be traced through the endnotes: some of these articles are anthologized in *Screen Reader 1* (London: Society for Education in Film and Television, 1977) and *Screen Reader 2: Cinema and Semiotics* (London: Society for Education in Film and Television, 1981). An important text not anthologized because of its length is 'John Ford's *Young Mr Lincoln*: A collective text by the Editors of *Cahiers du Cinéma*', trans. Helen Lackner and Diana Matias, *Screen*, 13: 3 (1972), pp. 5–44, which offers a close reading of the ideological operations of the film – though not without its own theoretical contradictions. The key text for semiotic film theory is Christian Metz, *Film Language: A Semiotics of the Cinema*, trans. Michael Taylor (New York: Oxford University Press, 1974). There seems to be no end to 'new' approaches to film theory, though often this work rehashes existing work without offering fresh insights. Robert Stam, Robert Burgoyne and Sandy Flitterman-Lewis, *New Vocabularies in Film Semiotics: Structuralism, Post-structuralism and Beyond* (London: Routledge, 1992) may not be the last word on the subject – though one might rather wish it were. Rather more useful, as it applies theoretical ideas to the analysis of specific films, is Jim Collins, Hilary Radner and Ava Preacher Collins (eds), *Film Theory Goes to the Movies* (London: Routledge, 1993), though even so the chapter that has best stood the test of time is Thomas Schatz's historical piece on 'The New Hollywood' rather than some of the essays on then-voguish films such as *The Silence of the Lambs* and *Thelma and Louise*.

There is an abundant body of feminist film studies. Histories of the representation of women in film include Molly Haskell, *From Reverence to Rape: The Treatment of Women in the Movies* (Chicago: University of Chicago Press, 1973; 1987), Marjorie Rosen, *Popcorn Venus: Women, Movies and the American*

Dream (New York: Avon, 1973), and Janet Thumim, *Celluloid Sisters: Women and Popular Cinema* (London: Macmillan, 1992), while E. Ann Kaplan, *Women and Film: Both Sides of the Camera* (London: Methuen, 1983) also considers the role of women in the film industry. More theoretical studies include Mary Anne Doane, Patricia Wellencamp and Linda Williams (eds), *Re-Vision: Essays in Feminist Film Criticism* (Frederick MD: University Publications, 1983), Annette Kuhn, *Women's Pictures: Feminism and Cinema* (London: Routledge & Kegan Paul, 1982), and Judith Mayne, *The Woman at the Keyhole: Feminism and Women's Cinema* (Bloomington: Indiana University Press, 1990). A major point of reference for these studies is Laura Mulvey, 'Visual Pleasure and Narrative Cinema', *Screen*, 16: 3 (1975), pp. 6–18, which is included, with other essays, in Laura Mulvey, *Visual and Other Pleasures* (London: Macmillan, 1989). Postcolonialism is less well served in the critical literature on film, though Roy Armes, *Third World Filmmaking and the West* (Berkeley: University of California Press, 1987) is a good introductory survey. On Third Cinema see: Mike Wayne, *Political Film: The Dialectics of Third Cinema* (London: Pluto Press, 2001); Jonathan Buchsbaum, 'A closer look at Third Cinema', *Historical Journal of Film, Radio and Television*, 21: 2 (2001), pp. 153–66; and Jim Pines and Paul Willemen (eds), *Questions of Third Cinema* (London: British Film Institute, 1989), in which several contributors argue that the Third Cinema paradigm can be extended to include 'alternative' film-making practices in the West.

▶ **Chapter 4**

The best starting points for discussion of film as a historical source are Paul Smith (ed.), *The Historian and Film* (Cambridge: Cambridge University Press, 1976), Karsten Fledelius *et al* (eds), *History and the Audio-Visual Media* (Copenhagen: University of Copenhagen, 1979), and John E. O'Connor (ed.), *Image as Artifact: The Historical Analysis of Film and Television* (Malabar: Robert E. Krieger, 1990). These collections include various contributions considering the nature of film as a historical source and the role of film in teaching history. For an excellent overview of 'Film as a primary source', see Chapter 1 of Anthony Aldgate, *Cinema and History: British Newsreels and the Spanish Civil War* (London: Scolar Press, 1979), pp. 1–16. The debates surrounding the emergence of the 'film and history' movement can be gleaned from the published conference proceedings, *Film and the Historian* (London: British Universities Film Council, 1968). Otherwise much of the important early work in this field is to be found in history journals. See in particular Nicholas Pronay, 'British newsreels in the 1930s: 1. Audiences and producers', *History*, 56 (1971), pp. 411–18, and 'British newsreels in the 1930s: 2. Their policies and impact', *History*, 57

(1972), pp. 63–72. The newsreels are also the subject of Luke McKernan, *Topical Budget: The Great British News Film* (London: British Film Institute, 1992), and K. R. M. Short and Stephen Dolezel (eds), *Hitler's Fall: The Newsreel Witness* (London: Croom Helm, 1988). Erik Barnouw, *Documentary: A History of the Non-Fiction Film* (New York: Oxford University Press, 1974; 1993), is the standard introduction to documentary film-making and remains useful. The history of film archiving is covered in Penelope Houston, *Keepers of the Frame: The Film Archives* (London: British Film Institute, 1994), and Caroline Frick, *Saving Cinema: The Politics of Preservation* (Oxford: Oxford University Press, 2011).

There is an extensive (and ever growing) critical literature on the representation of history in feature films. General studies include: Leen Engelen and Roel Vande Winkel (eds), *Perspectives on European Film and History* (Ghent: Academia Press, 2007); Marc Ferro, *Cinema and History*, trans. Naomi Greene (Detroit: Wayne State University Press, 1988 [1977]); Marnie Hughes-Warrington, *History Goes to the Movies: Studying History on Film* (London: Routledge, 2007); Marcia Landy, *Cinematic Uses of the Past* (Minneapolis: University of Minnesota Press, 1996); and Pierre Sorlin, *The Film in History: Restaging the Past* (Oxford: Basil Blackwell, 1980). More specific studies of particular national cinemas or historical subjects include: Sue Harper, *Picturing the Past: The Rise and Fall of the British Costume Film* (London: British Film Institute, 1994); Kevin J. Harty, *The Reel Middle Ages: American, Western and Eastern European, Middle Eastern, and Asian Films about Medieval Europe* (Jefferson: McFarland, 1999); Robert Brent Toplin, *History By Hollywood: The Use and Abuse of the American Past* (Urbana: University of Illinois Press, 1996); and Maria Wyke, *Projecting the Past: Ancient Rome, Cinema and History* (New York: Routledge, 1997). Finally, for a postmodernist intervention in the debate (albeit with the caveat that the author himself rejects the label), see Robert A. Rosenstone (ed.), *Revisioning History: Film and the Construction of a New Past* (Princeton: Princeton University Press, 1995), *Visions of the Past: The Challenge of Film to Our Idea of History* (Cambridge MA: Harvard University Press, 1995), and *History on Film/Film on History* (Harlow: Pearson Education, 2006).

▶ **Chapter 5**

The reflectionist approach to film and society is exemplified by Raymond Durgnat, *A Mirror for England: British Movies from Austerity to Affluence* (London: Faber and Faber, 1970), and Jeffrey Richards, *Visions of Yesterday* (London: Routledge & Kegan Paul, 1973). See also Robert Sklar's *Movie-Made America* listed in the reading for Chapter 1. Variations on this approach include: Robert A. Blake, *Screening America: Reflections on Five Classic Films* (New York: Paulist Press, 1991); Prem Chowdhry, *Colonial India and the Making of Empire Cinema:*

Image, Ideology and Identity (Manchester: Manchester University Press, 2000); and David W. Ellwood (ed.), *The Movies as History: Visions of the Twentieth Century* (Stroud: Sutton, 2000). The emergence of what Jeffrey Richards calls 'contextual cinematic history' is represented by: John E. O'Connor and Martin A. Jackson (eds), *American History/American Film* (New York: Ungar, 1979); K. R. M. Short (ed.), *Feature Films as History* (London: Croom Helm, 1981); Peter C. Rollins (ed.), *Hollywood As Historian: American Film in a Cultural Context* (Lexington: University Press of Kentucky, 1983); Jeffrey Richards and Anthony Aldgate, *Best of British: Cinema and Society 1930–1960* (Oxford: Basil Blackwell, 1983); and Anthony Aldgate and Jeffrey Richards, *Britain Can Take It: British Cinema in the Second World War* (Oxford: Basil Blackwell, 1986). These books all adopt a case-study approach, as do various articles in the *Historical Journal of Film, Radio and Television*. On the ideological strategies of American cinema during the studio period, see Richard Maltby, *Harmless Entertainment: Hollywood and the Ideology of Consensus* (Metuchen: Scarecrow Press, 1983). Richard Taylor, *Film Propaganda: Soviet Russia and Nazi Germany* (London: Croom Helm, 1979), and David Welch, *Propaganda and the German Cinema, 1933–1945* (Oxford: Oxford University Press, 1983), are pioneering historical studies of film propaganda, while excellent recent work in this field is exemplified by Jo Fox, *Film Propaganda in Britain and Nazi Germany: World War II Cinema* (Oxford: Berg, 2007), and Tony Shaw, *Hollywood's Cold War* (Edinburgh: Edinburgh University Press, 2007). Histories of censorship have focused largely on the 'golden age' of Hollywood when cinema was at its height as a social practice. See Gregory D. Black, *Hollywood Censored: Morality Codes, Catholics, and the Movies* (Cambridge: Cambridge University Press, 1994), and *The Catholic Crusade Against the Movies, 1940–1975* (Cambridge: Cambridge University Press, 1997), and Thomas Docherty, *Pre-Code Hollywood: Sex, Immorality and Insurrection in American Cinema 1930–1934* (New York: Columbia University Press, 1999). The British context is considered in James C. Robertson, *The Hidden Cinema: British Film Censorship in Action, 1913–1975* (London: Routledge, 1989), and Anthony Aldgate, *Censorship and the Permissive Society: British Cinema and Theatre 1955– 1965* (Oxford: Clarendon Press, 1995). Annette Kuhn, *Cinema, Censorship and Sexuality 1909–1925* (London: Routledge, 1988) is a comparative study of Britain and America.

There is an extensive literature of genre theory and criticism. Much of the early work on genre appeared in the form of journal articles: important texts include Tom Ryall, 'The notion of genre', *Screen*, 11: 2 (1970), pp. 22–32, Edward Buscombe, 'The idea of genre in the American cinema', *Screen*, 11: 2 (1970), pp. 33–45 – both from a special issue of *Screen* on genre theory – and Anthony Easthope, 'Notes on genre', *Screen Education*, 32/33 (1979/80), pp. 39–44. Many of the key texts are anthologized in Barry Keith Grant (ed.),

Film Genre Reader (Austin: University of Texas Press, 1986 and later editions), which also includes an extensive bibliography. Stephen Neale, *Genre* (London: British Film Institute, 1980) is both a critical survey of the first wave of genre theory in the 1970s and a contribution to the debate. Most genre studies have focused on American cinema. Thomas Schatz, *Hollywood Genres: Formulas, Filmmaking and the Studio System* (New York: Random House, 1981) is a very good introductory text, while Nick Browne (ed.), *Refiguring American Film Genres: Theory and History* (Berkeley: University of California Press, 1998) opens up the field with essays on some neglected genres and cycles. Important works of genre criticism include Jim Kitses, *Horizons West: Studies of Authorship within the Western* (London: Thames and Hudson, 1969), Colin McArthur, *Underworld USA* (London: Secker & Warburg, 1972), and Will Wright, *Sixguns and Society: A Structural Study of the Western* (Berkeley: University of California Press, 1975). For a critique of Wright's structuralist methodology, see Christopher Frayling, 'The American Western and American Society', in Philip Davies and Brian Neve (eds), *Cinema, Politics and Society in America* (Manchester: Manchester University Press, 1981), pp. 136–62. For an introduction to British cinema, see Marcia Landy, *British Genres: Cinema and Society, 1930–1960* (Princeton: Princeton University Press, 1991), and Alan Burton and Julian Petley (eds), 'Genre and British Cinema', special issue of the *Journal of Popular British Cinema*, 1 (1998). Richard Dyer and Ginette Vincendeau (eds), *Popular European Cinema* (London: Routledge, 1992) includes a selection of essays on European genres and cycles. There is an extensive critical literature on *film noir*: Andrew Spicer, *Film Noir* (Harlow: Pearson Education, 2002) provides a compact introduction to both the genre and the historiography. Paul Schrader, 'Notes on *film noir*', *Film Comment*, 8: 1 (1972), pp. 8–13, is the most important single text: it not only put *film noir* on the map of film studies but also argued for its relevance to contemporary cinema. Other useful studies include: Ian Cameron (ed.), *The Movie Book of Film Noir* (London: Studio Vista, 1994); Alain Silver and James Ursini (eds), *Film Noir Reader* (New York: Limelight Editions, 1996); R. Barton Palmer, *Hollywood's Dark Cinema: The American Film Noir* (New York: Twayne, 1994); E. Ann Kaplan (ed.), *Women in Film Noir* (London: British Film Institute, 1978); Frank Krutnik, *In A Lonely Street: Film Noir, Genre, Masculinity* (London: Routledge, 1991); and, especially, James Naremore, *More Than Night: Film Noir in its Contexts* (Berkeley: University of Califorinia Press, 1998).

► Chapter 6

Most histories of production have focused on Hollywood. Thomas Schatz, *The Genius of the System: Hollywood Filmmaking in the Studio Era* (New York: Pantheon, 1988) is one of the finest examples of archive-based research into the

US film industry. Other important work is represented by Edward Buscombe, 'Notes on Columbia Pictures Corporation 1926–41', *Screen*, 13: 3 (1975), pp. 65–82, and Nick Roddick, *A New Deal in Entertainment: Warner Brothers in the 1930s* (London: British Film Institute, 1983). Useful collections include Tino Balio (ed.), *The American Film Industry* (Madison: University of Wisconsin Press, 1976), Paul Kerr (ed.), *The Hollywood Film Industry: A Reader* (London: Routledge & Kegan Paul, 1986) and Janet Staiger (ed.), *The Studio System* (New Brunswick: Rutgers University Press, 1994). Neal Gabler, *An Empire of Their Own: How the Jews Invented Hollywood* (New York: Crown, 1988) is a somewhat impressionistic account of the movie moguls. See also the corrective view by Richard Maltby, 'The Political Economy of Hollywood: The Studio System', in Philip Davies and Brian Neve (eds), *Cinema, Politics and Society in America* (Manchester: Manchester University Press, 1981). There are many excellent case studies of the production of individual films: three of the best are Robert L. Carringer, *The Making of Citizen Kane* (Berkeley: University of California Press, rev. edn 1996), Charles Drazin, *In Search of the Third Man* (London: Methuen, 1999), and Sheldon Hall, *Zulu: With Some Guts Behind It – The Making of the Epic Movie* (Sheffield: Tomahawk Press, 2005). The Wisconsin/Warner Bros. Screenplay series (general editor: Tino Balio) is an excellent archive: each volume includes a contextualizing essay on the making of the film as well as the final shooting script, credits and extensive annotations.

The best starting point for historical studies of reception is Janet Staiger, *Interpreting Films: Studies in the Historical Reception of American Cinema* (Princeton: Princeton University Press, 1992), which includes an overview of reception theory followed by a series of case studies. Robert C. Allen, 'From exhibition to reception: reflections on the audience in film history', *Screen*, 31: 4 (1990), pp. 347–56, is another important foundational article for reception studies. Three volumes edited by Melvyn Stokes and Richard Maltby bring together some of the best research in this field: *American Movie Audiences: From the Turn of the Century to the Early Sound Era* (London: British Film Institute, 1999), *Identifying Hollywood's Audiences: Cultural Identity and the Movies* (London: British Film Institute, 1999), and *Hollywood Spectatorship: Changing Perceptions of Cinema Spectatorship* (London: British Film Institute, 2001). The most extensive recent research project into cinema-going is 'Going to the Show: Mapping Moviegoing in North Carolina', which has an open-access website at http://docsouth.unc.edu/gtts/index.html (last accessed 30.8.2012). Outside North America see the 'Cinema Context' database at http://www.cinemacontext.nl (last accessed 30.8.2012), which includes material for the Netherlands. Two major ethnographic studies of audiences and their memories of cinema-going are Jackie Stacey, *Star Gazing: Hollywood Cinema and its Female Spectators* (London: Routledge, 1994), and Annette Kuhn, *An Everyday Magic: Cinema and Cultural*

Memory (London: I. B. Tauris, 2002). For two contrasting accounts of cinema-going in Britain in the 1930s, see Jeffrey Richards, *The Age of the Dream Palace: Cinema and Society in Britain, 1930–1939* (London: Routledge & Kegan Paul, 1984), a social history based on primary sources including contemporary surveys of cinema, trade papers and fan magazines, and John Sedgwick, *Popular Filmgoing in 1930s Britain: A Choice of Pleasures* (Exeter: University of Exeter Press, 2000), which, in the absence of any box-office data, applies a statistical methodology known as 'POPSTAT' in order to rank the most popular films. Robert James, *Popular Culture and Working-Class Taste in Britain, 1930–39: A Round of Cheap Diversions?* (Manchester: Manchester University Press, 2010), considers cinema-going in the context of other working-class leisure activities.

Conclusion

Richard Maltby's assessment of the current state of film historiography is expounded in the introduction to a collection arising from a conference on film exhibition in Ghent in 2007: Richard Maltby, Daniel Biltereyst and Philippe Meers (eds), *Explorations in New Cinema History: Approaches and Case Studies* (Oxford: Wiley-Blackwell, 2011). Mette Hjort and Duncan Petrie (eds), *The Cinema of Small Nations* (Edinburgh: Edinburgh University Press, 2007) opens up some hitherto unknown national cinemas. And the emergence of research into 'Bollywood' is exemplified by M. Madhava Prasad, *Ideology of the Hindi Film: A Historical Construction* (New Delhi: Oxford University Press, 1998), Rachel Dwyer and Divia Patel, *Cinema India: The Visual Culture of Hindi Film* (London: Reaktion, 2002), Vijay Mishra, *Bollywood Cinema: Temples of Desire* (New York: Routledge, 2002), and – addressing the question of audiences in India and in the diaspora – Shakuntala Banaji, *Reading 'Bollywood': The Young Audience and Hindi Films* (Basingstoke: Palgrave Macmillan, 2006). Richard Maltby and Melvyn Stokes (eds), *Hollywood Abroad: Hollywood and Cultural Exchange* (London: British Film Institute, 2004) considers the overseas reception of US films. Sarah Street, *Transatlantic Crossings: British Feature Films in the USA* (London: Continuum, 2001) is an expert study of the distribution and reception of British films in the American market, while Mark Glancy, *Temporary American Citizens? Hollywood and the Americanization of Britain* (London: I. B. Tauris, 2013) considers the Anglo-American film relationship from the other side.

Index

Printed in China